Failing Forward *In* Saarland

Claudette E. Bouman

One Printers Way
Altona, MB R0G 0B0
Canada

www.friesenpress.com

First Edition — 2024

ISBN
978-1-03-830170-3 (Hardcover)
978-1-03-830169-7 (Paperback)
978-1-03-830171-0 (eBook)

1. *BIOGRAPHY & AUTOBIOGRAPHY, PERSONAL MEMOIRS*
2. *FAMILY & RELATIONSHIPS, PARENTING*
3. *TRAVEL, EUROPE*

We acknowledge the support of the Canada Council for the Arts.

Distributed to the trade by The Ingram Book Company

Testimonials for Failing Forward

Claudette Bouman's book, *Failing Forward*, is much more than a memoir. Rather, it is a mesmerizingly poetic exploration of life's wonders and difficulties, flowing seamlessly between the author's memories from her youth in native Barbados, her life in her adopted country of Canada, and her and her family's exciting but intimidating adjustments to being new temporary residents of Germany.

R.F. Cook, author of *The Eadaili and The Wanderer Duology.*

Failing Forward In Saarland is a beautifully honest examination of Bouman's time spent living abroad in Saarland, Germany. It does not shy away from topics such as language barriers, cultural differences, or family dynamics. Bouman manages to carry the past forward in her work, frequently referencing tales from her time spent living in Barbados, and later, Canada. The effect is an informative perspective on an ex-pat's life in Germany that is engaging and full of heart.

Jen Colclough, poet

A riveting book that I couldn't stop reading. Along with depicting challenges faced by a Canadian family while living for a year in Saarland, Germany, the author includes snippets of history and geography, which I found fascinating. Though I sometimes felt as if I was a voyeur peeking out my window into someone else's, I enjoyed every moment...

Cathy MacKenzie, author of *Wolves Don't Knock.*

Acknowledgements

This book began with notes I took in Saarland, Germany, from July 2013 through June 2014. Many people read early drafts of the developing manuscript and helped me to reach the finish line. The Writers' Federation of Nova Scotia (WFNS) awarded me an Alistair MacLeod mentorship, a massive boost to my confidence. Cooper Lee Bombardier gave me precious mentorship. Under the WFNS Manuscript Review Program, I benefitted from advice for re-vamping, re-visioning, and re-conceiving my writing. I'm grateful to the Canada Council for the Arts and Arts Nova Scotia for their financial support. Several people in the Dartmouth Evergreen Writers' Group supported my efforts every step of the way, delivering valued feedback and sage advice, especially Robert Cook, Phil Yeats and Cathy MacKenzie. Editors Marianne Ward, Rachel Cooper, Catherine Chapman, and Georgia Atkin did terrific work in advancing drafts of the manuscript closer to the book it is today. Each one, in her own unique style, offered comments and suggestions that shaped and pared down what was a runaway mess into a work more suitable for publication. I'd like to thank Céline Cusson, whose enthusiasm for this book never wavered after reading the very first chapters of the first draft. Catherine Finnemore and Jen Colclough offered generous words of encouragement from the beginning. Writer Jaimie Feldman gave straight-up, helpful ideas and reassurances early in the writing process,

as did Ray Schachter. Finally, I extend huge thanks to my family. Thomas and Leandra were full participants in this long journey as they lived and shared the Saarland year experience with me. My patient husband read and reread several drafts, serving as critic, reviewer, consultant on many things German, and agent. I'm inspired by Leandra's love of the written word, her commitment to emotional recognition and truth, and her wise insights. To my son Art, I owe a gratitude debt for his firm backing and strong belief in radical creative initiative. All together, they have been generous, tolerant, and just fabulous answering every call for assistance and putting up with the countless hours I spent completing this project.
To write this book, I relied upon my personal records, researched facts, when necessary, consulted with several people who appear in the book, and depended on my memory of the events at that time in my life. I have changed all names of individuals in this book except for my nuclear family to avoid identification and or embarrassment. Not all details are true to fact, as in some cases, I have changed particulars and events in order to preserve anonymity.

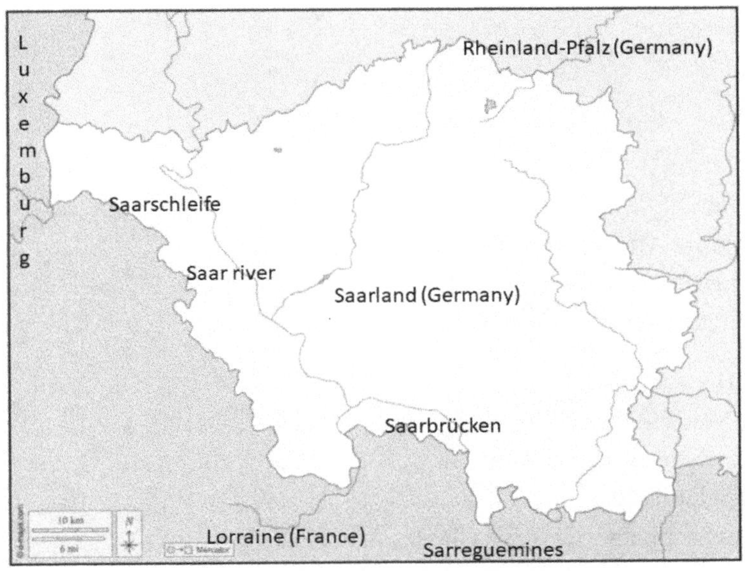

Source: https://d-maps.com/carte.php?num_car=6400&lang=en

CONTENTS

PART V

PART VI

PART I

1. Taking Off

As I stepped onto the plane, I took a deep breath. I hated flying. But my German-born husband was returning to his home country for a year-long sabbatical, and I, his Barbados-born Canadian wife, had taken a year off teaching to join him on the adventure. Our reluctant teenage daughter shuffled along behind me, looking morose. She would attend a new school in a new country, away from her friends and familiar surroundings. But at least it was a French-language school, and she was already fluent in French.

As for my own apprehensions about spending a year in Germany, did I mention I don't speak German?

Living abroad, away from familiar comforts and haunts—friends, home, car, favourite clothes, and walking trails—demands a champion spirit. As a small girl growing up in a small, crowded home without running water in tropical Barbados, I had no inkling that my life would take me to Canada and beyond.

Our family's story began when I crossed paths with Thomas Bouman, an energetic, floppy-haired German, at the University of British Columbia in Vancouver. We fell in love, got married, and eight years later, in 1998, relocated with two young children to salt-sprayed Nova Scotia. Fifteen years after that, we broke from work demands, daily routines, and familiar people and places to cross the Atlantic with our daughter for a year of renewal and fresh cultural experiences in Saarland, Germany, living there from the beginning of July 2013 to the end of June 2014.

Thomas and I hadn't chosen Germany on a whim. I'd visited that country six times between August 1990 and July 2011, well before our

2013–2014 stay. I'd been exposed to Germany, its language and culture, from my first visit there, vacationing with Thomas in the summer of 1990. It had been a giddy time getting to know each other and overloading a mere ten days to see Göttingen, Frankfurt, and Düsseldorf. We did more, streaking across Western Europe by car to visit Amsterdam and Paris, and then flying to London. My enjoyment of Amsterdam was marred by a breakfast of raw herring and onions but redeemed by a visit to a large indoor market, where I bought a beautifully tailored African dress and attended a South African play.

I fell in love with Göttingen, Thomas's university town, in Lower Saxony. We walked streets engraved with the names of famous scientists and decorated with a bust of Johann Carl Friedrich Gauss, a German mathematician. Thomas took the lead as tour guide, translator, and driver.

In December 1997, our children, Art and Leandra, joined us for their first visit to meet Thomas's mother, brothers, nieces, and nephews in Eutin, Northern Germany. We were embraced by the family's generous hospitality. In later family visits, their uncles and grandmother spoiled our children, and they romped on lawns and swam in nearby lakes or lazed at the beach. We were introduced to the *Strandkorb*, a bulky beach chair providing shelter from sun and wind. I loved Germany, its green, varied landscape, towns, museums, and deep history, but found the language a formidable barrier.

Our Saarland adventure was sparked by my husband's imagination. In 2008, at home with Art and Leandra, his travel lust burned bright. "What about a year abroad, in Germany?" Thomas said one summer's day out of the blue. His sometimes frizzy hair was curled in the day's humid air. He smiled cheekily beneath hooded blue eyes and a strong nose.

My eyes popped behind spectacles. "Wait, what?" The idea landed with a smack. I had loved every moment of my six previous visits to Germany, with and without our children. Thomas and I had yearned for the freedom of a long stretch of time without the usual work and family obligations. A treasury of possibilities opened up. I pictured myself engaged in a hearty fight to learn a foreign tongue and exploring historic European marvels, including celebrated museum collections.

"On my sabbatical leave in five years—"

"And with my deferred leave at the same time," I said, not missing a beat. "Yes. That would work."

"We have to get Leandra and Art on board. She'll be entering high school and Art will be on his own—work, university, whatever."

The vision took hold and grew. Thomas wanted his family to experience life in his cultural homeland, his *Heimat*. He looked forward to all the things he missed about Germany, most of all speaking his native tongue. We shifted from musings into concrete plans and began acting on them. Energized rather than put off by any tough task, Thomas knew how to engineer a year abroad. His sabbatical-year pay plus my deferred-leave pay, saved over three years, would give us the financial footing. Our financial commitments continued to include mortgage and car payments, financing our offspring's university hopes, and planning for retirement. Even so, the chance for me to drop the work routine and take off for distant shores rang out fiercely.

Leading up to our year-long stay, we'd done solid planning and reflection. We had to be able to afford life in Germany, and we needed to convince our daughter that she would enjoy our time there. (Art was in university and wouldn't be able to join us.) I felt ready to embrace discoveries and fresh experiences in a different country without over-thinking major obstacles. Was I capable of the dislocation, adaptations, and discomfort of a language barrier? I knew only that I would give it a good try.

Saarbrücken is the capital of the Saarland, a forested, southwestern German state bordered by France and Luxembourg. Named after the Saar River, a tributary of the Moselle, Saarland is part of the greater Moselle wine region. It is a small state, less famous than some of the other fifteen states that make up the Federal Republic of Germany and more affordable, which makes it appealing. Germany is a highly regionalized country with some cities being much more expensive than others. Housing and daily living costs in Munich or Hamburg, for instance, would be higher than in Saarbrücken. For continuity's sake, we planned for Leandra to attend a French school, as she was doing at home in Halifax. One of Thomas's colleagues had recommended the Lycée Jean de Pange just across the border from Saarbrücken in the small town of Sarreguemines, France. A bonus feature of our chosen city was Thomas's old university friend, Karl, who lived and worked in the forestry sector in Saarland. Thomas intended to make the year a working sabbatical to conduct forest research in Saarland's beech forests. I would have preferred Berlin, Hamburg, or even Freiburg, but when faced with practicalities like living costs, the proximity of a school for Leandra, the emotional weight of friendship, and a congenial research environment, my preferences gave way.

Starting with Karl, Thomas made calls connecting with people in Saarland about potential research projects. He explored housing and school options, following up with a catalogue of ideas, including, as usual, too-busy travel itineraries.

Decades earlier, at age sixteen, Thomas had started his international travel adventures, whipping across Western Europe and into Morocco. His passion for travel still beamed bright as a family man, igniting my own travel flames.

Leandra didn't much care where we'd live in Germany.

In the months leading up to our move, whenever her dad mentioned the year overseas, she suddenly needed to be somewhere else.

"Look, won't it be nice in Germany?" Thomas said, showing her a map.

"Oh, not now," she said, quickly brushing past him.

Another day he asked, "What shall we visit first in Saarland?"

"I don't know," she said, heading downstairs.

Another time, trying to whip up interest, he said, "I think you'll like your new school in France, Jean de Pange."

"How would you know?" She shot back, making for her room. "I have homework to do." The bedroom door slammed.

It disappointed me that Leandra hadn't caught our Saarland excitement. It nagged at us both, but we forged ahead, hoping she'd come around. Saarland contacts returned phone calls and emails extending an official invitation, a housing offer, and acceptance at the *lycée* in Sarreguemines.

Armed with his trusty German-engineered magnifying glass, Thomas took to studying his collection of European country and city maps, travel and train guides. "We'll go to Paris on the fast train and spend a weekend there," he enthused. "Aachen, in western Germany, is a must-see. And we definitely have to revisit Vienna."

Leandra, meantime, remained dead set against any major school change. I knew the lure of travel wrestled with her personal fears. Her dad would make tantalizing offers: "How about visits to Slovenia and England? What about a trip to Stratford to see a Shakespeare play?" She loved Shakespeare plays and would miss out on an entire season of Shakespeare by the Sea in Halifax. Still, for Leandra, the move to another country evoked nightmarish visions of being thrown under the social bus, on top of her worries about her education.

I was dealing with my own apprehensions. Would German immigration officials regard me as an unwelcome foreigner? I dreaded how I might be misperceived and treated as a Black woman, part of a small visible minority in a predominantly white Germany. Black people made for easy targets in countries where they stuck out with high visibility. Incidents of racial profiling abounded on the news and on the Internet. I couldn't be too naïve. Was I going to be safe in Saarland?

At a deeper level, my biggest fears were about failure to acquire the language. My knowledge of Germany—specifically its language, culture, and people—remained superficial even after several visits. On those visits, the land's natural beauty and rich historical and cultural variety first surprised and then intrigued me. But facing a year in Saarland tinged my excitement with apprehensions. I feared I would fail, that I would not gain enough German to communicate with ordinary Germans around me and live in the same way I enjoyed life in Canada. I felt incompetent, for unlike Thomas and Leandra, I'd never mastered a second language. Was it too late for me? Would I feel embarrassed if I could not make myself understood? I didn't want to look silly, didn't want my ignorance to be revealed. I feared I *couldn't* learn German. The vulnerability around this entire matter took me back to my schoolgirl attempts at learning Spanish in Barbados in the 1970s. In my worst imaginings, I anticipated making a humiliating spectacle of myself during German language classes.

My husband muttered reassurances: "You'll be fine, Claudette, don't worry." Or "You'll need to learn German. Do that and you'll love it." It helped my misgivings that some of what Germany represented to me was familiar—at the top of the list, a German partner, and next in line, prior visits.

One night, a week before our departure, all of Leandra's stifled emotions overflowed. After a significant family scene, one thing remained certain—we would go to Germany. What happened after that appeared fuzzy. Gosh, we'd already planned and organized so many things! But as parents, we could not deny the possibility of potential dramatic reversals resulting from our teenager's uneasiness. Would we need to turn around and head back home prematurely?

That night, instead of drifting off into easy slumber, Thomas and I stared at the ceiling wide-eyed. For the first time, I understood what Leandra was leaving behind: a world that had nurtured her as a child and sustained her as a teenager. She dreaded the uncertainty of what would follow.

As our departure for Germany approached, visions sometimes alarmed Thomas by raiding his night's sleep. Generous by nature, he shared every anxiety with me.

"What about a house-sitter? Should we rent it or pay someone to look after it? What about our valuables? Do we need another safety deposit box? What if a winter storm damages the house while we are gone? And what about the car?"

"Okay, what should we tackle first?"

My answers simply generated new Thomas questions and concerns. To my dismay, no amount of planning and preparation eased his anxieties. Exhausted, I responded to each additional concern, building my own expanding to-do list. Above all else, home ownership was the major concern. It took on a life of its own, morphing into a devil, threatening to halt our plans.

It took months to settle that biggest headache: a suitable home-sitter or a tenant? I quarrelled with Thomas, saying our tenant should pay us. He disagreed. He cursed at me and said, "You go find a paying tenant." I was shocked and hurt, for he rarely swore and, most of all, he *never* swore at me. Finally, we found our perfect home-sitter in one of Leandra's former teachers.

And then came all the other arrangements: insurances, automatic bill payments, house cleaning, clearing a space for the home-sitter, travel itineraries, car security, school plans for Leandra, financial arrangements for Art and our elderly parents, and on and on. A week before departure, one more worry sprang up as Thomas's head glided toward the pillow: "Claudette, we haven't yet made a will."

"Righto." All my pretensions at sleep fled.

"We could make an appointment to see a lawyer."

"Tomorrow? Bit late for that now. Let's write up a will, have it witnessed, and deposit it in our safety deposit box," I said.

"Yes, in Germany, these things don't always need a lawyer. People write wills and deposit them at City Hall all the time." I had learned from him that Germany could be a very legalistic nation, and remarkably efficient.

Well-organized to a fault, Thomas leaped into a whirlwind of activity over the next few days. For two days, we pored over will and testament templates and came up with a document that we signed, witnessed, and deposited. I composed a home-sitter's agreement. We made appointments with the bank and insurance providers, secured our accounts, stored our vehicle, arranged for home oversight, and made last-minute visits and calls to family and close friends. Well past midnight on the night before our departure, the gentle snores of a contented Thomas greeted my ears. We had managed the formidable catalogue of tasks and were finally ready for our journey.

In leaving, we were saying farewell to Art, who, with renewed grit, faced down a bachelor of arts degree at Cape Breton University. We were also parting from home, friends, neighbours, and everything that meant anything to us in Nova Scotia.

So here we were, three family members about to share the Saarland adventure together.

Leandra was an intelligent, cautious, and imaginative teenager, still growing into herself. Scared by moths in her bedroom at night, she'd cover them with big pillows rather than put them outside or squish them outright. She craved intellectual and social balance and found joy in books, the visual arts, film, and theatre. Those she balanced with practical arts, trying new recipes in the kitchen, learning to sew, and practising piano and flute. Never bored as a child, she chatted to herself as she sat in front of her dollhouse or in the backyard. She was independent and until now had lived a sheltered life as the second of two children, sibling to a big brother who was away at university. She'd inherited her foreign language abilities from her dad, not from me. They shared a similar generosity of spirit and contrariness.

Something quintessentially Northern German branded Thomas. He loved forests, beaches, and spaces emptied of people; disliked big cities and possessed an insatiable curiosity about the natural world. My partner could be contradictory, judgmental, and radically minded in economics, but conservative in social and family values. Although he seemed to miss nothing, he sometimes failed to take in the most obvious.

We each faced Saarland with a unique stance. Would Leandra make that teenage adjustment we had so carefully arranged for her? My husband would be fine. He'd be adapting to a different region from his Heimat on the Baltic Coast, where he'd grown up, and from central Germany, where he'd attended university. As for me, on one occasion, Art had confided to his dad, "Mom's going to be very lonely in Germany," a comment no doubt informed by his own experience while living there in 2010. It may also have had to do with my cautious nature. Was I taking too big a risk? Perhaps the answer to that question would determine the success or failure of our overseas gamble.

I was launching out on a journey of discovery. Contemplating that journey in hindsight, I've come across at least three metaphors for the land I would live in. In *Understanding Global Cultures* (1994), Martin Gannon says, "The symphony, rooted in the past and reined in the present by precision and synchronicity, makes an apt metaphor for modern Germany." An orchestra, like a society, comprises individuals who subdue their wants for the greater good (harmony) under the direction of a leader/conductor. Gannon posits that, perhaps because of Germany's history of shifting allegiances and borders, Germans have a deep longing for unity. I thought the metaphor held some truth. When Thomas was new to Canada in the 1990s, he spoke of how important social cohesion and consensus were for Germans.

In Steven Ozment's *A Mighty Fortress* (2005), a history of the German people, he presents Germany as a mighty fortress or castle.

The third metaphor is my own: Germany, as a sumptuous buffet or feast.

After twenty years of marriage, I'd concluded that all those evenings of my youth spent knitting and crocheting in tropical Barbados would have been better spent on language lessons, learning German. Back then, I had taught myself crocheting and how to make macrame plant hangers, tucking away my efforts when something more alluring called, dashing to the beach on vacation days, chillin' with the hill gang, or joining weekend dance parties. How could I know that I'd marry a man from Schleswig-Holstein, make Canada my home, and raise a family there? Growing up on a tiny island (I knew just how tiny after living on Canada's east and west coasts) meant that the odds had been stacked against the life I now lived.

In 1986, I disembarked a plane in Fredericton, having left Barbados for graduate studies in education at the University of New Brunswick. An insatiable appetite to travel to North America or live there abounds within the hearts of many West Indians. I was no different. This craving was fed by stories travellers told on returning home from such cities as New York, Miami, Toronto, or Montreal (*never* small rural places). Further, it was not uncommon to work alongside Americans or Canadians in Barbados. And so, I had long desired to travel, learn first-hand about Canada's peoples and landscapes, and pursue university studies for advancement in my teaching career. It helped that I knew and liked two Canadians, both from Ontario, with whom I had worked at the Barbados Community College in the early 1980s. I fired off applications to three Canadian universities. When the University of New Brunswick's acceptance offer arrived first, I jumped at it, heading to Fredericton in August.

That first, unsettling, but thrilling time in a new land was a test of my confidence and personal resilience, forcing me to rely on so-far-unproven inner muscle. Leaving the warmth and comfort of home, family, friends, and a secure teaching position to embrace, even temporarily, a new life in a foreign country scared me. I had often had difficulty accepting even small uncertainties in my life. I fought to beat back my doubts and fears. I secured my housing and changed apartments three times, which activated new and hitherto unproven reserves of spirit. Arranging suitable shelter had to be balanced with long, bitter days of academic grind.

My university studies progressed along with a homesickness that fuelled my desire to hurry back to Barbados. After a gruelling round of graduate courses in statistics, research methodology, and educational governance and supervision, I dug into a master's thesis, challenging my wits. From June to December 1987, I turned into a library and computer centre rat, often inhabiting them from ten in the morning until ten at night. Then, I would walk for half an hour downhill (local buses ceased running at nine P.M.) along lonely, dim residential streets to my rented room in a women's downtown residence, often bundled up against winter's bone-chilling bite.

Up to that point, I had felt heavily weighed down by being born into a low-income household, being female, and lacking positive family role models. For much of my childhood and youth, I hated my home life for its stifling poverty and harsh, visionless parents. Although by the mid-eighties I stood with pride as a teacher, my background hung about me like a drab winter coat worn in the heat of summer. Having never previously lived with people other than close relatives, I rapidly acquired enough social savvy to navigate roommates' irksome behaviour. A few of them would later become good friends.

My first New Brunswick winter dealt me a physical blow. New learnings were in store. One night, I fell with a bang to the pavement. Black, traitorous ice patches lay in wait on dark university car parks. Heavy spikes of ice menaced from overhangs. But winter wonderland landscapes of freshly fallen snow mesmerized me, and the winter of 1987 had heaps of it. I marvelled at sidewalks of tunnelled snow piled up shoulder-high on both sides, where only my head peeped out. Zipped up to my eyeballs, I marched to and from the university in wind chills that turned my legs into ice sticks. Then a letter from my mother arrived: "Wear stockings or tights under your jeans," she wrote. "I learned that from my sister-in-law in Maryland." What a laugh—winter wear advice from a woman who, in fifty-five years, had never set foot off her tropical isle.

I missed the brash, rowdy Bajan (Barbadian) manner and found solace among the university's small but jovial international student crowd of West

Indians, Nigerians, and Kenyans. I said yes to invitations such as, "Want to come over to our potluck on Friday night?" and "What about modelling and doing a Caribbean dance number for the annual Reggae Night event?" So much crazy fun. But that social buffer didn't ease the burning homesickness of my first Christmas spent away from the land of my birth. Sequestered in a stuffy room of cheap, student-shared housing, I estimated the distance south. It amounted to a really solitary time even amidst roommates' kind offerings of outings and warm apple crisp topped with dreamy whipped cream. The Canadian students and New Brunswickers I encountered in and around Fredericton were curious but polite and too often distant.

After seventeen months in Fredericton, teary-eyed but joyful, I clasped comrades close, said my goodbyes, and charted a route back to Barbados. But, to my surprise, I quickly grew restless there. I chafed under temporary lodgings with a younger sister and vexing conditions at my old workplace. I went to the Barbados teachers' loan assistance office and boldly asked to secure a loan for doctoral studies in British Columbia, Canada. Furnished with some first-hand knowledge about the Maritimes, its peoples, cultures, and weather, I yearned to live on the West Coast, in beautiful BC. A positive answer meant that after seven months, I again departed for Canada, resolving not to hurry home again this time.

By returning to Canada to pursue a doctorate in educational administration at the University of British Columbia (UBC), I had also ended a sour relationship. My freedom felt heady. Leaving a familiar, comfortable home place for new, foreign terrain would become an experience I repeated with our trip to Saarland.

Vancouver remains my favourite Canadian city, for there I met a wonderful man from Germany who would become my husband. On a research stipend from the German Academic Exchange Service, Thomas was visiting the forest science department at UBC. He cut a curious figure in the computer centre with shoulder-length, floppy curls and a springy step. Once the sparks flew, romantic trysts followed: a visit to Mayne Island, one of BC's Gulf Islands; and dates at local cinemas, restaurants, Stanley Park, and other dreamy Vancouver locales. All that romance made my required reading of scholarly articles for doctoral studies downright dull.

Married in 1990, we greeted our baby son, Art, a year later with mixed parental happiness and nerves. Living costs in one of Canada's most scenic but expensive housing markets positioned financial concerns as our top priority and dictated our next move. Imagine my reaction when Thomas held up a response to one of two or three dozen job applications saying, "I got a job offer in Swift Current!" Where was Swift Current? It was 1,527 kilometres east, roughly an eighteen-hour drive through mountains and prairies, not counting breaks. We danced around in glee, knocking over the coffee table and giving baby Art an awful fright.

My doctoral dissertation remained in grand disarray, and we stood on shaky financial ground when Thomas, our baby, and I set out for Saskatchewan. A great job and new work associates and friends at the Swift Current Agricultural Research Station awaited us. Bumping along inside the moving van, after passing through Banff National Park and with miles of flat prairie land stretching to the horizon, I could barely suppress tears at what I had left behind in stunning BC.

We lived in Swift Current for twenty months before relocating four hundred kilometres north to Prince Albert for Thomas's new job in forestry. I was also fortunate to find employment in my field. We enjoyed our work and social life among friendly folks—Woods Cree, descendants of early Black settlers, and other immigrants from the West Indies and beyond. In October 1997, we welcomed baby Leandra into our family, making six-year-old Art a proud big brother.

After six years in Saskatchewan, our final family move in 1998 brought us to Nova Scotia, where Thomas and I transplanted ourselves and rooted our children. I had cultivated professional contacts, joined a national education alliance, and networked with members of the Black Educators' Association in Halifax before making our pivotal move.

Within months of our arrival, my enquiries with teachers and officials at the Nova Scotia education establishment yielded positive results. One day, a year after my arrival, I walked into a junior high school classroom in Dartmouth with forced confidence announcing, "Good morning, grade eights. I am Mrs. Bouman and I will be your new homeroom teacher." That coveted new teaching position paved our path toward building a livelihood and life in our adopted home. We celebrated our heady successes with loud cheers of "*Prost!*" when Thomas accomplished a long-held ambition to teach at a university, accepting a professorship in the biology department at Cape Breton University (CBU). We settled in Dartmouth with Art and Leandra; Thomas commuted to CBU, four hundred kilometres away.

Meeting Thomas had changed everything when I became a wife and a mother of two. My focus changed from returning to my island birthplace to living a very different life of personal and professional certainty in Canada.

For me, living in English-speaking Canada, cultural and language differences had never created unscalable walls as I expected they could in Germany. I knew the language barrier would make an enormous difference in whether I experienced life in Saarland as a foreigner or thrived as a full, independent person. Nevertheless, I welcomed the risk, embracing the idea that failing forward has a utility. What was the worst that could happen? A premature end to our trip? Even that turnaround would put me further ahead than where I started out.

Failure in my overseas venture wasn't inevitable, but it was a distinct possibility. I didn't want to fail and wouldn't enjoy it, but adopting an attitude of failing forward meant I would accept my mistakes as stepping stones to future accomplishments. I would choose to use failure for the life lessons it taught me and apply those lessons to future efforts. Each failure would bring me new knowledge and personal growth.

By 2013, having lived in four Canadian provinces, I believed I possessed enough first-hand experiences as a foreigner and immigrant to provide the knowledge needed to effectively navigate new locations. Landing in New Brunswick had scared me into bolstering my courage. In British Columbia, the struggle to find housing gave way when international students helped each other. I nurtured friendships and mentorships among Canadian and international students that matured within and beyond my education department. I accepted invitations to socials, winter outings at Whistler Blackcomb and Cypress Mountain, Christmas parties, and even a baby shower (my own, when Art was born). Saskatchewan handed Thomas and me genuine employment opportunities. I felt strong pride in becoming sworn in as a Canadian citizen in Saskatoon. We were constructing productive, secure lives as our vision transformed from students into permanent residents. Saskatchewan taught me to face forward with optimism.

Building family life, setting clear, bright goals, and remaining open to life's rich possibilities paid me abundant rewards.

On the day of our departure for Germany, the booked airport taxi did a no-show. We had cut our landline the day before and possessed no cell. Thomas had made arrangements with the company and refused to call again. All they needed to do was dispatch a taxi for us on time. We found out later the taxi people had tried to reach us by phone; when that failed, they declined to send the car.

So, for an hour, we sat waiting in silence. Leandra, having not signed on for the deal, looked indifferent.

My stomach flipped as I sat there. What if we missed the plane? There's always another flight. At what cost and inconvenience? We can't miss this plane! "We need to get to the airport three hours before departure time," I almost yelled at Thomas. He was more nerve-wracked than I was. Leandra fidgeted with her carry-on.

"I know," Thomas said, displaying tense annoyance.

"What about David?"

Thomas rushed across the street to our neighbourhood friend, who offered his delivery van. A year-long trip required six large suitcases, a computer, three backpacks, three carry-on pieces, and handbags. Nerves awry, we bundled in for the trip to Halifax Stanfield International Airport.

At the newly renovated airport, mixed feelings washed over me. No one had come to see us off. In Barbados, there would be a ton of well-wishers, some hugging, some laughing, and others crying, wiping their noses on my fresh shirt. Leandra would weep into her grandmother's shoulder, saying, "Granny, I don't want to go to Germany. Can I live with you?" And her granny would hold her, rubbing her shoulders, making reassuring noises while eyeballing me. I clutched my handbag containing enough dimenhydrinate to sedate an elephant. I wimped out at flying, hoping not to hear the pilot announce: "We're currently cruising at an altitude of thirty thousand feet. You may now release your seatbelts, sit back, and relax." At six o'clock the next morning, we'd be in Frankfurt.

Leandra lounged. Her calm belied any lingering excitement or dread at the turn of events that didn't fit her worldview. We knew she loved new experiences, languages, and travel, but it would not be a peaceful year—unfamiliar country, foreign language, new school, new teachers, new classmates.

Thomas, dressed in khakis, had strapped a fanny pack (which Leandra and I absolutely refused to wear) with papers, passports, and a wallet to his waist. He gave off two contradictory airs: relaxed alertness. It was strangely anticlimactic after the past week's commotion.

I people-watched in the lounge area. Leaning on a wall, a nervous, wiry man wore dress shoes and new jeans. Nearby, a petite woman in Birkenstocks tried keeping in check a pair of blond girls wearing floral, bright cotton dresses. Two guys down the row of seats nattered away, one of whom wore a smart, black leather jacket and leather shoes, even in July. Having visited Germany, I was aware of a more formal dress code among Germans than the average Canadian. It seemed many older Germans loved leather shoes and real shirts, with sleeves and collars, in pastel shades.

When the boarding call rang out, my body rose, my face beamed, and my heart fluttered.

2. Frankfurt Airport and the Rails

Exiting customs, we faced a crowded, glittering hallway. We joined a promenade of rolling luggage, scuffing shoes, and trundling carts. Gleaming display cases along the concourse contained neat piles of fresh pastries—plunders (a croissant-style pastry) of quark, raspberry and apricot jam, almond flaked *Franzbrötchen* (a croissant filled with cinnamon sugar), plain buttery croissants, and raisin snails. Quark balls, pig ears, pretzels, and hazelnut bars bordered the edges. Warm, sweet aromas rose when I leaned in. Thomas pushed the luggage trolley and stopped at every display, looking for a Northern Germany treat.

"Your obsession with poppyseed cake can wait," I said.

"It's almost impossible to get it outside Schleswig-Holstein. It's not as good anywhere else."

We made our way down into the belly of the airport building, where Leandra and I waited while Thomas got train tickets. The next leg of our journey would take us to Saarbrücken, Saarland. We would face a tricky situation for our train journey, considering the mountain of luggage we had hauled all the way from Nova Scotia.

Leandra and I turned at the sound of running footsteps. Thomas held tickets high.

"Guess what these tickets to Saarbrücken cost!"

"Five hundred dollars?" Leandra replied. Her father's boyish glee was sometimes too much for her teenage soul.

"Family rate of forty euros."

"Wow," I answered. "Where in Canada could we get that?"

"Nowhere."

Leandra remained unimpressed.

A near-sonic boom and fast-approaching headlights in the dark tunnel announced the train's arrival. On board, we sat facing each other, a small table in between, convenient for the pastries and drinks we'd purchased at the airport. I settled in, relishing being transported and passing landscapes of abundant variety. Fellow passengers brushed past down the aisle. Anticipation or relief marked unknown faces at train stations.

"*Ihre Fahrkarten bitte.*" The train conductor asking for our tickets interrupted my reverie. A slightly built man in a neat blue uniform, he manoeuvred the narrow aisle with ease, wide legged, hands free. Drifting along and lulled by the sway, I stared out at the passing scenery—villages and neat hamlets and towns with red-and-black slate roofs decorated the countryside. Thomas and Leandra seemed half-asleep. It felt relaxing, almost magical.

Riding the rails turned into a favourite activity for the three of us.

Our Saarbrücken-bound train took a southwest route, crossing the Rhine River early on and then following one of its tributaries, the Nahe. Ribbons of water meandered down below in idyllic places, straight out of fairy lands. The train slowed to a crawl as it swung around tight bends, bypassing forested hills. Other times it raced through tunnels, exiting into bright landscapes of green, rolling vineyards. Well into the ride, Thomas pointed dramatically. "That's Bad Kreuznach. I almost moved *there* in grade ten. I wanted to stop school and go to the agricultural college."

Leandra leaned in closer, curious. "Why didn't you?"

"My father didn't like the idea, but he knew better than to argue with me. He set up a meeting with the director of agriculture in our home county who convinced me, given my good high school performance, university was a better path forward. I soon changed my mind."

We skirted places like Kirn, Idar-Oberstein, and St. Wendel. When we left Neunkirchen behind and approached St. Ingbert, Thomas knew we were closing in on our destination.

In 2011, we'd undertaken an eight-week vacation visiting Germany, Scotland, Austria, France, and Barbados. The German leg of the tour had taken us south to Freising and then north to the Baltic Coast for Thomas's mother's ninetieth birthday. We'd stopped in Saarland to visit Karl, Thomas's university friend.

Now I chugged past the familiar scenery that was just as spectacular as when I'd first seen it. And I had the promise of a year to delight in it. What would an entire year in Saarland bring? There'd be many opportunities to explore Germany and Europe, surely, but fresh contours would define my life, producing new outcomes. How different would a year be from vacationing briefly and being spoiled by Thomas's family with invitations and chaperoned tours? Living in an apartment would mean a change for us, too. And navigating daily life in a foreign language would be my personal hill to climb.

An announcement signalled time to step down at our journey's end. We'd been on the train for two hours, covering a distance of about 183 kilometres. The German buffet had begun by serving up one of my favourite delights: train travel. Why did it feel like I was stepping off a high ledge?

3. Saarbrücken Challenges

Travel-weary, we alighted at Saarbrücken Bahnhof, the city's central train station. With rows of shops on two floors, the station sold everyday fare, fresh pastries, books, and flowers. Via a spacious, high-ceilinged reception hall, it opened onto the city and a pedestrian zone where we hailed a taxi. After a long, winding route, the driver deposited us at the entrance to a small hotel on Mainzer Straße. Since our Saarland University guesthouse apartment would not be available until Monday, we had arranged this accommodation for two nights. We squeezed into an impossibly tight elevator with all our luggage.

A cozy city hotel, it stood on a busy street among ordinary, squat commercial buildings. From our windows, I spied a *Konditorei* (a café offering a wide variety of pastries), a fruit stall, and the entrance to a cobbled plaza across the street. The rumble of the traffic below beat at my chest. A glowering afternoon July sun struck at our windows, so we vacated the room to explore our new surroundings.

The hotel redeemed itself in the morning because of its prime location, handy to anywhere we wanted to go in our new city. Plus, it offered a delightful, robust breakfast buffet. Hearty, dark German *Brot* (bread) and crisp *Brötchen* (rolls) took centre stage. An assortment of thinly sliced meats ranged from cooked, cured, and smoked hams to *Mettwurst-* and *Leberwurst*-type sausages. We were tempted by supplies of butter, boiled eggs, sweet jams, local honey and cheeses, like Gouda and butter-cheese. And on a side counter, jars of Muesli, bran or plain oat cereals, milk, quark, and yogurts complemented the medley.

If we were to settle in Germany, I would have to cultivate an attitude of expecting the unexpected. Securing residence papers was high on our priority list. In 2012, I'd been warned by an acquaintance returning from a two-year stint in Hamburg that the German bureaucracy's appetite for paperwork quickly becomes insupportable. Official encounters would require fortitude.

Our adventures in Saarland started with a desire to open a personal bank account at *Sparkasse*—equivalent to a Canadian credit union and Thomas's ideological bank of choice—in the city's heart.

"Can we do this today?" Thomas asked a competent looking, sharp-eyed bank clerk.

She spoke German in crisp tones, telling him he couldn't open an account until he'd registered at the *Rathaus* City Hall.

"Okay, but we can't register at City Hall until we sort out our residence on Monday. We're getting apartment keys from Saarland University's housing office." He showed her a letter as proof.

The clerk was apologetic but repeated it was impossible to open an account without registering.

Blocked from completing his first task, Thomas's next desire was to fulfil the mandatory ID-cards requirement. German officialdom is serious about residence registration and IDs. Whenever citizens or residents arrive in Germany or move to live in a new location, they must register their new address. Registration documents are processed at the local city hall, but the paperwork arrives from Berlin. This means at least two levels of government: municipal officials, and federal authorities in Berlin track residents of Germany. Thomas had often railed about the absence of this registration requirement in Canada. How is it even possible that people move around at will in a country and it's not documented? A citizen registry is so important for elections, taxes, church contributions, everything, he'd say. It took him more than a decade living in Canada to accept that Canadian bureaucracy would never be as clear, efficient, or organized as the German culture he'd left behind in 1989. But now we were out of luck again, for the Rathaus was closed on weekends.

It seemed like the right time to go underground with our unfolding Catch-22 scenario. It began to resemble something straight out of the classic German film "The Captain from Köpenick." Thomas had told me the story, laughing. A man released from prison disguises himself as a Prussian military officer, recruits two blindly obedient soldiers, and occupies a Rathaus in Berlin to obtain his residence permit. Our frustrations signalled time for a breather and some comfort food.

"How about a treat from one of those neat Italian ice cream parlours in St. Johanner Markt, near Kappenstraße?"

Leandra, quiet so far, lit up. "Oh, yeah!"

We walked along pavement parallel to the Saarbahn rail tracks and past the landmark, neo-Gothic Johanneskirche (St. John's Church). We were in the St. Johann district, opposite the imposing sandstone Rathaus on the corner, also of neo-Gothic architecture. Turning right, we headed for the centre of the shopping district and walked toward the cobblestoned marketplace, which extended across busy streets, forming a popular, kilometre-long pedestrian shopping zone.

"Let's sit under these umbrellas," Thomas said. The July midday sun stung.

"Hello." An unsmiling waitress offered menus displaying dishes and glassware brimming with colourful ice cream and fruit concoctions. It wasn't going to be enough to say, "I'd like two scoops of chocolate ice cream." We had arrived in an ice cream paradise, where a banana split would have been too commonplace.

"These look so good. I'll have my all-time favourite, a vanilla *Spaghettieis*."

"Me too, but strawberry." Spaghettieis is a German ice cream dish made to look like a plate of spaghetti, and Leandra loved it almost as much as I did. Thomas ordered coffee ice cream with raspberry sauce and whipped cream, drizzled with dark chocolate.

We were sitting in the heart of Saarbrücken's Johanner Markt, a long, narrow public plaza. Featuring a decorative fountain designed by famous architect Friedrich Joachim Stengel, it's flanked by some of the city's oldest buildings. We tucked into our cold, creamy delights as pedestrians flowed by. German summer initiation rites were not that tough to endure after all. I was falling in love.

Bright and early Monday morning, Thomas, Leandra, and I met the world scrubbed clean. A favourable Rathaus encounter, new resident IDs, a Sparkasse bank account, and apartment keys all hung in the balance. In the busy city centre, we surveyed a plain, white-plastered, three-storey stone-and-glass building attached to the city library. We entered the noiseless corridors of City Hall and went into a tidy citizen registry office.

The room hummed with quiet efficiency. We had climbed stairs to a pleasant second-floor hallway lit by fluorescent lighting and natural light from a row of large windows. The walls were pale blue. A haughty receptionist sat at a desk to our left, and on the right, an automatic photo machine and a ticket dispenser stood against the wall. A row of chairs faced the machine, where three or four men sat, waiting. Ahead, a roomy desk and extended countertop hindered any further public intrusion into a greater space, with about twenty desks topped by computers. Half a dozen employees stared at screens or consulted documents and colleagues, a phone echoed softly nearby, and paperwork rustled faintly.

We sat down. Alert, watchful people were present, staying put for the same prize, *Personalausweis*, or German ID cards. Thomas and Leandra (who is both a Canadian and a German citizen, thanks to being born in Canada to a German parent), were in the right spot. I came to learn that I, being non-German, had come to the wrong office.

A young man with piercing blue eyes and a crewcut welcomed us to his desk. I witnessed Thomas's quick interview exchanges. I understood little of the actual words and followed the motions and gestures to glean meaning through intuition. Here, where German was required, I expected to act the role of spectator. It was a part I dreaded having to get used to in the coming weeks.

First, we needed to feed an automatic machine with enough money to spit out photos for ID cards. I tried to look awake and think spirited thoughts, but it was no use; my face showed every hour of sleep I'd missed over the past week, resulting in a snapshot that resembled a cross between a convict and a grandmother. As Erma Bombeck says, when you look like your passport photo, it's time to go home. I swore to cut up that ID card the moment I departed Germany. Leandra's photo was cute and perky, and Thomas's was fine in an okay sort of way.

Thomas charmed his way through the interview with the clean-cut, astute clerk. He answered innocuous questions about eye and hair colour, height, and occupation; provided proof of our address; and filled out forms. He was ready, organized with his portfolio of passports, invitation letter, and marriage certificate opened up before the smooth-mannered official. I observed the poise of fluency in his prompt answers, a marvellous thing.

In Canada, Thomas spoke with confidence in official settings but often asked for things to be repeated. Certain words or local vernacular caused his forehead to crease in puzzlement. Sometimes it was a problem of understanding others, and other times it was a problem of being understood. On occasion, I was surprised by the relatively ordinary words that were still unfamiliar to him, like "noose," "dank," or "goad." He knew a mountain of botanical and scientific jargon, and it annoyed the hell out of him when he met an English word he didn't know. Sometimes people asked him to repeat himself because of his "European accent." He kept being devilled by the English "v" and "th" sounds. After twenty years, "veil" came out as "whale" and "north" as "norse." I found his German accent endearing as he did my Bajan accent.

The friendly civil servant at the citizen registry liked Thomas's answers so much that he gave him a welcome-to-Saarbrücken gift. It included vouchers for the local zoo, symphony recitals, and the famous operetta by Johann Strauss II, *Die Fledermaus*. We left to await the arrival of IDs for him and Leandra from Berlin. But what about me?

In the end, I comprehended the term *Ausländerin*, a female foreigner, assigned to me. It meant being transferred to Frau Schulte, at the *Ausländeramt*, the foreigner's office, in a distant location. Just her name alone gave me the shudders, on top of the fact that she would decide whether I warranted a year's residence in Germany.

4. An Encounter with Frau Schulte

As a foreigner, you'd better know your German before applying for a German residence card in Saarland unless you have a cellphone with built-in GPS. Even my German husband, who was experienced with bureaucratic entanglements, found the trip to the Ausländeramt—located at the very end of a cul-de-sac, tucked away on the outskirts of town with no signage—adventurous.

Old German cities, like many in Europe, are not necessarily organized on a grid pattern from north to south and east to west, like, say, Vancouver or Saskatoon. Saarbrücken, not a large city, has a spider-web structure that, even six months later, Leandra and I found challenging to navigate. It was with a misplaced sense of complacency that Thomas, Leandra, and I set out on our mission to find Frau Schulte, furnished with an inadequate, tiny city map.

Our destination was located on Lebacher Straße. In order to reach it, we covered a distance of six kilometres in unfamiliar territory. We took a ten-minute bus ride from our guesthouse to downtown. We passed attractive, spacious homes in an upscale residential area and got off at the busiest tram station in the city, near the St. Johann market, the Johanneskirche, and the Rathaus.

Saarbrücken was heavily bombed during the Second World War. Over one thousand people were killed in raids, and over eleven thousand homes destroyed, along with 75 percent of the city. Apart from the striking historic church and City Hall, which had survived the bombardment, much had been rebuilt. On foot, we passed plain, unadorned business fronts with dim overhangs, restaurants, and apartments buildings in white plastered style, rebuilt in the post-war era. Large department stores like Karstadt and structures like Kongresshalle, built in the 1990s, were of clean lines and plenty of glistening glass.

It took us a good hour to locate the Ausländeramt. We entered the building, scrambled up a flight of stairs, and stared into a small waiting room where an electronic monitor, an automatic photo machine, and several patient people stared back, all with a pensive expression as if painted by the same wistful artist.

Sitting there catching my cool, I wanted my palpitations to cease before Frau Schulte summoned me in. In my imagination, she'd turned into a formidable figure at the centre of Saarland's bureaucratic web. Although the waiting room possessed a window, only the merest hint of a hot, thick brew blew in.

Leandra looked as if prickly heat consumed her from the top of her curly mop to her hot feet. She was angry at everyone and no one that afternoon. Thomas stayed buoyant, taking on every hitch with his usual upbeat enthusiasm. He was, however, beginning to grow a bright red mask, the effect of too much summer sun.

We sat watching people come and go—a Romanian family here, a Russian family there, and a Chinese couple—all in a fascinating mosaic. Whoever claimed present-day Germany wasn't multiethnic? When a Ghanaian woman fell short of change for the automatic photo machine, Thomas leaped up, producing the needed amount. For her photo, she posed with a braid standing straight up in the middle of a beautifully coiffured head.

When our number chimed on the electronic display, we stepped into Frau Schulte's office. Nervous about my lack of German but hopeful, I faced her. She represented my first up-close encounter with German bureaucracy, and she held the power to make me instantly glad, sad, or mad.

When Thomas mentioned this power of hers, Frau Schulte scoffed at her bureaucratic control over the entire immigration process. Stylish light-brown hair framed a finely sculpted face. After friendly greetings that eased my tension, she asked me to complete an application form.

"*Sprechen sie Deutsch?*" she asked, smiling. Did I speak German?

"*Nein*," I answered, too quickly. No.

"But my Frau is taking a language course at Saarland University in August," Thomas said quickly in German. Frau Schulte's expression flashed from hesitancy to openness. I wondered how often Frau Schulte had to face prospective immigrants who knew little to no German but who wished to stay and integrate into German life. It wouldn't be easy for her to decide whether to allow them to stay, no matter how compassionate her outlook. Still, she looked pleased with my intention to tackle German in a classroom and the fact that I understood her initial basic question. Responding with a word in German showed something of my willing spirit. But she knew nothing of the jitters hiding beneath my brave mask.

Then a surprising exchange brightened my outlook. Thomas reported that our fifteen-year-old daughter was German. She would live in the city and attend school in Sarreguemines. That piece of information served Frau Schulte well, and the rhythm of the interview shifted. My residency could now be approved, not because Thomas and Leandra were themselves citizens but because Leandra, as a minor, would need her mother's ongoing support in Saarland. I felt the pull of the earth spinning and sensed myself shifting from the periphery where I had been placed in the auspicious air of the Rathaus. Now I was being pushed into the centre of the immigration universe. The term *Ausländerin* did apply but not as intentional exclusion. Frau Schulte decided in my favour.

What a perceptive, warm woman Frau Schulte turned out to be, the opposite of my expectations. The frustration and suspense of being relegated to a different, far-off foreigner office to sort out my residency status collapsed into sweet relief. Perhaps we two women in the family could do the Saarbrücken-Sarreguemines thing all by ourselves after all.

Before sitting in Frau Schulte's office, I had learned that by German bureaucratic rules, our marriage wasn't official, even after twenty-two years. The German appetite for authorization extended beyond what we considered authentic proof. When Thomas had said, "Our Canadian marriage certificate is not enough," I had answered, "Are you kidding me?" But he wasn't joking. Instead, he said something about fake marriages. Being able to produce a Canadian marriage certificate as supporting evidence counted for little in Berlin. In anticipation mode, Thomas had troubled the German Consulate in Halifax before leaving for Germany, requesting an official stamp to uphold our legal documentation. Still not enough. We needed authorization from both Foreign Affairs Canada in Ottawa and the German Consulate in Toronto. Then Thomas had to send translated documents to Berlin for final confirmation. Had the critical approval come through from Berlin, it would have been enough for Frau Schulte. Without it, she leaned on the parent-child support reason to allow my year-long stay in Saarland.

When the notice arrived from Berlin three weeks later, we had to return to Frau Schulte's office to get my ID card. Unfortunately, neither Thomas nor I knew quite how we'd found the office the first time. Again, it took us a good hour to find the same building.

A thin, business-like woman with shoulder-length, dark-brown hair had swapped places with Frau Schulte. After preliminary intros, she handed over my residence card. A heavy weight fell from my shoulders. Looking at the solemn clerk, I said, "Now I won't have to carry my passport everywhere." She shook her head and said, "Unfortunately, you'll still need to always carry your passport."

Shrugging, I rose to leave. *Oh well, I'm living in Germany after all!*

PART II

5. Our New Home and Émilie

Our furnished apartment in Saarbrücken was on the eastern outskirts of the city, off a busy stretch toward the autobahn, on Meerwiesertalweg. Up an inclined driveway, obscured from street view by thick foliage, stood the concrete, three-level building of nine apartments with no elevator—fairly common in Germany. The apartment building was directly opposite the entrance to a wildlife park, Wildpark, and a few minutes from Saarland University. Well situated, in Thomas's opinion.

In the 1960s, the Humboldt Foundation had established dozens of guest houses for international scientists and scholars at universities throughout Germany. Unremarkable in pink and grey colours, the three-level square building typified post-war German architecture. The ten steps from the parking lot to the building's entrance led to another fifty-six steps that tested my vigour whenever I lugged groceries and full laundry baskets upstairs.

One of the first adjustments we had to make was to the apartment. Embracing strange or even uncomfortable situations in new living quarters requires flexibility. The size and arrangement of a new kitchen and bathroom called for a major mind shift. I balked at the absence of familiar spaces, kitchen equipment, and special cooking and baking ware. Thomas, on the other hand, could live like a prince in a tent for most of the year. He loved camping. When we first met, he'd shown me a tent. "What are we doing with that?" I asked.

"We'll tent on camping grounds in Germany, the Netherlands, and France."

I never said, "Oh no, we won't," but my face must have conveyed loads, meaning we never camped even once.

On our first Monday in Saarbrücken, Thomas located the on-campus housing office and secured the apartment keys. The exterior of the building belied its interior. I right away delighted in the indoor spaces. Natural light from large picture windows fell on the walls of the bedrooms and sitting room.

Spacious, with two large bedrooms and a generous bathroom, the apartment had a large enough kitchen to accommodate a small side table for four. *Space is going to be important, if we're to survive each other's nerves for a year.* The bedrooms were coated in light yellow, while the sitting room had walls of subtle lilac. Leandra's eyes widened and her expression changed from hesitancy to enthusiasm as she moved about. "This is nice," she murmured, going into one of the bedrooms, claiming it. "I like this apartment. This room's bigger than mine back home." Her only prior contacts with apartments had been her dad's in Cape Breton and her brother's. Those cramped, uncomfortable residences had begged for vigorous scrubbings.

Thomas beamed. "Like it?" he asked. "I couldn't believe how quickly I got it with phone calls to the university housing office."

"Nice. But look at those trees blocking the view to the street." I understood scaring up good, affordable shelter anywhere in Germany took determination and luck, but still, the view.

Paying me no mind, he added, "Isn't this wonderful?"

We heard steps and turned to greet a stranger. "*Hallo, Ich bin Émilie,*" said the wiry, animated manager of the guesthouse. She shook our hands with force as Thomas did introductions. "Hallo, we're from Canada." He launched into German, switching to French when he discovered Émilie lived in Forbach, in nearby France.

"This apartment is lovely," I said to her. "And so large." Émilie had come to welcome us and lay down basic ground rules. She showed us around, issuing cheerfully toned, no-nonsense instructions in French. Between Leandra's and Thomas's translations, I cobbled together the essentials.

Émilie paused just outside the larger bedroom. A bulky, pink-beige wall closet faced the door. Two single mattresses, fitted together into a low, pine bed frame, were positioned in the room facing a window and a glass door leading to a tiny balcony. Two small wooden nightstands with cute lamps accessorized the bed. The yellow of the walls matched striped bed linens, duvets, and square-shaped, flat pillows.

She said to leave the bedroom furniture in the bedrooms because it was heavy and she was alone cleaning. *I love this room, but the bed, divided down the middle. And those pillows...* Thomas had told me how his childhood sleeps were tormented by large, down-filled pillows flattened to a hardened lump that gave zero support to his head. (After Émilie left, Leandra said, "Those are the dumbest pillows ever," and I winked in agreement.)

Émilie moved to pause next at the kitchen door. She asked that we not put hot pots or pans on the kitchen countertops, except on the stone portion. "This is very, very expensive," she said, tapping the ubiquitous pink-beige veneer covering the kitchen counters and everything else wooden in the apartment—tables, sideboards, closets. We should otherwise use the heavy glass cutting board kept in the bottom cupboard, which she stooped to pull out. "Kitchen utensils are here," she said, pulling open more cupboards and drawers. "And here's the refrigerator." She tugged an off-white, neat cupboard door to reveal a fridge, one-quarter the size of the refrigerator left at home in Canada.

She demonstrated with a press, turn, and turn back the gas stove's safety feature, adding that she cleaned once every week. Her cleaning day for us was Wednesday. *That's something to remember on Tuesdays, before Émilie waltzes in. The apartment is so freaking clean and spare, almost sterile.*

Leandra, Thomas, and I moved in sync with Émilie's motions, actions that she must have performed countless times for past tenants. Leandra soaked it all in, uncertain about an unfurling future in this space. As for me, I was somewhat intimidated by the thought of having an energetic *Putzfrau* in every week to clean our living quarters and observe our living habits. How could she not? In Nova Scotia, we'd never considered such a service. The evident upside would be less cleaning for me. But a cleaning lady constituted a mixed blessing and would require steadfast tolerance and co-operation.

Émilie said she changed the bath towels and kitchen cloths each week, and every two weeks she changed the bed linens.

"We'll leave you to do your work on cleaning day," Thomas promised. He was fine with all the vows of cleanliness and efficiency. "Where shall we leave the towels and bedsheets?" he asked.

She told him to strip the beds and leave the linens in the bedrooms. The towels and kitchen cloths we should put in the laundry basket on Wednesdays outside our apartment door. She added that she cleaned, but doing dishes, pots, and pans was not part of her job. She was very plain-spoken and sure of herself; I wanted her litany of instructions to dry up.

I glanced at Leandra, wondering how her thoughts must be racing ahead, as she calculated the volume of cleaning up after herself she'd have to do. Her cozy room in Nova Scotia brimmed with childhood souvenirs and treasured gifts. She rarely ever had it set in smart order, resulting in sporadic battles with me whenever I urged her to tidy up—roughly three times a year. Now she'd be expected to keep her room straight biweekly.

Despite our misgivings, during the months ahead we fell into a smooth routine. We cleared floors and kitchen counters and stripped beds every second week. We met the cleaning-up-before-the-cleaning-lady-arrived test, and I experienced satisfaction in doing so.

For our entire stay, Émilie's *joie de vivre* remained charming, but she stood firm on household expectations; she was no pushover. Of us three, I was the one who met her the most, when she worked in the apartment building for other tenants. "*Guten Tag*, Mrs. Bouman," she'd greet me. And another time, "Here's a Phillips radio for news and weather reports." She helped Thomas practise his French, telling him stories about her hometown of Forbach, her work experiences with the university, and the education experiences of her two daughters.

As clean and sparkling as we kept the apartment, it just wasn't home. It took weeks before it felt like a comfortable, livable space, probably something to do with its too sanitized, concrete, sparse décor. More maddeningly, I couldn't find a comfortable enough spot to lounge, read, and relax in for any length of time. Granted, a formidable, wooden, two-piece set stood in the living room, a heavy, grey-blue, three-seater sofa covered with a blue blanket and a matching armchair—but it didn't exactly scream relaxation.

I wondered how those pieces ever made it up fifty-six steps for, no matter how hard I pushed, I failed to dislodge them from their rooted spots. They would bestow *goadies* (the Bajanism for a hernia) on anyone. I concluded that they must have been carted up by a crane, entering the apartment through the wide balcony door. On both sides of the sofa's expanse lay cushions of indeterminate hue. Large framed prints with inoffensive floral designs hung above them.

An expandable wooden dining table, with essential pink veneer, and a waist-high sideboard completed furnishings in the living room. The attractive sideboard held glassware on one side and three large empty drawers on the other. Those empty drawers were vital spaces and eventually filled up beyond capacity with a mix of significant papers, receipts, and trash that Thomas found hard to separate from until the urgency of our departure. As long as his papers remained tamped down, nothing peeping out, Thomas was content. Any notices, letters, or documents he couldn't find teased him by hiding in those once-empty drawers. They became dumping grounds and treasure troves, because everywhere else had to be maintained in pristine order. At the same time, they yielded answers to questions like: "Claudette, where's the invoice for the phone?" or "Where's the address Anna wrote down for us?" or "Remember the welcome package that clerk at City Hall gave us? Are the tickets for the Saarland Zoo in there?" They reigned supreme in a concealed mess amidst an apartment culture of shipshape cleanliness.

Several months earlier, I'd peered over Thomas's shoulder in Nova Scotia as we searched Google Earth to satisfy my curiosity.

"Where's the place we're going to stay?"

"Here, look."

I couldn't believe my eyes when the best computer images presented two tiny, blurred rooftops, a postage-stamp-sized parking lot choked by forests, and farther off, a university complex bounded by yet more forests.

One of those small, hazy buildings was the apartment building, and the other housed an entrepreneurial start-up centre. The fears of a Bajan girl materialized. Nothing but woods—beech trees and the occasional red oak or chestnut—encircled our building. I couldn't help but think of the familiar German fairy tale of Hansel and Gretel getting lost in the dark, frightening woods. Disappointment knocked at my chest since our environs looked dark and depressing. Seclusion was not something I excelled at. Where were the city views?

"You mentioned two options for housing. Wasn't one downtown?"

"When I booked, that was taken. This one's way nicer."

"Huh? How would you know when you haven't seen the other?"

"It's noisy downtown." Often hyper and nervous, Thomas was annoyingly calm and self-satisfied. But being churlish wasn't going to help me. Since I was stuck, I'd have to work on my attitude to discover and learn to tolerate the forest's secrets.

Our bedroom window offered a forested prospect. One morning, lying in bed, I frowned at the thick, grey-green trunks in my way. I rose from the bed to gaze out. Shading beech saplings, bushes, and wild plants, thirty-metre trunks drew my eyes upwards toward a green crown. My favourite scenery conjured up landscapes of hazy, far-off hills and fields, dotted with pine chalets and scurrying rivers. In my fancy, people and nature waltzed. Thomas had picked this spot to be "in the green," wrapped by trees. For him, the trees were the view; for me, they blocked the view. No other contrast could illustrate the stark difference between us as a couple than our loves of different landscapes.

Soon Thomas and I started taking forest walks, without Leandra, except once when we bribed her. That one time, on a summer Sunday afternoon, went something like this:

"Leandra, would you like to join us for a walk?" her dad asked.

For her, rambling for the pleasure of it held little appeal. She was goal-focused, had to be going somewhere. "Where are you going?"

"Around the Schwarzenberg for an hour or so," he said, referring to the forest.

She hollered through a shut bedroom door. "No, thanks."

Thomas doesn't often take no for an answer; he made a quick switch. "How about a walk toward the ice cream parlour on Ilseplatz then? And who knows, Barbarossa Bakery may even be in the cards."

It worked, for we heard a stir behind the door and it creaked open. Who cared that our shift in direction around Schwarzenberg cut our walking distance in half? Spaghettieis and bee-sting cake are barefaced con artists.

In mid-July 2013, Thomas and I ventured out for the first time into the dark Schwarzenberg Forest of my overactive imagination. My childhood is shrouded in fears of dark and unfamiliar places, especially woods. I didn't think I could trust anyone we met in secluded woods here in Saarland. Fear of the unknown, of all my familiar fears, has always been my steadiest companion. Many forested places in the world are not safe. I would never enter deep forested wilderness in Nova Scotia, as I fear bears and coyotes.

When we first started walking the Schwarzenberg trail behind our apartment, I felt a twinge of fear as we set off but faked nonchalance. I never admitted it to my husband, not wanting to appear foolish. My pluck paid off. Twenty minutes in, at a forest junction, we stumbled upon hiking signposts pointing every which way to a network of trails crisscrossing Saarland and leading toward a wider Germany. I never thought I'd encounter a forest crossroads with signposts displaying the exact distance to various towns and cities. It impressed upon me the reality of a natural, parallel world.

Thomas asked directions of a passerby in order to avert getting lost. The man said to keep to the circular trail to the university's lands and back to the guest house. As we pushed deeper into the woods, the tall, dark beech, spruce, and pine trees loomed. The north side of the forest looked eerie; I half expected to hear the hoofbeats of phantom horsemen. My imagination pictured shadowy figures crouching behind treelines, set to encircle us, the impudent interlopers. Nevertheless, we plodded on, my heartbeats thudding in my ears. We met no one at all for the next thirty minutes.

My heart lurched when we rounded a bend on the north side of the mountain, for below to the right rested a village. It was Scheidt, inside a hillside at the bottom of a small vale. Red-and-black-slate roofs contrasted against white walls fringed by green foliage. Garden beds of petunias and geraniums bordered stone houses. Farther off to the right and up ahead, we faced a sweep of black, forested mountains.

A rush of traffic broke the silence. Twenty metres below, through thick shrubs, I glimpsed a road. It dissected Scheidt, leading toward Saarbrücken and beyond. My qualms subsided in a heartbeat.

We're not alone. All felt easy. No need to dread strange woods, as any good Bajan would, inhabiting as they do an island cleared of woodlands.

Islanders loved the commotion of being among others and found safety there; they feared the isolation of lonely wilderness. In deep Canadian wilderness, my thoughts would turn to black bears, coyotes, and even grizzlies. In wilderness-rich Nova Scotia, coyotes had attacked and killed a young woman in Cape Breton Highlands National Park once. Thank goodness no such wild creatures lurked here, ready to pounce on guileless wanderers. Images of us being lost forever to civilization vanished as we turned left, onto the east side of the university lands.

Walking uphill, we passed a multilevel garage near the science department and skirted the campus before re-entering forests. Our route led back to Humboldt House. A nearby beech-covered hillside would become research grounds for Thomas in a few weeks. He would search there among leaves and soils, amassing samples, coming to know the trees individually, as if by name.

Familiarity bred a measure of contentment, allowing me the respite of nature available to people who love forests. In time, I grew to enjoy our nature walks around Schwarzenberg, though never to Thomas's extent. At first, my well-developed *yuk*-antennas tingled when I met any strange new crawlies in the woods. I had fallen back into the hole of childhood, where my nightmares were populated with red-ant swarms, millipedes, and centipedes that moved slowly on a sea of creepy legs over every nasty thing in their path. If they landed on me, they could deliver acid-stings or bites. With my growing admiration of Saarland woods, I surprised myself when even the ubiquitous black dung beetles carpeting the forest floor, initially evoking my disgust, now fitted in perfectly.

Over the next months, I discovered the many moods of the woods that Thomas already knew from experience and training. They teemed with activity. People ambled, jogged, and biked there. A variety of animals, chief among them birds, dodged about canopy and floor. Thomas told me that where he grew up, wild boar, faced at night, induced the greatest fear in rural folk until the return of the wolf. The Central European boar, native to Germany, has coarse hair, tiny beady eyes, and sharp teeth and tusks connected to powerful jaws. Thomas heard stories of wild boar attacking humans, causing serious injuries and, on occasion, death. He worried about chancing upon them on our hikes. They left plenty of evidence of nocturnal foraging.

Digging for mast (nuts, roots, and acorns), boars ploughed long stretches of trail. I witnessed this throughout the fall, winter, and spring. Tearing up forest soil, they churned the earth as surely as if yoked oxen had run through. We never met them out on our jaunts, but one night Thomas heard piggy grunts. "Come quick," he waved. Below our balcony in near inky blackness, on the parking lot, a sounder of five boars wagged their stick tails on fat bodies, nudging for mast as they moved. (Boars are social creatures, and a group of them is called a sounder.)

Nonetheless, the forest became a sweet quiet haven for us as it was for the Saarländer we encountered there. People sought out the vast shade of the forest canopy at all hours of the day, alone and in the company of pets and human companions. It dawned on me that these woods were safer than most urban streets anywhere, and I wished the same beauty and serenity could be transported around the world for all people to discover and explore.

In August, Thomas saw a tiny black shape perched inside the flue of a chimney on top of a pavilion shelter used by picnickers.

"An owl," he said, pointing. Skeptical that he could pick out from a distance such a tiny, reclusive creature, I climbed down a steep slope off our trail for a closer look. On approach, the creature pulled its body down to disappear inside the chimney. But I marked its presence for several weeks afterwards on our daily walks, as one would acknowledge a friend.

In October, golden beech leaves fell upon our heads like confetti from heaven. Birds sang louder and sweeter in the Schwarzenberg Forest. Sounds of the woodpeckers' jack-hammering became music to my ears. Little birdie ground hoppers, no bigger than butterflies, flitted in the undergrowth. A pair of amorous pigeons circled our guesthouse daily, cooing and purring, before winging off. Higher in the heavens, buzzards and other birds of prey spun before making a sudden downward swoop and a fatal foray.

When I was a child and young adult, forests were never my first go-to for recreation. Back then, I romped on green fields, occupied backyards, and lounged on coral beaches amid the clamour of friends. Now, I looked forward to walks in an old beech forest preserving natural cavities where owls, bats, and wild boar found refuge and breeding spots. Hiking among the stately trees of Schwarzenberg Forest behind our apartment energized and soothed me.

6. Saarbrücken and Saarland

Soon after settling in Saarland, I visited a lively downtown, ready to explore and take in my new surroundings. A stifling mid-afternoon heat had set in. Criss-crossing a wide plaza, commuters ran from the central railway station to the tram stop; some jumped onto buses or slid into taxis, others waited. Clumps of youths slouched, drinking beer and scuffling. Behind me, shoppers streamed up and down the pedestrian zone. A sleek electric Saarbahn tram blew by. I loved it, ready to settle into this city boasting such a clean transportation option. If only Halifax had trams like Saarbrücken, most challenges of parking on a choked-up peninsula would vanish. Here was an offering to sample from the real German banquet, including daily rides in a tram from Saarland to France.

I absorbed the signs of urban life around me, scurrying commuters and shoppers clicking on cobbled streets, multi-storeyed shops, buses rumbling to stops, and trains fanning out, connecting to major European cities. It reawakened the child in me, one who had enjoyed St. Barnabas Church bus excursions to picnic spots around Barbados. North Point, Bathsheba and East Coast Beaches attracted busloads during lazy vacation times. Using public transportation here would enhance the regard I held for Saarland and Germany and reinforce a sense of social bonding with fellow commuters.

Saarbrücken is a walkable city, and I loved crossing the cobblestoned market square, the plaza alive with vendors, customers, and tourists on a stroll towards the Saar River. Though unpretentious and small in comparison to larger, wealthier cities like Frankfurt, Hamburg, and Munich, Saarbrücken possesses historical treasures for anyone ready to search them out. Standing on land that predated the existence of the "old" nations of Germany and France, where various periods of human settlement were layered on like a palimpsest, taught me first-hand the complexity of Western Europe's history. Thomas revelled in it, but he too admitted so much was unrecorded, unknowable.

One of Germany's sixteen *Länder*, or states, Saarland is shaped like a small-headed, fat-bodied dinosaur, bumpy all around, and encompasses 2,570 square kilometres. The relatively small (in Canadian terms) province of Nova Scotia, at 55,284 square kilometres, is more than twenty times larger than Saarland. Both populations hover around one million.

Saarland challenged an anglophone outsider like me to get to know its special place in a federal Germany. Saarland's history is complicated. Twice in the twentieth century, allied powers separated it from Germany. These separations occurred from 1920 to 1935, as the Territory of the Saar Basin, and again from 1947 to 1956, as the Saar Protectorate.

Most Saarländer live and shop in Saarbrücken, the capital and largest city of the state. The Saar River, which gives the region its name, flows through this lively administrative, commercial, and cultural centre next to the French border. The city came into being after the 1909 merger of Saarbrücken, St. Johann, and Malstatt-Burbach, the traditional industrial and transport centre of the Saar coal basin.

Our alternative to shopping in Saarbrücken was Dudweiler in the opposite direction from downtown. Dudoplatz, the town plaza, possessed a quaint, old-time square at the centre of narrow residential, sometimes winding, cobbled streets. I thought this town charming; Thomas loved it for its small size and industrious, intense local shopkeepers. Independent bakeries, fruit and vegetable stores, organic food and butcher shops, a Netto supermarket, a post office, a bank, and a no-frills clothing store framed the square, giving it a commercial air. Regular bus service connected Dudweiler to surroundings areas. Seven kilometres from Saarbrücken and three kilometres from Saarland University, Dudweiler was best known for its proximity to Saarland University. It was where Thomas's host professor granted him a shared working space as Saarland University owned labs, office spaces, and student residences there.

Thomas loved the high-energy, resolute shop owners, in no time at all, coming close to feeling like a regular engaging with operators. "Most of all, I want to support those small independent businesses rather than always going to the big box superstores." He purchased a Yamaha digital keyboard from a musical instruments store for Leandra there within two weeks of arriving in Saarland. Later, he bought special items: "A genuine Solingen nail file at a Drogerie, a daily *Frankfurter Allgemeine Zeitung* newspaper, and fountain pen ink cartridges at a *Papier-und Schreibwarenhandlung*." I had to get used to a German "Drogerie" (drugstore) not selling medicines but a wide assortment of cosmetics and toiletries resembling Canada's Shoppers Drug Mart—without the pharmacy section.

In a nostalgic mood, my new friend Anna, who I met one morning at Saarland University, once said, "Dudweiler used to be so much more vibrant than what it is now." Within thirty-five years, the population had shrunk from 29,000 to 19,600. She was saddened by the change in fortunes. We learned from an older disgruntled local how everything was now centred in Saarbrücken to the neglect of Dudweiler. She had been forced to travel daily for seven kilometres to Saarbrücken for work.

From Thomas, his friend Karl and Anna, I heard about the historic significance of coal mining and steelmaking. Saarland reminded me of Nova Scotia with Sydney Mines and other coal mining towns. Decline in coal mines and steelworks in Nova Scotia depleted local economies. Saarland also closed its coal mines. It still produces steel and has had a long history of developing other products that brought some wealth to the region, including pottery, optical instruments, machinery, and construction materials. A major contrast between Saarland and my home province is that while Saarland lies in the heart of Europe, a continent of five hundred million people, Nova Scotia is situated on the northeastern periphery of North America and is sparsely populated. In hindsight, I regret not visiting a coal mine or mining museum in Saarland.

A week later, on an unhurried Saturday in the city, I leaned over a stone bridge checking the Saar's emerald waters. That bridge dated back to Roman times, about the first century CE, as part of a road from Metz (eastern France) to Worms (western Germany). In a city guide, I learned that road crossed a north–south route from Trier to Strasbourg on the river's right bank. On the ancient road was a settlement called Vicus Saravus (Saar village). The bridge was a good example of the presence of ancient history all around me. I imagined legions of Romans trekking across long stretches of these lands, building forts, roads, and bridges as they went.

Thomas and I rediscovered daytime life outside the strictures of work. One day during our first month, we strolled along the bank of the Saar River to attend a beer garden and festival where we listened to folksy music and ate waffles. Over several months, we visited historic landmarks in and around the city. Another striking stone bridge spanning the Saar was built in 1546. We explored the lovely Gothic Church of St. Arnual, in the St. Arnual district of Saarbrücken. It was a former Augustinian monastery dating back to the twelfth century.

As an example of the complexities of historic migrations, the St. Arnual district was once the settlement area of a tribe called the Mediomatricians. They were Celts in the area of what is now eastern France, Saarland, and Rhineland-Palatinate. Today's Metz, in France, emerged from what used to be its capital.

The attractive eighteenth-century Saarbrücken Palace and monuments in the colourful St. Johanner Markt dominated the old city landscape. Along with the palace, Prince Henry William built a number of churches, including the baroque Ludwigskirche for Protestants and the baroque basilica for Catholics on the other side of the Saar River. I asked Thomas why the need for two similar churches designed by the same architect, Friedrich Joachim Stengel.

"The eighteenth-century sovereign was Protestant. His people were Catholics. Keeping different religions at peace cost a lot," he said.

"And that's not cynicism, it's fact?"

He nodded. A long history of Catholicism versus Protestantism shaped this landscape.

The neo-Gothic Lutheran Johanneskirche with the highest tower of the city (seventy-four metres) served as an excellent orienting point. It stood in the heart of downtown, near the bustling pedestrian zone and tram station.

Picturesque St. Johanner Markt and surroundings were of a basalt-stoned plaza, *Gassen* (tight gaps or closes), inner courtyards, and ancient looking buildings reminiscent of medieval marketplaces. Specialty clothing and shoe boutiques lined the plaza side by side with affordable restaurants like Kartoffel House. I fell in love with the old-world market square where, three times a week, buyers scrutinized pears, apples, berries, potatoes, leeks, baked goods, sausages, meat, plants, and bunches of bright flowers sold by small, independent vendors. Leandra was captivated by the second-hand bikes.

Another downtown attraction, the *Staatstheater*, was destroyed in the Second World War but reopened in 1948. A pallid sandy colour, its plain plastered architecture was unspectacular. It bulged at the front, ringed by a forbidding circle of sixteen hefty, six-metre-tall pillars. A great many windows shone from the front and sides. On a visit for the opera *Die Fledermaus*, Thomas, Leandra, and I enjoyed the rounded lobby with impressive floor-to-ceiling glass panels around the central auditorium and stage, though in the crush at intermission, the lobby felt claustrophobic, choked by the crowds.

Another weekend, we wandered through Saarland's art museum, spread across three sites. We stopped in at two, the Old Collection and Moderne Galerie. A white, three-storey, historic administration building next to Saarbrücken Palace housed the Old Collection. I stood transfixed before paintings by seventeenth-century still-life painter Abraham Mignon. I found his rendering of grottoes and of nature's gifts—game, fish, flowers, and fruit—startling in their impact. The museum also surprised us with an exhibit of a thick, intricate gold necklace once owned by a Celtic duchess.

Moderne Galerie, integrated into the Saar riverbank, displayed *Great Gaia*, a contorted outdoor sculpture of silver silhouetted against a green lawn. Thomas disliked the contemporary works inside. "Conceptual art doesn't even begin to describe it," he scoffed. A standalone chair and a video of a train travelling without end were but two examples. I, too, found the "subjective photography" puzzling. I preferred classic aesthetics, techniques, and materials in art.

The foreignness of German place names, street names, and historic references froze my brain and twisted my tongue, making them hard for me to remember. Standing on the banks of the Saar River and touring ancient bridges, museums, churches, fountains, and market squares opened up a world of history and culture. I marvelled at this country, which the Celts and Romans had occupied for centuries before giving way to the Germans and the French.

In 2021, at home in Nova Scotia, I pulled out a German map. "Why is Saarland carved out of Rheinland-Pfalz?" I asked Thomas.

"It's not. Let me show you." He grasped his old historical world atlas, and we squinted at pages of finely printed illustrations of tribal Western Europe dating back to pre-Roman times. Before long, I was lost. Mapping and remapping of Western European boundaries ran rampant for centuries. Thomas explained we were looking at the results of conquests, migrations, and settlements over millennia, the rise and fall of tribes, duchies, and empires. These regions changed hands over and over again. At some point, firm country and provincial boundaries emerged. "It's a mixture of long history, different language groups, and politics, to name a few factors," he said.

I couldn't help comparing Saarland's history to that of my two homelands. Historically, the Amerindian Barrancoid people were the first settlers to make Barbados home. It was then settled and colonized in the 1620s by the British, and it remained a British colony until independence in 1966. In comparison, neighbouring St. Lucia exchanged between the British and French fourteen times between 1663 and 1814. Canada's oldest British settlement, St. John's, Newfoundland, dates back to 1497. Saarland has a deeper, more varied, and layered history involving Celtic, Roman, German, and French conquests, civilizations, and occupations. What a wealth of learning lay within my grasp, even without easy access to the language.

7. To England

In July, the three of us piled into a car and hit the road for England. We planned to stay in Reading, using it as a base to launch out and explore Salisbury, Stonehenge, Stratford-upon-Avon, Bath, and London. Place names and characters from Jane Austen's life and novels rose up before Leandra. Thomas suggested driving through the night to reach the early morning ferry at Calais, in northern France. "I don't want to drive for the first time in England at night going to Brighton and Reading," he said. Leandra and I also saw enormous value in arriving in daylight to enjoy the English scenery. Off we went, in a rental car. I supplied Thomas with a steady source of water and snacks as he focused on the road and we whistled along via France's Route Nationale.

I squinted as we swished past grassy meadows, fields lush with bushy beets, and wheat flagging in gentle night winds. Arrow straight rows of vines in vineyards ranged beneath the face of a midsummer sky. The sound of the car's tires droned soothingly. I have little memory of the landscape because of the night, but sometimes we turned through tight, bumpy, cobbled streets. One such turn, around midnight, took us through a small place close to Cambrai, where we stopped for refreshments at a no-fuss café. Curious villagers, all men, observed us as we ordered drinks, lounging outside in near tropical night air. We reached the ferry terminal in Calais at dawn, well before departure time.

The English customs officer, a woman with an easy, round face, and darting eyes examined our passports and handed back Thomas's and Leandra's without so much as *pickin' she teet'*. Then she piped: "Claudette, how long will you be staying in the UK?" Born in the island bizarrely referred to as "Little England" ever since Bajans had joined British armed forces during the Second World War, I was outraged.

Wait a minute. Why am I being singled out and treated differently? Is this a Black thing? Does this lady think Thomas is bringing Black women with Canadian passports into good old England to land on the dole? And then I thought, *Would she single me out like this if she knew how much I adore Elton John?*

I bit my tongue and answered with a polite: "For six days, just like my husband and daughter."

"Thank you. Enjoy your trip."

"Thank you." I gave her a nasty cut-eye.

I was thrilled at my first crossing of the English Channel, even as a secret fear of the sea gnawed at my insides. A superstitious mother fostered it in me. She often warned me and my siblings as we bolted to the beach, "Remember, the sea doan have nuh back door." Now, my joy overwhelmed my fear for the moment.

Boarding the ferry ahead of time, very early in the morning, I must have looked as bedraggled as I felt.

My thoughts zipped to long ago when my older brother, Theo, brimmed with excitement at becoming a brand-new seaman on a cargo ship out of Bridgetown, Barbados, heading for Liverpool, England. Returning after his first stint out, he brought back a small red-and-white vinyl record player and a stack of singles, among which was a song called "Crocodile Rock."

For the next few months, the little red-and-white record player did hard duty. Luckily, Theo didn't mind me playing it. To begin with, he avoided home whenever he could. He spent his spare time chillin' up the hill with a trusty gang of boys who, like him, knew little of what to make of their lives pierced through with deprivations.

Nobody at home had ever owned a record player, and having a record collection was a true novelty. Such possessions belonged to the rising working and middle classes, prosperity that simply did not fit the Gittens family just yet. Sometimes life was made bearable by the American pop tunes regularly aired on the non-stop local Rediffusion radio broadcast.

Our family's chattel house in Barbados, a sleepy grey with white trim, sat on a ground sill allowing entry to a dank earth cellar from the backyard. Our mother sometimes stored yams and sweet potatoes there. Inside, the house was stifling, without any real sense of coziness or personal possession. Constructed of pine, the simple chattel house comprised two gabled roof sections. A small front part served as sitting, recreational, and dining room during the day and transformed into a bedroom for two boys at night. In the second part, three girls had the luxury of sharing a bed and bedroom. On either side of the hallway, cardboard partitions separated us girls from the grown-ups' sleeping arrangements on the other side.

When we were still children, before we moved into this area farther away from the crowded environs of Bridgetown, we all slept in one bedroom in a one-roof house. Back then, our parents slept on the bed, and we four children (baby number five had not yet arrived) slept in a row on bedding made up of worn-out clothing and sheets on the floor. The older children's feet stretched out under the bed.

That was all in the past. Ever since relocating to the airier St. Barnabas, the potential for moving up in the world stared my family in the face. Roomier residential lots had become available in the area through a government relocation plan, and when their opportunity came, my parents snatched hold.

Living in St. Barnabas meant a new school, different neighbours, and new playmates. I accepted the challenge of a fight the very first week in my new school, Pine Primary. I vigorously traded blow for blow as an initiation rite, not about to take spiteful Beverley's last lash, as I'd been taught at home. Stern-faced teachers tugged us two Tasmanian devils apart, dragging us off to the headmaster's office. There we were both promptly and suitably rewarded by Mr. Husbands's thick leather strap and rebuked for hitting each other. No questions were asked, just lashes and admonitions generously and deftly extended. I felt a rage in my bosom I hardly understood, for betrayal by school authorities signified the worst punishment. I wished for the courage to kick headmaster Husbands in the shins and run home on my seven-year-old legs, never to see him or that unfair school again. But at home, other, stiffer consequences would have followed such an act. Parental understanding could only be longed for. Why did my parents never ask what happened?

Life proceeded. In 1963, the newest and last member of the family arrived, little Katie with velvety smooth skin and curly, soft hair. The baby was an inconvenience, requiring 24/7 care, as any newborn does. My mother, Adella, Della to friends, had endured the pregnancy, anxious to shed the fetus within her. Existing below the poverty line all her life, she was eager to work again as a domestic, a field labourer, a janitor—whatever became available. My father, Andy, worked at the island's ironworks foundry in Bridgetown. When it closed in 1968, two years after national independence, peril emerged from the shadows. He prowled the scorching streets of Bridgetown, looking for an available, steady labour job for months. He finally found it a year later as a porter for R. L. Seals and Co., the island's largest food distributor.

When Katie turned two, she was parcelled up and dispatched without ceremony to live with an aging paternal aunt and her common-law husband so that my mother could keep working. Such informal family arrangements ran rife in Barbados then, and they still do. It was an arrangement that suited everybody except sad little Katie, who would grow into childhood missing her big brothers and sisters. Auntie Glenda loved the little girl's warm, innocent presence, showing affection by giving shelter, keeping her clean, and spoiling her with, among other things, the creamy breadfruit cou-cou and salt fish Katie loved. Once a week, Uncle Eric bundled her into his taxi-car for a road trip and a home visit. Katie's excitement couldn't be contained. "Why dat yar following we yar?" she'd squeal, twisting her neck at any random car that happened to trail them at the time. At three she couldn't yet say *car*.

When Katie was four and a half, my mother dressed her in a royal blue school uniform she'd sewn herself, marched her down through the neighbourhood gap, and deposited her at the door of the reception classroom. Della then promptly disappeared from view, hiding behind a tree. She was afraid school authorities wouldn't admit Katie because of age and avoided confronting the unsmiling, rude reception class teacher. Upshot was, Katie started school at age four. With no love for cute little kids, the rough-mannered teacher cast Katie a hard glance and ordered her to sit down and be quiet. Katie didn't cry even though her shiny, patent leather shoes pinched.

I was by now in the last stage of primary school, wishing that I didn't have to mind a little sister who knew nothing about the inner workings of catty girl cliques and the cool moves of ten-year-olds. This sisterly caregiving caused embarrassment. Taking Katie's hand, I'd walk her home for a quick bite at lunchtime, then walk back through the school gate to spend the rest of the lunch hour trudging the scruffy school grounds, towing my small charge. Astonishingly, it never occurred to me to play with her. My friends and peers, meantime, competed in energetic counting games, hopscotch, and Simon Says. Others, against parental advice, walked along the front road to meet the little-girl boss of us and escort her back to school as the "queen bee" we accepted her to be. My two older siblings, Theo and Cheryl, already attended two different secondary schools kilometres away. I, the third child, stood as an uneasy centrepiece, occupying a middle ground. Mackie, a year younger than I, attended my primary school in class three. But I hardly saw anything of him in or around the schoolhouse. He kept to his own group of wild ones tearing around.

By the time I left Pine Primary a year later, Katie, now in Infants One class, showed more ease at school. The head woman in charge of serving milk and biscuits at break offered to look out for her, as no official break or lunch-time supervision existed. Mackie was still at the school, but he was unreliable. Katie would trail the short distance to school with him, return home for a drink of syrupy lemonade and a piece of white bread covered in corned beef at lunchtime, and run back to school again for the afternoon session.

By age fourteen, I had settled into a dual life—one at home where I barely tolerated my parents who knew nothing about *anything*, and another at school where friendships thrived, and I learned about a different way of living from the hell I felt trapped inside. I depended on the island's well-developed public transportation system to travel to and from Foundation Girls' School, way out of my neighbourhood. At first, the school's atmosphere and practices seemed alien, far removed from the familiar ways of home and neighbourhood, but after three years, I felt a close affinity to my friends, peers, and teachers. There I basked in a spirited, stimulating glow, absent at home.

I admitted to no one, least of all to myself, that I felt more at home at school than at home. I felt straitjacketed there. Especially with my sweat-stained, morose father in the house—he scared me. A tall, spare-boned man, his big hands thick with fingers, hung at the end of strong limbs. A strained tension tied him and my tired mother together, its roots deepening with years of unrequited dreams, mostly on my mother's side. Admonitions rained down on our heads for common childish mistakes, and gentle words and praise were boulders in his throat. Sometimes my betrayal cut like a sharp blade, but I just covered it up, lying to myself. Why was I born into the wrong family?

We all regretted my older brother, Theo, throwing away an opportunity for a decent education. He hated school, did nothing brilliant, and made a point of failing every single subject he attempted. He got into spectacular trouble, fought, stole money, lied about it, and regularly got thrashed at home. There seemed to be no end to the troubles he rained down upon our mother's long-suffering head. One day, he took it into his puny brain to run away. He ended up living briefly at a cousin's, Maria, who wanted nothing to do with sheltering a teenage boy. She stomached him for a few days but turned him in the direction of home at her first chance. She desperately begged my mother not to beat Theo when he arrived home.

"Spare him, Della," she pleaded. It didn't work. The motto in our little house said: "Hard ears, you won't hear? Hard ears you will feel!" And so said, so done. It was bend or be broken.

Still, what was to be done with this boy, fast turning into a young man? If warnings, scoldings, and lickings didn't work, what would? Enter fortuitous, casual fate.

In the working-class neighbourhood lived a few men whose outer trappings marked them as doing fine for themselves and their families. Their houses appeared larger, grander, crowned by haloes of soft light. These men met the steady, envious gazes of their neighbours proudly, head-on at every turn, for they happened to be among the first to acquire indoor plumbing in the early '60s. Meanwhile, whenever a member of the Gittens household needed to do a number one or number two, they sat in an outdoor toilet with a wooden seat over a reeking hole in the ground. Sporadic application of lime directly into the pit latrine did little to alleviate a seething, robust mass of cockroach invasions, especially at night. Childhood nightmares abounded where the main actors crept over my nether regions while doing my private acts. But the children of the fortunate men always wore beautiful, store-bought clothes and sometimes showed off gold wristwatches. Their fathers either worked on ships docking at the Deep-Water Harbour in Bridgetown as merchant seamen or as seasonal farm workers in a heavenly country called Canada.

Someone, their identity lost in the muddle of informal neighbourhood gossip, relations, and connections, informed our mother about the possibility of Theo going to sea. It was likely Nester, up the hill, living in one of those newly built, affordable wall houses for government workers begrudged by others not so fortunate. Several years later, Nester would help Della again, this time securing work for her as a janitor, cleaning Pine Primary School, which we had all attended.

The solution for Theo to work as a seaman sounded nothing less than amazing. It would get him out of the house and the neighbourhood where all he did was hang around up the hill, at best bullying younger boys and at worst pelting small stones at girls who ignored his wolf whistles. After hangin' out, he'd head home to eat or sleep. A seaman's job would set him straight, help him learn some discipline. (Mona, a beloved cousin, counselled Theo wisely: if he didn't listen up and mind the senior sailors, he could get thrown overboard and drown at sea, with no one asking any questions.) Best of all, he could earn good money to help out at home and eventually become self-sufficient. One small snag, resolved only by the passage of time, reared up, blocking the way of hopes and dreams: he had to be at least sixteen.

At the time this amazing idea surfaced, Theo had just turned fifteen and, not surprisingly, he continued being fifteen for a long, hairy time. But with the help of Trevor, an experienced seaman, mother and son readied all the necessary papers, suffered life's vicissitudes, and waited. They awaited not only his next birthday but also a ship that would hire him on as a novice sailor. The once plentiful supply of sailor jobs on shipping lines from Liverpool, Bristol, and Nova Scotia seemed to be drying up. But eventually, Theo's ship did come in. He was hired and sailed off into the horizon from the Deep-Water Harbour, close to picturesque Carlisle Bay. I don't remember the name of the shipping line, the date, or the time he disappeared off the west coast of the island. I was in school on the big day.

Theo's job was to be a mess boy, cooking and cleaning in the kitchen for sailors on board. He loved it, although he never spoke much about it at home. It afforded him an expansive kind of freedom he'd never before experienced. Now in his hands existed real independence and opportunities to work and see the world at the same time, visiting port cities in England, the west coast of Africa, and other places. As arranged prior to departure, he started sending some of his earnings back home monthly for saving. At the time, the early '70s, it seemed like loads of money. He must have worked on a British shipping line because his pay came home in British currency. When it was changed into Barbadian dollars, each pound equalled $4.80.

When Theo arrived home after several months at sea, he was loaded with cash, treats, and cool things—clothing items, cute handbags, and that small red-and-white record player. A pile of vinyl records spilled out as we tore through his baggage. Among his record collection were double-sided singles by Elton John. "Daniel" was melancholic, just plain sad, and "Goodbye Yellow Brick Road" gripping and nostalgic. Now, right here at home were records I could play and sing along to until I knew the lyrics by heart, not having to wait forever to hear my favourite Motown tracks played on the radio when everyone else came running to listen and loudly join in. For me, hypnotic songs assuaged the life of want in the same way frequent churchgoing did for the older women.

Playing those songs over and over again, I grew to love them all, but my favourite became "Crocodile Rock." After school or on weekends, whenever I could, I'd creep to the player sitting on a small mahogany coffee table in a corner of our front room. I'd lift the hard, clear-plastic cover with the arm and needle underneath. Freeing a vinyl record from its paper sleeve, I'd set it on the black turntable. I'd blow dust from the fragile needle, position it gently on the waiting record, and switch on the player. It played with batteries, as our house had no electric power until 1978, when my mother, my siblings, and I moved out for good. Sometimes the batteries were dead, and then I'd suffer a pang of disappointment. When they worked, paradise reigned, surrounded by a wall of sound.

I loved "Crocodile Rock" for its crazy, upbeat lyrics and wicked melody. I didn't know who this Elton John fella was, but he could surely rock a tune. It caught the heart and soul of a teenage girl who yearned to be free of constraints, scarcity, and daily griefs. I imagined myself holding hands and skimming stones with a beautiful boy and wearing tight dresses on Friday nights at forbidden house parties, regular events in near and far-off neighbourhoods. "Crocodile Rock" was echoed in a song that came a little later, "December, 1963" or more familiarly, "Oh, What a Night!" by The Four Seasons. Those kinds of pop songs stirred my teenage pot, mixing roiling imagination with adolescent desires. They conjured up a world parents stubbornly denied their teenagers but which lived on as ever-so-romantic, fun, and free. Freedom to be, to ride around in an old Chevy, steal kisses, and do even more with a handsome young man after a rollicking time rocking round the clock. Wasn't that every young girl's dream?

But even inside the driving, insistent beat of the melody, the lyrics changed. It wasn't always going to be, *oh, what a night!* with romantic trysts and helter-skelter getaways, doing a thing called the crocodile rock. In the song, years passed and something essential died: Suzie took off with some foreign guy, leaving behind the singer with only mere memories of never having known a better time. In the disappointing world of St. Barnabas, a dream of infatuation with a gorgeous beau gave way to daily reality and hard truths. What was to be done at home around those miserables, an alcoholic father and a severe, glum crone?

Time solves everything, and one even survives the worst case of teenage angst. Theo's job as a seaman permitted the purchase of land and the building of a new house that appeared large, grand and crowned by haloes of soft light. But his personal life affected a confused clutter for a while before settled family life arrived in the person of a dynamic new wife. Even so, modern conveniences reached the Gittens: electricity, refrigerator, television, and indoor plumbing, all sans our father, who stayed on in the old house. I fought my way through college and university, eventually accepting a teaching position. Lucky Cheryl acquired and advanced into a job right out of high school in the fast-growing daycare sector. Katie grew into a fine, independent woman, changing jobs every few months for a time until she secured a demanding position with a profitable supermarket in bustling Bridgetown. Mackie's life hung in the balance; not everything fell into place. For a while, he resembled a piece of driftwood tossed onto the Constitution River. With time, he matured, adopting that big-boned stature of our father. As a popular market man, he sold vegetables, fat sweet potatoes, chunky yams, and leathery-skinned breadfruits from a Suzuki van parked beside the city's Lower Green Market.

The small, ever more forlorn chattel house still rested squat on its ground sill, crumbling quietly around its last occupant. On hushed nights, our old man, Andy, could be heard moaning about the good times he never had and that he guessed he never would. That worn out, cheap record player and the feverish times spent singing and dancing to "Crocodile Rock" were all but forgotten.

The ferry crossing from Calais to Dover took ninety minutes, filled with more of a weary commuter crowd than hyper tourists. Although seeing the white cliffs of Dover took my breath away, what followed was a tiring journey navigating country roads and byways to Brighton. Along the way, quaint red brick homes peeped over shoulder-high hedgerows, and mansions were well hidden behind acres of treed lots. Our brief time in Brighton left impressions of crowds, a bazaar on a pier, and taking photos outside the Royal Pavilion. The best part was a relaxing sit-down in the café of the Brighton Museum and Art Gallery.

Then we rushed away, Thomas in a panic that I shared to avoid London traffic and reach Reading before nightfall.

Reading was a perfect launching pad for what we wanted to do. On day two, we found the location of a school Jane Austen had attended and explored a museum of rural English life brimming with pre–Industrial Revolution tools and equipment. We were charmed by the dry humour of a young man there who remarked Reading's best asset was that it possessed countless connections by rail, bus, and car to other places, making it a great place to get away from. We caught a heaving train to London to walk famous streets and shopping districts, sightseeing and touring historic locations and museums.

Thomas looked relaxed, the pressure of driving off his shoulders. I was loving it, having much more fun than navigating in a car. Nevertheless, when we disembarked at a packed London station, I felt a sudden rush of confusion and loss of bearings in the swarms. I was learning how much large crowds and cities disoriented me. Leandra's eyes shone, for London lit her up. Thomas oriented us with a map that Leandra grasped in a few seconds while I tagged along.

Leandra wanted to go inside Westminster Abbey, but her hopes were dashed by crazy-long queues. No one hated queues more than her dad. She and Thomas then went inside the National Gallery on Trafalgar Square for a few hours. I sat on the wide concrete steps, my back to massive concrete pillars. A group of youth sat nearby, munching from boxes of Chinese takeout and chatting. It was all I could do to stop myself from stretching out to lie down. I gazed across the way toward the centre of the square where two fountains commemorating long-dead British admirals displayed elaborate sculptures of mermaids, mermen, tritons, and dolphins. I was so whacked I could not focus on any one thing for long. I let my mind wander.

I had heard so much about Trafalgar Square from Barbadians who had moved to England. The British Nationality Act of 1948 gave citizens of the United Kingdom and its colonies status and the right to settle in the UK. That and encouragement from British government campaigns in Caribbean countries led to waves of immigration. Between 1948 and 1971, nearly half a million people moved from the Caribbean to Britain, which faced severe labour shortages after the Second World War. They were responding to the need for workers in the transport system, postal service, and health service. Many Barbadian immigrants had faced overt, stark racism for the first time in their lives in the cruel "mother country," and, like people who had experienced war, often preferred to keep their private hurts to themselves.

After the National Gallery, Thomas, Leandra, and I took leave from the crowds, boarding another crammed train heading back toward Reading. Leandra groaned when she turned to leave. Wistful, she was forsaking all the sights of this megacity after having had the time of her life. She'd glimpsed only a bit of the immensity of London. For me, one day in London had been enough and Thomas, not a lover of big cities or crowds, had endured it for our sakes.

Over the next five days, we set out for adventures to Bath, Salisbury, and Stonehenge, joined a theatre audience in Stratford-upon-Avon, and travelled to Oxford. Salisbury and Bath were the highlights of the England tour for me. Salisbury Cathedral easily ranked as one of the most stunning church buildings I'd ever seen, up there with Notre Dame of Paris and the Dom of Cologne. We learned a dash of its history from an enthusiastic, cheerful greeter at the cathedral door. Wearing fancy red and gold regalia, he pointed out fine art on the ceiling and encouraged visitors to peek at a copy of the famous Magna Carta sealed under oath by King John at Runnymede, on the bank of the River Thames. As I had learned long ago in college history in Barbados, the charter of rights was imposed upon a harassed King of England by a group of his not-so-submissive subjects. People of all descriptions and ethnic origins strode through the doors and were drawn to a glass case bearing the document as if it was the most precious diamond in the universe. Leandra ate up tales of Salisbury as fast as they escaped the speaker's lips. On the suggestion of the greeter, she and I sought out the adjoining bookstore. I bought local resident Edward Rutherfurd's *Sarum*, a meaty historical novel tracing the turbulent history of England over a period of ten thousand years.

We next made a visit to Stonehenge, in a chaos of construction, tourists, and food trucks, before heading to scenic Bath. The historic Pump Room, serving as a tea shop and restaurant adjacent to the Roman Baths, was a must see for Leandra. We stepped inside a large grand chamber room with rounded recesses at both ends, one for musicians. I admired its ornate touches, cream walls and high-ceilinged grandeur. Quiet reigned. A couple dozen tables, gracefully laid out, awaited missing customers. Leandra and I went next into the baths, joining dozens of people to observe in wonder hot springs still spilling out after millennia.

With much longing on Leandra's part, we left Reading in the wake of our return ferry crossing. Driving back to Germany via France, we stopped at Reims Cathedral, a welcome break before we hustled along on the Route Nationale, devouring tarmac through northern France, back to Saarbrücken.

8. The Sprachkurs - German Classes

Never knew before what eternity was made for.
It is to give some of us a chance to learn German.
– Mark Twain

As August edged closer, a nagging fear grew within me. Going back into the classroom, this time on the wrong side of the teacher's desk, and trying to master a foreign language at age fifty-six was going to be a steep hill to climb. *Too steep?* Leandra was scared too.

Leandra and I shared a common cause in our misgivings. But our points of view differed on the social chart. Her worries sprang not from having to learn or use a foreign language, whether German or French; she was fluent in French, having attended French school since kindergarten, and she wanted to learn more German. Her fears arose from leaving home, friends, and school and being surrounded by strangers in a new school setting. I, on the other hand, was not scared of meeting new people; a teacher is, if nothing else, a people person. I was frightened about being tongue-tied when I didn't know what to say or how to say it in German, of looking silly when I made mistakes. Social and emotional safety rugs were being pulled from under Leandra's feet. The security rug being yanked away from me was the English language. These anxieties underpinned our lives in Germany.

"August ends in anguish" is how I defined my experience with *Sprachkurs*, the conversational German language course offered at Saarland University. International students arrived early on registration day. Next day, we nervously met at breakfast tables in the university Mensa.

If I asked "Where's the Mensa?" on any university campus in Germany, people would know instantly that I meant the cafeteria. Thomas, Leandra, and I would take advantage of our university guesthouse status to "feast" at the Mensa, a unique institution rooted in German university culture.

After our student breakfast, we completed an online, hour-long language pre-test, which would be used to divide students of a similar level into teaching groups. Leandra and I had taken German classes in Halifax. We attended one ninety-minute evening class a week, participating in little-to-no German during the rest of the week when preoccupation with work and family life absorbed me. It didn't help that Thomas hadn't made a sure effort to teach us German, much to his mother's dismay, and the raised eyebrows of traditionally minded folks we met in Saarland.

While working through the pre-test, I became overwhelmed. After half an hour, I tried to return to a previous page and got knocked out of the exercise. I panicked, tried to restart, and ended up being the last one out of the room. With a sinking feeling, I knew I'd botched it. Next day, when the student crowd waited to be sorted into groups, I was among the last to be called, assigned to the class of beginners. It was humiliating. I didn't land in the same group as Leandra, who had made it two rungs higher up the language ladder. "Oh, mum!" she said, giving me a sympathetic look when I told her what group I was in. I saw relief in her face, too. She was liberated from her mother, at least for Sprachkurs.

During weekdays in August, I attended classes from 9:00 A.M. to 3:00 P.M. with a noon-hour lunch break. The exception was on Fridays, when classes ended at 1:30. My classmates and I were introduced to basic conversational German. I grabbed hold of the chance to become acquainted with fellow Sprachkurs participants from around the world, ranging in age from eighteen to twenty-four. Friendly and curious, the group of five comprised two young women from Italy, a young man from Portugal, a female Chinese student, Joyce, studying law in England, and myself.

I really liked that our class joined all Sprachkurs students for planned social and cultural events like visiting Metz and Trier and for a wine-sampling trip. One Saturday morning in early August, Leandra and I and forty other students waited on the university plaza, chattering. Mere weeks into our year in Germany, we boarded a bus for a cultural experience: a scenic tour of Saarland ending with a *Weinprobe*, a wine-tasting.

Sitting by myself, I viewed the unfamiliar landscapes, villages, towns, and fields. We travelled north, passing through Saarlouis, Dillingen, and Merzig to reach Mettlach, where we paused to view the Saarschleife, a tourist attraction that's also known as the Great Bend in the Saar. From a lookoff in a lovely recreational park, we looked far down below at the ribbon of the Saar River making its U-turn amidst rugged terrain and rich greenery.

"Look at that! Isn't it beautiful?" one of the student tour guides said.

"Wow!" I replied. From high up behind me, voices drifted down. A skywalk among treetops ended at the great bend. *I wish I could see it from up there.* Leandra chummed with a cohort a few years older than her. After two intense weeks of classes, lunches, and group activities, she mingled easily with Joyce and company. From the Saarschleife we were bused on to historic Trier in Rheinland-Pfalz. Founded in 16 BCE, Trier is Germany's oldest city and an important site for ancient art treasures and monuments. The student guides showed us Roman ruins, a museum, and the Porta Nigra, the best-preserved city gate from the ancient world. One memorable fact about the city was that Karl Marx was born there in 1818.

Toward early evening, our bus carved its way through slopes of vineyards, pulling up to a tidy, garden-like entrance. We stepped into a spacious wine cave, its dim interior cool and spotless. As we settled at heavy wooden tables, the wine master introduced himself and gave us a list of white wines, mostly Rieslings. He then moved step by step up the list, pouring a steady stream for sampling with the help of assistants, everything said in German. In all, I must have tried six different wines, with generous helpings of cheeses, sausage, ham, and chunks of black rye bread. Under the influence of too much alcohol, Russian and Mexican groups rivalled each other in jolly and loud singing.

I sat with five young women, a merry mix from Brazil, Russia, Spain, and Italy. I could make out Leandra on the far side of the cave, pretending to be motherless with teenagers from Holland, England, Tunisia, Italy, and Georgia. She told me later, "I'm only fifteen, and they were offering me all kinds of wine. Nobody cared." In Nova Scotia, she wouldn't even have been allowed into this kind of establishment. I noticed she showed remarkable restraint, refusing to touch any alcohol. Her thirstier table companions divided her spoils among themselves. They became increasingly merrier and louder as the event went on, as did I.

To seal an unforgettable event, I bought ice wine for Thomas, whom we'd left behind at the apartment. By coincidence, I sat with a student from Moscow on the ride back. Julia, a quiet woman of fine build, looked to be in her early thirties. She taught English in Moscow. She described the steady increase in homelessness in her city as unemployed people poured in from outlying rural areas. "It's becoming more and more dangerous to travel alone at night. My boyfriend meets me after work to walk me home." She displayed an alert, intelligent manner. Her hopes of immigrating to Germany had been dashed. "My older sister lives here with her family, but my application for residence was rejected last year."

In 2013 and 2014, thousands of Europeans and people from other countries considered Germany an economic mecca. I saw this reflected in the composition of my German class. Europe's open borders allowed easy movement of people across that continent, legally and illegally.

In full darkness, Leandra and I stepped off the bus at the university to pick our way home through a corridor of cathedral-like trees. "How did you like that?" I asked her.

"Oh, it was so much fun. Joyce and the other girls are really nice."

Unruffled by personal safety concerns, we arrived at our apartment bearing the gift of *Eiswein* for Thomas.

"It's been lonely without you two. Good to have you back," he said, squeezing Leandra and me in a tight embrace. Our apartment was beginning to feel like home.

Before the Sprachkurs course started, I'd anticipated meeting new people, learning German, and challenging myself in a new setting. Soon, I badly missed my colleagues back home, mature people my age. Among my course mates, motivations varied. Two students already had close German friendships, thus their rush to acquire language fluency. The Italian girls' attitudes diverged. The younger one, Carlena, turned out to be a fashionista and a half-hearted dabbler. Why was she in Saarbrücken again? For her, this German language thing seemed too much like climbing a sand hill, so why try too hard? Her friend, Sofia, possessed a brain as sharp as flint, grasping and nailing language lessons effortlessly, but she pined for her fiancé in Italy and couldn't wait to rejoin him. Carlena, meantime, talked with liveliness about partying, zoning out in class as if willing herself invisible to our instructor, who kept calling on her to participate. I liked my course mates, but I had trouble relating to them beyond the classroom; our interests diverged by age, life experiences, and culture.

Joyce, our vivacious Chinese classmate, struggled with German like me, but she came in every morning exuberant, greeting us with a loud, cheerful "Guten Tag!" She'd then ask each student and the instructor how we were. Her pet pastime was shopping downtown, where she was drawn to the DM-Drogerie Markt like an iron particle to a magnet. She'd tell us, "DM's the best. Yesterday I bought lots of cosmetics for only ten euros." Another time she exclaimed, "C&A is having a sale on clothes, so I got two pairs of jeans for only fifteen euros each." She knew the German word for a special, *Sonderangebot*, long before the rest of us.

Led by three different instructors at different times, the month-long lessons progressed sometimes with hiccups and sheer awkwardness. The casual, shaggy-haired male instructor, fortyish, displayed remarkable teaching skills and patience with us, a band of rather lacklustre students. His persistence in helping us catch German verbal endings using a playback button on a recorder is seared into my memory. In the final week of the Sprachkurs, under his direction, all students contributed to a course magazine in German that we felt good about.

Halfway through the course, I sensed a party mood growing among participants. This was intensified by repeated no-shows from the youngest and second member of our instruction team, who admitted to us once she'd slept through three alarms. This poor example of professionalism and commitment bugged me. It didn't fit my image of disciplined, hardworking Germans. Were things different in Saarland?

As an educator, I would never skip classes except for valid reasons. On those days when our instructor made a no-show, I felt a mixture of relief, disappointment, and anger. Relief because learning the language sometimes smacked of self-inflicted torture, disappointment as those absences didn't meet my expectations, and anger that she dared to not show up to teach a course for which I'd paid a premium.

Our third instructor, a short, perky, mature woman, did her best to animate the group to reach the course objective: practise speaking the language.

I emerged from that Sprachkurs better aware than ever of my inability to wrap my head around German grammar, pronunciation, and sentence structure. My flailing Bajan tongue all but broke, failing too often to co-operate in tongue-twisters. I sometimes laughed when my feeble linguistic attempts tumbled out. When the course ended, the sun shone brighter in the Saarland sky and the stomach butterflies I'd experienced for four weeks receded to landscapes as distant as the Canadian Rockies.

On the final day of the course, August 30, a shock at home erased all thoughts of learning to speak German. Thomas collapsed on his way back to bed from the bathroom. Although I was standing right beside him, holding onto an arm, his body was so slick with sweat that he slipped out of my grasp and fell full length onto his back.

For a few days beforehand, he had complained of feeling weak and unwell. Nevertheless, he'd marched through his tasks gathering leaves and soil samples from nearby forests, meeting academics in the geography department of Saarland University, visiting Leandra's school in France, and treasure-hunting for textbooks and school supplies. He'd also asked me to inspect a strange red spot on his upper left arm and talked nervously about Lyme disease. Lyme disease was prevalent in Germany, and forest workers were tested yearly for it. As a visitor, Thomas did not qualify for such a health test. Furthermore, he'd joked that none in our little Bouman clan was permitted to fall sick while in Germany. We had Canadian insurance coverage but not German, so perhaps he tempted fate. It made me think of the old adage my Bajan grandmother uttered to reckless youth: "Man proposes; God disposes." Or as Thomas said in German, "*Der Mensch denkt, Gott lenkt.*"

On August 29, returning from Sarreguemines with Leandra, a pale Thomas confessed, "I don't know what's wrong, but I don't feel well at all."

"That's no good. Should you just go to bed?"

"Do I have a temperature? I feel chills." I touched his feverish head. Alarm set in for both of us. We possessed neither aspirin nor a thermometer, so I headed out to the nearest store.

Outside, dashing down the driveway, I thought my best bet was to hop a bus for the nearest Netto Marken-Discount grocery store, less than five minutes away. In the evening, with only one bus going by on the half-hour, a fifteen-minute walk could be faster. When I inquired at the store, I realized what a naive Canadian I was. Grocery, convenience, or department stores do not sell over-the-counter drugs, not even Vicks VapoRub! Meanwhile, their shelves are bursting with alcoholic drinks. For aspirin and a thermometer, I'd have to find an *Apotheke*, a pharmacy. All of this I heard in English, thank goodness, from the store supervisor who gave directions to the nearest pharmacy, a ten-minute walk away. My ramblings took me past two empty Apotheken, firmly closed at six P.M. It was now almost seven. *What should I do?*

A renewed sense of urgency pressed me on as I pictured Thomas tossing hot and heavy on the bed, probably unconscious on my return with useless aspirin and a ready thermometer. An uncomfortable feeling settled while I walked those unfamiliar streets and eerily quiet residential byways off the beaten track to the city centre. Frightening memories from my childhood and youth surfaced. German Shepherds would snarl as my siblings and I took shortcuts through upper-crust Belleville and Culloden Gardens in Barbados. Would they do the same here?

Looking above the housetops, I oriented myself toward the Johanneskirche, its spire rising, pointing like a comforting finger heavenward. *Thank you!* Pacing towards downtown Saarbrücken, I found a pharmacy open for emergency hours on the busiest street in the city, Bahnhofstraße, the train station street. A kind female pharmacist served me, speaking impeccable English. After a brief wait and a short bus ride back, I walked up Fuchstälchen (fox hollow), that scenic but dreadfully steep driveway leading up to the apartment building. Thomas measured his temperature, found his fever to be low grade, swallowed an aspirin, and slept.

I wish the story had ended there. Thomas woke up the next morning feeling crappy with fever and chills and a raging headache. And then the collapse. He went down squarely, smacking the back of his head on a night table. I thought his head must have split open. The effect of the blow, Thomas said later, was "to do the trick of knocking the headache right out of my head."

With such a tumble, all sorts of crazy possibilities again reared up. In full-on panic, I raced downstairs to find the ambulance emergency number pasted next to the letter boxes, shrieking at Leandra to watch her dad. Leaping up fifty-six stairs, I made an emergency call, trying my best (all in English) to convey the urgency of the matter to the calm first responder at the other end. That responder could not grasp my pronunciation of Fuchstälchen however hard I tried. My communication failure was frustrating and pathetic at the same time. Fifteen-year-old Leandra stood gaping at me. After this went on for moments that felt much longer, Thomas rose like a battle-hardened soldier and gave precise directions to the ambulance personnel. How he managed to maintain his consciousness and composure could only be described as a miracle.

Within ten minutes, ambulance attendants appeared, took vital signs, asked key questions, and transported Thomas and me to a nearby hospital. "Please don't use the blue strobe lights or siren," Thomas told them. His medical emergency added up to half a day in hospital for blood work, observation, and final diagnosis of a viral infection and dehydration by an Eastern European doctor with somewhat limited German. *Really, doctor? Was that it?*

It took a full week for Thomas to regain enough strength to feel like his old self. For that week, he rose feebly from bed at night to change sleeping clothes drenched in sweat. We both exhaled in relief when his illness did not develop into anything serious or debilitating. Except for the large bull's-eye rash, many of the common symptoms of Lyme disease, such as fever, headache, stiff neck, and flu-like symptoms, fit viral infections. "I think I probably caught a bug on the ferry leaving Dover for Calais. Remember, I ate stale clotted cream and a scone. I've felt slightly sick ever since."

I raised my eyebrows. "How could food make you sick a month later?"

He shook his head, unconvinced. "Don't know, just haven't felt right ever since that ferry from Calais." And so, his questions lingered.

Weeks later, Thomas and Frau Schmidt, Leandra's piano teacher, spoke about infectious diseases and illnesses, he speculating about the cause of his viral infection. "Isn't that strange? I missed work last week because of sickness," Frau Schmidt told him. "My symptoms were fever and body weakness." She then shared a story about a disorder she'd suffered that enhanced my skepticism about physician expertise.

Two years prior, Frau Schmidt had gone to see a doctor after suffering swollen joints and stiffness, reducing her mobility. Her doctor diagnosed multiple sclerosis, which she scoffed at and sought a second opinion. The second physician recommended a wait-and-see period after a close questioning. A key question he asked her was, "Have you been to a swimming pool recently?" She said, "Yes, I went one week ago to the Calypso pool." It's a huge, sexy, indoor swimming complex in Saarbrücken. The doctor said he'd seen several patients with similar symptoms after swimming there and right away diagnosed a pool bug. Later, Thomas said to me, "See why I never trust swimming pools? They can be cesspools for collection and spread of infections." Curious to see the impressive recreation facility, we visited the much-advertised Calypso swimming, sauna, and wellness paradise in Saarbrücken, but we never dared to swim there.

Even one year after his ordeal, Thomas, with a quizzical brow, asked, "What made me sick in Saarbrücken?" The physician's medical diagnosis appeared to be little better than an educated guess.

I was flooded with grateful relief when Thomas bounced back to full health and we returned to facing normal daily challenges and indulging in overloaded travel tours. A year-long stay in Saarland necessitated that Thomas, Leandra, and I maintain excellent health. Until Thomas fell ill, I'd taken that precondition for granted. What I never took for granted was that living in a foreign country demanded I make myself understood to ordinary Germans. In an emergency, I would become dependent on Germans who knew English. That fact exposed my weakness. I needed to learn the language of the land. If only desperately wanting to succeed at something made it happen.

If matters had taken a more serious turn with my husband, we may have been forced to make a hasty end to our overseas plans. Leandra and I could not have negotiated Saarland life without Thomas. He knew everything we needed to know or knew how to find out what we needed to know. He'd wrung two German citizen IDs and a foreigner residence card for us out of bureaucratic meetings and he'd shaped our comfortable housing arrangements and smoothed our banking transactions, all because he wanted us to experience German life and culture. We needed him to be well in order for us to do that.

His sudden illness had alarmed Leandra just as much as me, but by the evening she had returned to her natural teenage spirits—as her attitude at the Sprachkurs end-of-term party, later that evening, revealed.

The half-full bus blew by Leandra and me at the stop, accelerating up the hill toward the university.

"Wait, what the hell? Why did he do that?" I asked, confused. It had been an upsetting day for us with Thomas's ordeal and hours spent at the hospital.

"The bus wasn't even full," Leandra said, as our eyes followed its course.

Now two months into our year in Saarbrücken, I felt fairly at ease, going and coming by public tram and bus. I even yelled *"Hallo!"* to the bus driver when he tried to pass our Wildpark stop. A vexing feature of living in the well-hidden Humboldt guest apartment was that bus drivers either assumed no one resided behind the dark trees or that whoever lived back there needed no public buses. Thankfully, for me, it never came to the panic I witnessed of one of a steady stream of new students.

The young Middle Eastern woman, apparently unable to speak any German but in danger of being bused all the way up to the university, yelled, "Let me off! Please! Let me off!" She looked terrified, causing the driver to halt suddenly, jolting the passengers. Two cheeky young boys on their way home from school sniggered into their chests at her alarm. They must have wondered what real danger was there if all she had to do was to walk for a few minutes back toward her residence? Perhaps her fear was brought on by being a stranger in a new land with no mastery of a foreign tongue. I related to her panic.

The Sprachkurs staff had organized a final social for students. Leading up to an evening of partying and food, students, guided by an instructor, created a booklet that told simple stories and showed off the German phrases we'd learned. Our "Course Newspaper for the University of Saarland" featured several stories, including *Heidelberg Exkursion* (Heidelberg Excursion), *Einkaufen im Zentrum* (Shopping in the Centre), *Wir sprechen über Stereotype* (We Talk About Stereotypes), *Ägypten: Ein Porträt* (Egypt: A Portrait), *Angekommen in Saarbrücken* (Arrived in Saarbrücken), and *Treffen in der Heimbar* (Meeting in the Residence Bar). In photos, we, the participants, beamed with pride at our efforts—and our happiness that the torture was over. I missed the class presentations slated for that morning, but planned to briefly attend the celebratory party in the evening with Leandra.

Samplings of various international foods and drinks promised to top the evening's agenda. Leandra had attended classes while her dad and I awaited medical attention. Later, she asked, "What shall we bring to the party?"

"I'm in no mood to make anything fancy, so let's make sandwiches; we've got roast beef, ham, and brie." I wasn't sure what would be considered Canada's national dish. I thought of poutine, but it would've been hard to pull off in a snap. I grew up on Barbados's national dish, spicy fried or steamed flying fish or salted cod sauce on a bed of cornmeal and okra cou cou. Again, not an easy dish to whip up, especially since I've never cooked cou cou myself.

We bolted out the door for an evening of celebration with me still bothered by the day's events, Leandra looking happy, and I hoping we'd timed it for a quick bus. But instead of stopping, the bus breezed by like a trade wind gust during hurricane season. Luckily, ten minutes later, another bus arrived, resulting in no actual delay.

The party pulsated, thick with people, spicy food aromas, and loud voices and laughter. By Bajan standards, if not Canadian, we were good on time. The story of the night belonged to a group of merry Mexicans who'd attempted to board a bus downtown bearing large pots from which aromas of peppers and other spices escaped, something not done in Germany. Denied entry by the bus driver, they good-naturedly resorted to taxis. When they finally arrived, everybody knew. Amidst cheers and merriment, they held high their pots of Mexican rice, corn casserole, and pork stew spicy enough to burn a hole in the palate.

Coupled with a buffet of dishes, the availability of a wide assortment of alcoholic drinks throughout the evening generated shriller and rowdier youthful liveliness.

In this madness, Leandra held back, as curious as a kitten about the splashes of alcohol and unabashed revelry. I faced a predicament: she was too young to be left behind to fend for herself at a youthful drinking party, and I was too concerned about her dad to party into the early morning hours. I knew Leandra loved the festive, young energy and didn't want to leave, but after about four hours, I pulled her aside.

"The last bus past our apartment leaves in half an hour, at 11 P.M. We should get it."

She looked like she understood, saying a curt, "Okay." As the time drew near, she made no effort to untangle herself from a gaggle of half-drunk people led by Joyce in an ecstasy of freedom from restraint. *These people she's known for one month. Her dad's lying sick at home, after being at the hospital today. I wish I could just leave her behind to walk home or take a taxi.*

But I knew there'd be a reckoning at home with a father alarmed about the dangers of drinking and darkness for his young daughter. I alerted her that I was leaving for the bus stop and hoped she'd follow. She didn't. *But I can't leave without her.* So, I stayed. Seconds before the bus departed the university grounds, and after I'd yelled several cross promptings at my daughter, she and I sprinted and caught the bus just in time.

We gave each other the silent treatment on the short ride home and during the cardiac workout up the driveway. We found a weak but contented Thomas in bed. He rested easier, knowing everyone in our family was safe at home. Leandra had signalled her desire to spread her social wings wider, sans maternal protection, but I wasn't ready to let her venture too far alone.

9. Public Broadcasting: Mostly Fun TV

Standing in our bright apartment living room, Thomas ripped open the official-looking envelope and scanned the contents.

"What's that?" I asked, scrutinising the paper by his side. We were only two months into our life in Saarland.

"It's a request from a federal agency to pay fees for radio and television broadcasting."

"But we don't even have a decent radio or TV," I said, puzzled.

"It doesn't matter if you get these services; every German household has to pay," Thomas said, in an end-of-story way.

In Barbados, as early as 1963, my dad had owned a small blue-and-white transistor radio we weren't supposed to touch, which he used to tune in to the Caribbean Broadcasting Corporation (CBC) and shortwave radio. As teenagers in the 1970s, my siblings and I heard local and international news and listened to Motown pop songs on privately owned Rediffusion, for which my mother paid $2.75 weekly. When, in 1978, our family could afford a television, we watched lame TV programs in the evenings. Programming was mostly local news and American shows and movies on the government-owned CBC network, which was available without charge. The explosion in electronic and digital technology over recent decades has transformed everything to do with radio and television and has left people of my generation staggering to keep up.

In a large federal nation like Germany, public broadcasting represents a complicated landscape.

"How do news stations and television channels operate in Germany?" I asked Thomas, out of naïve curiosity. He answered, but I would be hard pressed to explain to anyone what he said. A little while later, I asked again. After he explained it a second time, I thought, *My God! It requires a Ph.D. to comprehend the organization of German radio broadcasting and television networks!*

"What's ARD?" We were relaxing in the sitting room in Saarland on a Sunday afternoon. Diffused light lit up a patch of pale blue sky.

"It's public broadcasting here. ARD means *Arbeitsgemeinschaft der öffentlich-rechtlichen Rundfunkanstalten der Bundesrepublik Deutschland*," he said, grinning.

My jaw dropped. "What?"

Thomas explained ARD is a network of Germany's regional, public-service broadcasters. Established in 1950 in West Germany, ARD represents the common interests of decentralized, postwar broadcasting services.

"In Germany, broadcasting services are government supported but not government owned or operated," he said. He told me they are run by boards representing churches, political parties, labour unions, and other public interests. Although the programming is not free of political bias, and some private broadcasting is permitted, commercial and ideological content does not dominate the airwaves in the same way as in Canada or, more so, in the USA.

"Sounds like people here get more objective news." I liked the idea.

I learned that the ARD is huge, perhaps the world's second-largest public broadcaster after the British Broadcasting Corporation (BBC), with a budget of 6.3 billion euros and twenty-three thousand employees in 2014. Its money comes chiefly from mandatory fees from every household (thus the request letter to us), and municipal government. For an average household, the fee is about eighteen euros per month, although those on welfare do not have to contribute.

This organization and its broad range of civic support provides trustworthy newscasting that reflects federated Germany's politics. Any North American paying attention must be impressed by this nation's diverse, high-quality public broadcasting.

I understood less of the subject of Germany's radio and television broadcasting than I let on. In the mornings, the battered transistor radio interrupted our breakfast with news reports. After that commenced a litany of *Staus*, or kilometres-long traffic jams, around the country. In January, I listened to weather reports about the mild Saarland temperatures we enjoyed, compared to wintry Nova Scotia. Anything more lay well beyond my understanding.

Late one morning in September, our apartment buzzer sounded. It was too early for Leandra to be back from school. "It's Karl," a voice sounded through the intercom. "Oh, yes, come on up," Thomas shouted. We heard slow, heavy footsteps and then frail Karl stood at the door with a cheerful expression. A slightly built man with a receding hairline and a bit of a belly, Karl was red from exertion. An old Göttingen University pal of Thomas, he was a big part of the reason we'd landed in Saarland. Julia, his curly-haired wife with a gentle face, had not come with him.

"Hallo, Karl. Come in. Wow! You didn't have to haul that upstairs. I could've come down," Thomas said. "Great to see you!"

Grey-haired Karl marched forward with a sixteen-inch, older-model Phillips television. He winked at me, saying in English, "All this guy here thinks about are trees and more trees. Claudette, you may be able to use this. It's no use to us sitting in storage."

"Thanks, Karl. That's so kind." *Perhaps I can pick up some German from TV shows.*

Leandra cheered for the TV as much as I did while Thomas feigned indifference. "I didn't like that Karl had to carry that TV up here," he fretted, thinking his friend had pushed his luck, overtaxing himself, as he battled serious, longstanding health issues. Karl brought over the TV because he took a look at Leandra and me stranded in the woods and thought "social isolation."

With seven available channels, Thomas and I elected to watch the news. *Heute* and *Tagesschau* served as evening highlights; but Friday nights topped my entertainment list when *The Voice of Germany* came on, followed by *The Voice of Kids* on channel seven. Thomas dubbed it "the American channel" because of its "light" programming. We sometimes caught a fascinating nature show, but I never paid enough attention to the schedule to watch that consistently.

The Voice of Germany became the most amusing show ever for Leandra and me, with Thomas refusing to watch on principle. Contestants sang the most terrible American pop songs. Over the course of many weeks, they were whittled down to the last six performers when sometimes the worst singers won.

"I'm rooting for Emily," I told Leandra. "Who'd you like to win?"

"I like the sixteen-year-old girl singing Miley Cyrus's songs. She has a great voice."

We were neither surprised nor upset when the unlikeliest prevailed—a mature bearded guy with a huge, Joe Cocker–type voice. Coaches and TV judges for the contestants included Nena, the German actress and singer-songwriter of "99 Luftballons" fame. Their compliments and comments for the singers sounded so cheesy. Leandra would wait to double over in near hysterical laughter at *"Das war unglaublich gut!"* (That was unbelievably good!) and *"Es war ganz, ganz toll!"* (It was really, really super!) We couldn't get enough of it, anticipating a much needed end-of-week comic relief.

Thomas's artificial indifference toward the TV didn't last long. Soon he couldn't neglect the evening *Tagesschau* broadcast under any circumstances, lest the vast stretches of Germany's civilization and forested lands spin out of magnetic orbit.

Sometimes, just for fun and the sheer hell of it, I flipped to a cooking show. In an interesting online article, Roger Boyes claimed that a quiet revolution had occurred in German eating habits since the 1990s. An example of typical German cuisine used to be *Grünkohleintopf und Eisbein mit Sauerkraut* (kale stew and pork knuckle with sauerkraut). Farmers' food, it was a single warm dish, sturdy enough to keep physical labourers going all day. In turn, *gutbürgerliche Küche* (home cooking) was traditionally a robust three-course dinner, with plenty of gravy, dumplings, and red cabbage.

To show the change in German eating, a German woman, Juliane Caspar, was appointed editor-in-chief of the French *Michelin Guide* in 2008. She became the first woman and first non-French national to occupy that position. German daily meals were becoming less meat-heavy, and fish was back, not always buttered. German chefs were including more vegetables, fewer potatoes, more pasta, and more flavourful sauces.

Boyes declared that cooking shows were not just popular in Germany, they had become chic. Thus, Jamie Oliver's kitchen implements and recipe books flooded the market. Much of the cuisine change seemed to be reflected and driven by television chefs. A new wave of chef shows was turning cooks like Tim Mälzer, Johann Lafer, and Nelson Müller into TV celebrities. Boyes said cooking had been made sexy and competitive to men. Nelson Müller, of Ghanaian descent, became well known to the German TV audience. He presented his own TV show, *The German Master Chef*, based on the original UK show *Master Chef*.

Thomas showed no interest in watching cooking shows, and Leandra had little time. I kept to simple but nutritious meals when I braved our kitchen: potatoes, rice, lentils, beans, pastas, tomato sauces, fresh vegetables, and fruits. We munched on German-style meat patties (*Frikadellen*) served by a forceful apprentice meat sales clerk at my husband's favourite Dudweiler butcher shop. Among our breakfast choices were hot cereals, eggs, various breads, cheeses, ham, pancakes, and crepes.

We kept family mealtime as a priority. The nourishing food from our kitchen contrasted with the skill and creativity of the famous TV chefs. On a special occasion, Thomas prepared white asparagus in late April with tiny, fresh potatoes and prosciutto. Peeling the asparagus was a pain (for me, not for him). Another time, he bought *Rouladen*, thinly sliced top round roast beef cut and rolled by a real butcher, with bacon slices and spices buried inside. Whether preparing simple or fancy fare, a sense of my own good fortune living in Saarland often overwhelmed me.

Back in the day, my mother was a good cook and loved cooking for a family of seven. Sundays gave her precious time to prepare a genuine spread. She'd start at noon with a little help from my older sister or me. (Our two brothers disappeared or hung around, timing mealtimes perfectly.) By 3 P.M. she'd laid out bowls of steaming rice and peas (or beans), creamy oven-baked macaroni pie, oven-roasted chicken, thick beef and vegetable stew, and/or fried pork chops. Lettuce, avocado, and cucumber salad, and tomatoes, sometimes homegrown, added colour and flavour.

On weekdays, we would eat our main meal in the late afternoon. I loved coarse cornmeal pap, with evaporated milk swimming on top, covered with shredded coconut and spoonfuls of dark cane sugar. Sometimes our mother fried bakes (doughnuts) and fishcakes or, on occasion, rolled out fat, moist pancakes as delightful surprises. Treats included soda crackers and tangy, imported New Zealand Anchor cheese on Friday or Saturday nights. On Sunday evenings we ran up the gap to purchase pillowy coconut turnovers still warm from the oven at a neighbourhood bakery, a jump away.

How I sometimes missed those good Bajan foods and Sunday afternoon meals, never the same after I moved to Canada. Some key ingredients couldn't be found, and I lost the desire to reproduce island food that didn't taste the same as back home.

And, of course, those dishes and treats were nothing like what we were enjoying in Germany.

PART III

10. Federal Elections 2013

It was a warm August evening. Thomas, Leandra, and I strode up Saarbrücken Centre's shopping district to Schillerplatz 1, an elegant, modern building of rectangular forms and glass. It sat among posh hotels and upscale office blocks, fronted by a paved expanse that led to wide steps. Mirrored ceilings reflecting white light lured us into the foyer. Tall windows at the back allowed a good view of the city. A lavish chandelier in the middle sparkled as chatter erupted from scores of people dressed in smart evening attire, mingling at small round tables and sipping drinks.

We stood in the pride of Saarland, *die Kongresshalle*, opened in 1967 and expanded and moved in 1995 to its current location. Divided up into halls and foyers, this facility of three levels holds conferences, ceremonies, galas, musical performances, and theatre shows. The atmosphere tingled with glamour. It was my first visit to this building and my first theatre outing in Saarland.

"What a beautiful stage and back panelling," I said to Thomas and Leandra as we took our seats toward the back of the great hall. "It's golden under the lighting." I silently wished we'd gotten seats closer to the front, but the stage was raised high enough to see it. In front of us, rows and rows of black chairs were filled with people. Behind us up high balcony seats made a half circle. The Congress Hall seated 1,300, and we were there to see a modern version of "The Three Musketeers."

"How about a play at die Kongresshalle?" Thomas had asked a few weeks earlier. He didn't have to ask twice for Leandra and I shared a passion for theatre, attending Neptune Theatre and haunting Shakespeare by the Sea summer theatre performances in Point Pleasant Park in Halifax.

Discovering our new city meant, among other pleasures, experiencing live theatre. A memorable moment in *The Three Musketeers* leapt out at me when the country bumpkin exclaimed *"Mein Pferd!"* (My horse!) He had missed his prized gift of a lame horse—from his beloved deceased father—that reappeared late in the play. The character's country charm contrasted with sophisticated city life and the corruption of city slickers. Even I discerned that his courage overrode his naïveté, in time endearing him to the king and his fellow musketeers.

What a wonder for me to be able to follow a foreign-language play and laugh along with the audience at comical moments. I pretended I was watching a mime. "What's *Eure Majestät*?" I whispered to Thomas after a few references. "Your Majesty," he replied. *It's so obvious. Why didn't I think of that?* I suppressed my urge to ask for too many translations. I understood little of the dialogue but challenged myself to follow characters' actions. Leandra faced the same predicament, but she never once asked for a translation. At the end, she said she'd loved the play. Did she have a higher tolerance for an unknown language, or was she better at it than I was?

That same year, we landed in the high drama of German federal elections, my first time to experience German elections up close. Electioneering consumed the nation with the voting date slated for September 22. Politicians, media pundits, and the general public predicted Angela Merkel's party, the Christian Democratic Union (CDU), would win the most votes, making her third-time chancellor in a coalition government. Taking a bold stand, Merkel rejected tax increases proposed by the opposition.

Around me I saw and heard a torrent of election slogans, TV debates, advertisements, placards, and emotional appeals for a better, stronger Germany. Colour-coded posters displayed party affiliation: red for the Social Democratic Party (SPD); green for the Green Party; yellow, pink, and cyan for the Free Democratic Party (FDP); light blue for the Alternative for Germany (AfD); and black and blue for the Christian Democratic Union of Germany (CDU) and the Christian Social Union in Bavaria (CSU) respectively, the union centre-right parties of Germany.

I spotted simple placards promoting "Angie" and "*Die Wahl*" (the vote). One slogan read: "*Bleib cool und Kanzlerin wählen*" (Keep cool and vote for the Chancellor). Others for the CDU translated into "Relieve the middle class," "Successful together," and "Good for Germany." Some slogans of the right-wing populist AfD said: "New Germans? We make them ourselves"; "This alternative is not kosher!"; and "Stop Islamization." One hot Saturday afternoon, we bounced into the Piraten party under bright orange tents in the crowded pedestrian zone. They handed us pens and posters in a fair-like atmosphere.

Peer Steinbrück was the chancellor candidate of the Social Democratic Party and Merkel's main challenger. One of his billboards showed a bone-weary Merkel and her coalition partner with the slogan, "Best government since reunification? Vote for change now."

Merkel's government took heat for bailing out European countries such as Greece. She campaigned on Germany's unemployment record, which fell to a two-decade low during her chancellorship; progress toward a balanced budget; and the eurozone benefits accruing to Germany's export industries. The opposition piled on questions about her legacy and her potential successor. She appealed to voters to support her against Euroskeptics, people against increasing the powers of the European Union.

Economic crises stacking up among eurozone members like Greece, Spain, Portugal, and Italy in the first decades of the twenty-first century meant future economic bailouts by wealthier European countries. The German economy was thriving, and people from countries surrounding Germany looked to it for better economic prospects. Migration and refugee crises loomed, exacerbated by wars and political instability in Syria, Libya, Afghanistan and various countries in Africa. Also, Germany has had, since the 1960s, a visible and growing Turkish immigrant population, not fully integrated into its political and social life.

When Thomas heard Merkel planned to appear in Saarbrücken at the Kongresshalle, he asked, "Do you want to join me for a political show?" Neither Leandra nor I had seen Merkel in person, so I said yes. Leandra hesitated, as she had little real interest in political events. She said afterwards that she had been dragged along to another parent thing.

"Look at this crowd," I said as we approached the Kongresshalle, where we'd enjoyed *The Three Musketeers* a few weeks before. "We should have come earlier. I hope we get seats inside." A stage with massive screens and speakers towered above the crowd. The air buzzed with energy. Intensity lined the faces of people milling around and streaming in one direction. I felt nervous about getting separated. A seething mass of humanity jostled toward the main entrance and into the lobby. Inside, I grabbed Leandra's hand and Thomas clutched mine, leading the way. Swallowed up by the crowd, we caught a fleeting glimpse of Merkel's profile as she waded through on her way into the hall, flanked by security guards. She smiled with tired eyes. It was wonderful to be there, but Thomas pushed for us to get closer to the hall.

A calm, watchful security man blocked us from entering an already capacity-filled auditorium. Thomas told him, "Why don't you get the party hacks out and let some undecided voters in? That would be better for Merkel and her party's chances at the polls." To his astonishment, the security guard at the door looked past him. I had no clue what Thomas had said at the time, but when he later translated for me, I chuckled, admiring his gumption. He's nothing if not provocative, and just loves participating in the political fray.

Outside, surrounded by a crush of people, we stood under a dark sky to join hundreds watching the political speeches on screens. We heard Annegret Kramp-Karrenbauer, Minister President of Saarland, speak before introducing Merkel. People listened with fixed force, paying out civil applause. After an hour we left, clattering over paving and then cobbled stones.

"What was Merkel's message to the locals?" I asked Thomas.

"Reassurance that the Saarland would remain self-standing—that there's no push from the federal government for a union of small Saarland with the larger neighbouring *Bundesland* of Rheinland-Pfalz."

"Oh. Is that an issue?"

"Yah, yah, always. Especially at election time."

The electioneering continued with little relief. Thomas did on-the-spot interpretations for me. CDU's slogan "Together successful" emphasized national unity from a popular party. CSU's "Bayern. Strong in Berlin" did not apply to Saarland, appealing instead to a large centre. SPD's "The we decides" emphasized social unity of a popular party not leaving anyone behind. FDP's "Only with us" stressed a specific small-party profile.

Bündnis 90/the Greens' "And You?" was aimed at the individual voter. Die Linke's (The Left's) "100% Social" stressed social fairness. I thought several of the slogans concise, subtle, and clever, especially the Greens' "And You?" and the SPD's "The we decides."

On Sunday, September 22, I welcomed deliverance from political campaigning. On election day, always a Sunday, Thomas pulled on a dress shirt, khaki slacks, navy blue corduroy jacket, and new Clarks leather shoes he'd bought that summer in England. He set off alone to cast his ballot in the German federal election for the first time in twenty-seven years. When he left to walk through the nearby Schwarzenberg woods, he carried an air of satisfied expectation and pride. He voted at a neighbourhood high school polling station. Leading up to the event, he'd said often enough, "I'm so happy to be able to vote in this election." As a university youth, he'd been involved in protests against nuclear power. In him, passion for politics and current affairs burned bright.

Keen to follow every detail of the election results, Thomas turned to the old, battered radio for daily updates and, in the evenings, he switched on the still older TV for *Heute* and *Tagesschau.* So many political actors entered the complicated German political arena, I found it hard to make sense of it all, like a struggling math student learning calculus for the first time. But the two big parties were accounted for: the Christian Democratic Union and its sister party in Bavaria, the Christian Social Union (CDU/CSU), and the Social Democratic Party of Germany (SPD). Several smaller contenders like The Greens, The Left, The Pirate Party Germany, the Free Democratic Party (FDP), Alternative for Germany (AfD), and even a Nazi party had all vied for the electorate's attention.

In the end, the results threw up a mix of affirmation, surprise, and just plain shock. Together, Angela Merkel's Christian Democratic Union and sister party CSU finished with a total of 41 percent of the vote. The SPD received 25.7 percent, and the others ranged from The Left with 8.6 percent to AfD with 4.7 percent.

In Germany, a party must take at least 5 percent of the vote to sit in the *Bundestag* (parliament). The shocker was the FDP (the Free Democratic Party) missing the mark and getting booted out of parliament after having formed a coalition with Merkel's CDU party in the previous government.

Predictions followed that the SPD would form a grand coalition with the CDU to share government. Leading up to the election, negative perceptions swirling around SPD's leader Steinbrück about his large speaking fees and appearance of corruption discredited his party. The Alternative for Germany (AfD) made rapid gains as a new party; Germany's bona fide right-wing party had just barely missed out on winning parliamentary status.

From his reading of the political coverage, Thomas thought results gave huge relief to many Germans for the time being. Fast forward to 2017 when AfD gained 12.6 percent of the vote (translating to ninety-four seats) and to 2021, where it slipped to 10.3 percent (eighty-three seats).

For a bit of context, Germany manages to squeeze 83.2 million people into 357,022 square kilometres, while Canada's population of 38 million inhabits 9,984,670 square kilometres; Canada is about twenty-eight times larger than Germany. The burgeoning refugee crisis in Europe fired up AfD's popularity. Many more migrants and refugees enter Germany yearly than Canada, with numbers greatly fluctuating. This fluctuation renders German politics volatile.

Non-stop coverage of the bargaining chips being traded around the big coalition table dominated radio and television news for months. In German politics, all major parties must be allowed their say, and by Bajan and Canadian standards, negotiations tend to be mind-numbingly protracted. By December, Merkel's party reached an agreement with the main opposition party, the SPD, to form a coalition.

In the same month as national elections in Germany, I received a surprise in the mail. As new year-long residents in Saarbrücken, Thomas and I were invited to participate in upcoming municipal elections. That the notification arrived addressed to "the woman of the house" gave me a moment's introspection. *But why?* I was a foreigner and couldn't yet speak enough of the language to avoid facing the embarrassment of being misunderstood.

"It's not a big deal," my husband said. "It's because you're the most senior in the household." What a backhanded compliment. "It's really important for things to be well-defined in Germany. The eldest in a household is considered the head of that household." *Why is a head needed? Why can't it be mutual?* Despite my questions, I had to acknowledge that Germany's policy, which contradicted traditional, biblical doctrine and the dominant patriarchal ideology in many countries around the globe, fit my personal outlook on how the world could be better run.

11. Leandra's School in France

Leandra faced the rigours of another school day in Sarreguemines while I accompanied her across the French border purely for the pleasure of it.

Passengers packed the yellow Saarbahn car filled with blended odours of bath soaps, deodorants, shampoos, and conditioners fanning up my nose. Two rows of commuters faced front, divided by a narrow aisle. Standing riders scrunched in close, people swayed, tall ones clutched ceiling straps, children grasped metal poles. At 7:30 A.M. we rubbed shoulders with sundry passengers, some with glowing faces, a few sleepy, lulled by the tram's rocking. Workers wore paint-stained factory overalls, business suits, blazers, ties, or dark-coloured skirts and dresses. Elementary kids with heavy backpacks knocked gamely alongside too cool for school high schoolers.

In Saarbrücken we lived in the west beyond the west. On any given school morning in September, we claimed spaces on the Saarbahn as it rushed toward Lorraine. On the way, it passed idyllic German villages with peculiar names that I mouthed silently, like Brebach, Büdingen, Güdingen, and Kleinblittersdorf. I cast an eye down the line as we flashed past clumps of trees, grassy meadows, nearby or far-off buildings, and cozy homes. Sometimes the way was lined with trees, other times the Saar River glimmered.

For moral support and love of riding a posh commuter rail, during the month of September, I accompanied Leandra to Sarreguemines where she attended Jean de Pange school. For me, it was holiday travel, a guilty pleasure, but then Leandra still resented being compelled to go to a new school in a foreign land from an equally foreign home base. Altogether, the morning trip took an hour. The first part of the journey was a ten-minute bus ride into the heart of Saarbrücken, where we boarded a tram to cross the border into Sarreguemines, riding half an hour. After alighting the tram and walking briskly ten minutes up a steep incline that crossed over a train bridge, Leandra arrived at the school's gated entrance.

Sarreguemines is the French spelling of the city that Germans call Saargemünd. It is located in the Moselle Department of Lorraine in north-eastern France. Sarreguemines, with a population of about 20,000, is the centre of an *arrondissement*, or administrative district. The name reflects the merging of the Blies and Saar Rivers at the city's location. As with many places in Europe, the sister cities of Saarbrücken and Sarreguemines share a long history. Pertinent historical details are not lost; older French and German citizens possess long memories.

History details that Sarreguemines was passed with Lorraine from the Holy Roman Empire of the German nation to the Kingdom of France in 1766. One hundred and five years later, it was transferred to the 2nd German Reich with the Treaty of Frankfurt following the Franco-German War. From 1871 to 1918, it formed part of the German imperial province of Alsace-Lorraine. It was returned to France after the First World War. Thomas heard first-hand resentments about French occupation from those who remembered occupied Saarland after the Second World War. In the spirit of European unity, politicians now refer to the surrounding landscape encompassing the Saarland, Lorraine, and Luxembourg as the Saar-Lor-Lux region. We travelled through its gorgeous undulating countryside by train and car, unrestricted by the need for passports or visas.

Rich coal deposits and a thriving coke and steel industry shaped the economy of this region for centuries, but, like similar industries in Cape Breton, Nova Scotia, new economic bases were needed after decline. In many locations, I saw evidence of Saarland's steel power. Good examples stood out at the Saarland University. At the university plaza and main bus stop stood a 15-metre-tall parallelogram of steel bridge girders that twisted depending on the angle from which one viewed them. Buses drove around this column in opposite directions. Near the famous Hermann Neuberger Sports School, stood an indoor arena with huge exterior steel trusses. On our frequent hikes, Thomas and I walked behind one of the two steel-supported university parkades.

Like German and French residents, I benefited from the proximity of Saarbrücken and Sarreguemines. I never got used to the reality that we lived in Germany, and Leandra went by tram to school in France. It felt magical.

In this thrilling setting, why did Leandra weep in the bathroom after school? Was that normal? How bad could her daily experience be? It wouldn't have helped to ask Thomas; he was just as helpless as I was to relate to Leandra's French high school of 1,200 students. A continent of quirky teenage faces greeted her in the courtyard after she leapt from the tram and raced across the overpass.

Each morning, hikes up and down granite stairs, trudges across cobble-stoned yards, and entrances to gaping classrooms lay ahead of her. Vigilant *surveillants* (student-supervisors) pounced on tardy students even as no cozy nooks, familiar hallways, or library hideaways beckoned her. And where was that awesome North American convenience, a locker to rid herself of the wretched gorilla backpack loaded with kilos of textbooks? The school board in Lorraine had issued students a one-hundred-euro book voucher in August, and an efficient parent association had distributed textbooks to be collected at year's end.

When I asked after the first day, "How was school?" I got a stare back with a shrug. I noticed her red nose and eyes and pressed no further.

The Saturday after the first school week, Leandra and I were out shopping at C&A, Primark, and Karstadt having left Thomas behind at home. We stopped at one of my favourite spots, the train station café, for a bite.

Aromas of fresh breads sprinkled with a variety of seeds and grains tickled my nose and tempted my appetite. Chocolate, almond, and butter croissants competed too. "Hallo!" A focused, creased-face attendant greeted us at the glass counter. She bustled behind assorted trays of cold cuts from ham to wursts, garnished with cucumber and tomatoes slices. "One cheese croissant and sparkling water, *bitte*," I said. In a flash, my order was ready. Five customers lined up behind us at this popular spot. Leandra ordered, "An almond croissant, *bitte*. And an *Apfelschorle*." She found that fizzy water mixed with apple juice quenching.

We took our food and settled into the small eating area. A curious young woman in a wheelchair eyed us, not averting her eyes. Two guys in tradesman's gear at separate tables chomped. A backdrop buzz of train station noises rose and fell, people sauntered and sometimes dashed. Just outside the doorway, a group of male youths hung out, smoking and teasing.

We munched yummy, delicious train station pastry and turned to school talk.

"Even the food at school is strange." I looked at her, startled. French schools served gourmet meals by North American standards, actually by any standards. The lunches had multiple courses, starting with a vegetable, like a leafy lettuce salad, a cucumber tomato salad, or beets. A warm main dish included another veggie accompanied by sliced roast beef and baked potatoes, veal with mushrooms and broccoli, or breaded fish with cauliflower. Her dad had paid her full lunch cost for the year up front. "I don't like those weird sauces." She thought for a moment. "But this is supposed to be some kind of great opportunity for me, right?"

I nodded. "I wish I'd had this chance when I was your age."

"But you'll never know. Will you Mum?"

"Right, I'll never know," I nodded, still hoping she'd be glad she'd done this one day.

When Leandra started at Lycée Jean de Pange, geared up and ambitious as usual about school, she faced fear and confusion. She decided not to let social antics and foreign customs prevent her from succeeding in a performance-driven education system. Thomas said her schooling reflected the admiration of Germany's economic success that the French aspired to match. It was based on the German obsession with *Leistungsgesellschaft*, a society organized on efficiency and performance.

Our daughter's Bajan-German intuitions told her that she lay at the mercy of a school system that could rebuild her better after knocking her down first. I didn't know this at the time, but later she put it together for herself and for me based on her experiences with the regimented school structure: long days, tough grading, high work volume, grand teacher expectations, and unvarnished candour. In her memory, every day of the first week was a nightmare painted with uncertainty, frustration, and tears.

No path opened up other than the one requiring her to dig deeper into inner reserves and become a fighter.

After another week of tears, we faced a decision-making juncture together. Should we pack up, leave Germany, and ship back to where we'd come from, or would Leandra tough things out?

One evening after supper, we sat under golden lamplight. I faced the sitting-room picture window, Thomas at my right and Leandra across from me. Outside was all forest shadow, for fall had arrived. Leandra had delayed her arrival at the supper table. "Leandra, how about giving this Saarland experiment another two weeks, then we revisit?" Thomas asked, holding her gaze. "We can leave for Nova Scotia if this is too much for you." I gave her a sympathetic nod, which she returned, and we left it at that for the time being.

In early October, when Leandra turned sixteen, I knew she'd be happy if we returned to Canada, but we had arranged for home-sitters to keep our house for the year, rent-free. "Leandra, do you remember that your grade eight teacher and her partner now live in our house?" Thomas asked, for it was necessary to broach this uncomfortable reality.

Leandra's head jerked up. "Oh, yeah." She'd almost forgotten.

"What would it be like for them if we kicked them out a few months after settling in?" her father asked.

"Oh." She was lost in thought for a long moment, then said, "I'll try my best to make it," she said.

"Are you sure? We can go back home even if it's inconvenient for them and us." Thomas always needed firm assurance. I knew he meant it.

"Yes!" she shouted.

I'd been silent until now. "That's great, Leandra, if that's what you *really* want. But remember, we can always go home."

"I'll try to get through it."

I didn't realize I'd been holding my breath until I exhaled. Thomas didn't look relieved yet, but Leandra's generous nature was rising. I held her close, and she broke away to go to her room. Thomas still looked very serious, but I thought things were starting to shift. I hoped she was disappointed not disheartened, and that time and new routines would fetch us a remedy.

Twice on her trips to school, something unexpected happened. One morning, a large chap with a wide arse in paint-stained workman's overalls almost sat in Leandra's lap at the Johanneskirche tram station. He claimed the same seat every morning at 7 A.M., waiting for the Sarreguemines commute. Offering no apologies to anyone, mule-like his attitude declared, "Just bugger off and go somewhere else!" And people did exactly that, far away from him.

The very next day, we hit a snag, complicated by the language barrier and my insecurity. A running notice on the announcement board at the tram station read: *Schienenersatzverkehr zw. Kleinblittersdorf u. Saargemünd wegen Störung auf D.B. Strecke*. Puzzled, Leandra and I checked each other, boarded the train when it arrived, hoping nothing bad would happen.

"It doesn't look good," I whispered to her. She shook her head, her eyes wide, but I felt too shy to ask anyone anything. Mistake.

That morning there was a major disturbance on the line between Kleinblittersdorf and Sarreguemines with the tram ending at Kleinblittersdorf. When the train stopped, not going any further, I swallowed hard and scrambled up. I asked a friendly, vigilant female passenger what was going on. She indicated in brisk English that everyone must get off and wait for a connector bus. No directions I could see announced where such a bus waited or when it would arrive. German bus drivers, unlike those in Barbados, are not necessarily unfriendly souls, but then everything seemed so obvious. Their eyes and actions spoke, revealing aloofness. I imagined them thinking, *Can't you read German? And if you can't, then why are you here?* Leandra and I dashed about, frantic with unanswered questions and concerns, like two lost Canada geese. Leandra would be late for school, and those mean *surveillants* would doubtless pounce.

A few bus drivers eyed us, either not knowing or not wanting to know what ailed us two strange birds. Two options appeared feasible: wait or walk. I felt an acute urge to do the latter but knew that option to be unwise because of the time squeeze. It didn't help that we spied the friendly female passenger disappearing with a cluster of people across the train tracks, along Kleinblittersdorf streets, likely heading off to a nearby workplace. I considered taking a taxi, but I was always the frugal one. Thomas would have done it in a heartbeat; he had no problem spending money he had.

Reason prevailed—walking would worsen our delay. "We'll wait for the connector," I said to Leandra, who looked anxious but followed my lead.

After twenty-five anxiety-inducing minutes, the link bus arrived. We hopped on, riding for fifteen minutes to a destination back of the Sarreguemines train station where several people waited. Leandra was forty-five minutes late for an 8 A.M. start so she sprinted up the hill, her heavy backpack keeping time. She told me afterwards how irritated she'd been having to report to the *surveillant* for a late note to enter class. I turned to reboard the bus back to Kleinblittersdorf for the tram to Saarbrücken. What a morning.

Lesson learned? When you see a running announcement that has *Störung* (disturbance or disruption) in it, ask a question about what's happening. Lose your reserve no matter how self-conscious you feel. Reveal your ignorance to the universe so that you can learn. Embrace new or surprising incidents in a foreign land or face tiresome inconveniences.

12. A Friendly Encounter

September brought perfect fall weather and bright new beginnings. It offered a welcome pause after my humbling university language course and our travels to England, and before the start of classes with the *Volkshochschule*, an adult education institution. I decided to explore the nearby university campus.

Saarland University is a public, modern research university located in Saarbrücken with the medical department in Homburg, a town thirty-six kilometres northeast of Saarbrücken. Established in 1948 in Homburg in co-operation with France, the university comprises eight faculties that cover the major branches of science. Due to its unique history, operating at one time partly independently and linked to France by economic union, the university promotes a European vision. The Saarbrücken campus lay within easy walking or even easier busing distance of our apartment.

On this September day, a fast walk took me through beech woods and past a red, rubberized, Olympic-sized running track bordered on one side by a large indoor arena strengthened by a gigantic steel-framed roof. Steel, the ever-present symbol of Saarland prosperity, reminded me of the French politician Clemenceau pressing the American president Woodrow Wilson to give France control over the Saarland in the movie *Paris 1919*. "Mister President," he said, "I want the Sarre."

The contested land, pulled back and forth between France and Germany, made for a fascinating history. As an anglophone new to the region, I didn't immediately clue into the effects of these border changes. My husband, the history buff in the family, helped me fill in the gaps.

"France occupied the Saarland twice after the First World War and again after the Second World War," he said. "The second time, they just seized it. Turning military barracks into Saarland University was an attempt to make the capture acceptable for Saarländer."

I already knew a referendum held in the late 1950s showed a majority of Saarländer wanted the Saarland to become a state in the German Federal Republic.

"Language is key to a people's identity and country," Thomas added, warming to the topic.

"How so?"

"In the past, the Vosges Mountain range was the barrier between France and Germany." He said a linguistic boundary is reflected in treaties dating back to the ninth century, when the Holy Roman Empire created by Charlemagne was carved up by his descendants. At that time, cities such as Metz and Strasbourg were located well within the territory that became known as the Holy Roman Empire of the German Nation. During nine centuries, various reigns of rulers moved the boundary of France eastwards. This expansion was reversed in 1871 after the Franco-German war. It was reversed again in 1919 after the First World War.

Thomas confessed, "Being an admirer of French culture, I had a hard time accepting the mixed political history of Alsace-Lorraine. When bus drivers and people in Sarreguemines heard my accent, they spoke to me in German."

"So, the border marks a boundary, but not so for French and German citizens of the region," I said.

"Traditions are sometimes more important than tidy political decisions."

On my right, I passed a cafeteria fitted with wide glass panes and an airy patio roomy enough to seat fifty. To the left, I peeked through glass at an empty Olympic-sized swimming pool. I skirted a sandy volleyball court, strolling past the university's largest library. Ahead, I saw the main way through which a steady flow of city buses swung. Near the bus terminal, an artist had undertaken the mission of erecting that twisted, iconic steel artwork. If I continued walking along the bus route that passed through the university, I would leave its grounds and be on the way to Dudweiler.

The campus brimmed with young, energetic local and foreign students. I envied their energy and good fortune. In fresh air, several students waited at nearby bus stops or lounged outside or inside a busy coffee shop with bright red fixtures. The university bookshop, science buildings, and a convenience store populated the area down an incline and to the far right. Nearer on the left, a sprawling green lawn fronted a low brown building, a student union café. I had arrived at the central plaza, the beating heart of the university campus, an easy meeting point for anyone on a date or an appointment. Up a tiresome hill loomed the Mensa, an ugly, three-storey, squarish building built in 1970 of raw, exposed concrete in the architectural style of brutalism. It seats 1,200 and serves about 3,500 meals every day.

But today, I had no interest in exploring the stretches of this university community with its anthill occupants and imposing structures. Nor was I on any schedule, although I was on a date with destiny unknown to me at the time. Having thrown over my day job for a year, I greeted the idea of hanging out in the campus coffee shop on a Wednesday as a rare indulgence. My observation powers sharpened, and I savoured opportunities to be still and watchful without the worry of restive students waiting for me in a classroom, ruled by bells. I bought a newspaper to use as camouflage. The occasion demanded a reward of coffee and a treat: Saarland's delicious bread and pastry options.

Sipping coffee, I tried to make sense of the words spread out before me on the front-page of the *Saarbrücker Zeitung*. I later learned from my husband that a local gang had barged into a popular Croatian restaurant in town, perhaps extorting protection money. The owner succeeded in barricading himself in the men's toilet with a gun before the police arrived.

Having followed through on a recommendation from one of my instructors in the conversational German class to try that very restaurant, Leandra, Thomas, and I had enjoyed a splendid meal there in August. We ate smoky pogacha bread, flavourful *Ćevapčići* (skinless meat sausages), potatoes fried to a golden wonder, and grilled lamb chops accompanied by Balkan sauerkraut.

"Would you like my liqueur, Thomas?" I asked after the skinny, child-sized waitress had served it at the end of our meal.

"Mine too?" Leandra put her shot glass in front of her dad.

"You mean I have to finish three shots?" His eyes gleamed as he shifted in his seat.

"No one's twisting your arm, Dad."

Passing one glass under his nose, Thomas sniffed. "It has a wonderful fruity aroma. A Croatian brandy made from ripe, blue plums. Are you sure you don't want it, Claudette?"

"Positive." So, Thomas faced the onerous task of finishing three shots of traditional Balkan liqueur, *Slivovitz*, a brandy digestive. He did so with gusto, loving fine food and knowing more about wines and alcoholic beverages than I could ever remember. Three more attempts to dine there fell through, as this popular place overflowed with patrons.

Now at the university cafeteria, I persisted with my newspaper, becoming aware that I was being watched. A woman with a curious expression sat across from me, enjoying a sandwich. Eye contact could not be avoided. The lady said *Hallo* and something else in German. It may have been as simple as *"Sprechen Sie Deutsch?"* (Do you speak German?), but at that instant, the little German I did know flew straight from my brain and made a direct line for Nova Scotia.

"Sorry, I don't know any German," I said, hoping that would be enough. But this outgoing spirit was nothing if not keen, switching to English. After all, we were sitting in a coffee shop in an international university where the average German, Saarländer or not, spoke some English.

We started chatting. Her name was Anna, and she lived about half an hour outside Saarbrücken. She drove into the city to take Spanish and Italian classes at the university, to shop, and to see and be seen. A retired teacher, Anna had many interests, among them music, travelling, and learning languages. She spoke about the university, Saarland, and her life. In turn, I gave her a condensed version of my life story and told her I lived with my husband and teenage daughter nearby and that we were spending a year away from home in Nova Scotia.

"And so, where do you stay?" she asked.

"At the university residence, in Fuchstälchen. Across from Wildpark," I said.

"Uh huh. That's a secluded spot. And your daughter, how old is she?"

"Almost sixteen. She's going to school in France, at Lycée Jean de Pange."

"Uh huh. Why so far away? That means she has to take the bus and tram every morning."

"She's attending a French school in Nova Scotia, so it's good to have her attend school in France to continue with the language."

"But there's a French school right here where she can learn German. Why doesn't she go there?"

"Oh, is there? I didn't know. Not really sure why."

"Would you like to see the French school and find out if Leandra can go there? It would be better for her. She could make friends with teenagers close by and meet Germans her own age. It's the Deutsch-Französische School. Really close."

"Okay, if it's not too much trouble."

"Let's go then. My car's parked in the university garage down the hill. We'll drive there."

As we walked along, Anna joked, "Don't worry, you're not being kidnapped."

"Oh, I'm not afraid." We laughed.

We became fast friends. I learned that Anna missed her husband, who had passed away some years earlier from a heart attack. Her adult son lived and worked elsewhere in Germany and younger sister, a music teacher, lived nearby.

"And you, Claudette, what do you do in Canada?" She asked as we walked.

"I teach at high school."

"What luck, to meet a teacher from Canada! What's that like, teaching in Canada?"

"Nothing like what I'm doing today, hanging around in a coffee shop on campus." We laughed again, like old friends already.

"Right. You said you arrived in Canada as a student. Where from?"

"Barbados, in the West Indies."

"Oh, I've always been so interested in how people live in different parts of the world." It had started out as an ordinary day, and out of nowhere, popped up a new acquaintance. At first, the encounter felt overwhelming as Anna charged in to solve the German school affair, not in need of a fix, but I greeted the chance to meet a woman from Saarland and to learn from her about the country. I wanted to know how her alternative school suggestion would go.

After a short ride through posh residential boulevards with gated driveways, we arrived at a three-storey building tucked amidst neat hedgerows and plush lawns. Walking into a bright lobby with high ceilings, we greeted a uniformed student and, after a brief wait, were ushered into the spotless, roomy office of an administrator. Her manner was somewhat frosty. She offered us seats as she took hers behind a wide writing desk of light wood. Speaking German, Anna explained the situation about Leandra and the desire to see her attend school with equal opportunity to learn German and French. To be sure, Leandra's German did not reach high school level, and to throw this overachiever into grade ten classes requiring German would be catastrophic. She'd be compelled to learn lots of German before understanding concepts and content in given subjects, leading to a bonkers year. As it stood, it already felt like that for us, even though she was being taught in familiar French.

Sitting unruffled and efficient, the dress-suited administrator spoke in German, which Anna translated for me afterwards. She didn't approve of students dabbling. One year would not be enough for serious study at her high school, reputed as a school for high achievers. After grade nine, an equal number of classes were taught in French and German. Slender and graceful with a German-French accent full of professional-ese, she sat even taller. Not all students fitted the school's exacting academic demands. Her lips moved little, as if in a secret code, but her hands worked at her desk. What evidence was there that this lady's daughter would succeed here? she'd asked Anna, throwing me a glance. It would be best for the student in question to continue where she was, as she would be returning to Canada after grade ten and any more academic disruption at this point would prove unnecessary and undesirable.

I viewed the exchanges with alert interest but felt a bit like a misfit, as the discussion showed no real need of my input. The impromptu meeting came to a polite, decisive end when the speakers stood as if lifted up by one mighty hand.

Once we were out of earshot, Anna related much of the conversation to me straight away. What ticked Anna right off was the presumption of "dabbling." "Why not even consider a trial run?" Anna fumed. "How can a German citizen be denied entry into a school teaching in both German and French, in Saarland of all states? The arrogance!"

Nonetheless, the result was as dry as laundry spread out on the grass in the scorching sun. Leandra was denied admission at the Deutsch-Französische School. With this unlooked-for skirmish settled, the status quo continued, and from my vantage point, things looked no worse than they appeared before Anna's charge. "It's just fine, Anna. Thank you. No harm done," I said.

What sweet relief that Leandra didn't have to change schools. We'd just settled the crisis of not having to return to Canada because of her lonely existence in an anonymous school, with no friends, strange teachers, and weird sauces. I had agreed to accompany Anna out of novelty and the pull of a new acquaintance. Later, when I said to my family, "Hey, guess what happened today?" they reacted with surprise at first. Thomas and Leandra agreed that it was a generous attempt by Anna to broaden our knowledge and understanding of Saarland's education possibilities, aimed at German language acquisition, but it was best for Leandra to remain right there at Jean de Pange.

A gregarious woman, Anna had swooped in, extending warm gifts of invitations and connections, and I seized upon them. Meeting her turned out to be a terrific chance event. I reaped rewards of friendship, new experiences, and knowledge venturing out into Saarland. One genuine friendship vanquished the prospect of isolation outside my immediate family. It gave more texture to my foreign life, making the connection to the new landscape feel concrete and real.

In July 2016, my family made a return visit to Saarland, and we attended Anna's birthday party, which she'd postponed so we could be there. We're still in touch today by phone, cards, letters, and email, exchanging book titles for good reads.

13. At College in People's School

Whenever the literary German dives into a sentence,
this is the last you are going to see of him till he emerges
on the other side of his Atlantic with his verb in his mouth.
– Mark Twain

What are those two women gabbing about? I wondered about the pair sitting in front of me on the bus. Observing two cool university types next to me at the bus stop piqued my nosiness. *Are they doing a post-mortem on their latest engineering exam?* And in the supermarket, I thought, *What's the manager saying to the employee restacking containers of quark?* These people weren't looking at or talking about me. That wasn't the point.

They were talking about things that interested them, gave excitement, made them laugh, glow, or scoff. Back home, snippets of strangers' conversations about the weather, lunch dates, upcoming concerts, and sales at the local grocery store circled and enriched my universe. Faced with the reality of daily life in Germany, I dreamed. Wouldn't it be wonderful to wave a magic wand and have all that German spoken around me made clear? Wouldn't it be grand if I could read and talk about German poetry and literature with Anna and the teachers at the Volkshochschule? In Germany, a Volkshochschule is a cross between a community college and an adult-learning university but it does not grant degrees.

For me, trying to learn German was like walking in spiked heels on a beach of sea-rounded rocks, every step fretted by painful, inevitable stumbles. American author and satirist Mark Twain made two attempts to learn German, at ages fifteen and forty-three. In his 1880 essay "The Awful German Language" in *A Tramp Abroad*, he explores the vexations a native English speaker encounters when trying to learn German. Twain takes a swipe at linguistic gender in German, saying, "Every noun has a gender, and there is no sense or system in distribution; so, the gender of each must be learned separately and by heart. There is no other way. To do this, one has to have a memory like a memorandum-book. In German, a young lady has no sex, while a turnip has. Think what overwrought reverence that shows for the turnip, and what callous disrespect for the girl."

I prodded Thomas about this witticism. Frowning, he answered with a cryptic remark, "I think Twain doesn't fully understand the *neutrum* for girls." Umm, neither did I, and life not being eternal, I felt no need to linger for more of Thomas's insight unless I planned on permanent residence in Germany.

I thought if exceptions to German grammar and spelling rules operated anything like they did in English, they would match the relentless dandelions erupting in our front yard every spring. I couldn't win with German or with nature, as there would always be one more rule and one more dandelion. As my time in Saarland stretched out, I became more mindful of the advice a friend of Twain's offered him: "Speak in German, Mark. Some of these people may understand English."

I quickly picked up where to break German words into syllables for proper pronunciation and liked to indulge in it as a game. This sounds easier to do than it is for someone new to German. For instance, an easy English word like *linked* to an English speaker is made up of the root word *link* and the suffix *-ed* indicating past tense. And it would be pronounced as one syllable. If we heard anyone pronounce it as *lin-ked*, we would hear the mistake right away.

Acquiring German, with its many long, indomitable words, involved learning to decode where natural syllable breaks and stresses occurred. It became a tricky but fun exercise, one of the drills I came to enjoy. Place names could be a mouthful, like our apartment's location in Fuchstälchen.

This name, divided into Fuchs-täl-chen, was hard for me to say because of the *ä* vowel modified by an umlaut. Kleinblittersdorf, on the other hand, broke into Klein-blit-ters-dorf and slid over my tongue.

Thomas remains convinced that it's hard to waffle in German. In contrast, English provides copious opportunities for ambiguity and downright lies because the speaker can always cop out by saying, "That's not what I really meant! I was joking." Is he right? Whenever I used the word *just*, as in "just salad," for my husband it always meant *only* or *merely*, as a put-down, rather than *simply* or *purely*, as I sometimes meant it. For comparison, translated literally, the German phrase *So ist es nun einmal* is "So is it now once." A sensible translation into English says, "It is what it is." One of the hazards of translation is potential loss of meaning.

Learning *ein bisschen Deutsch* (a little German) in the Volkshochschule amounted to flight in my imagination after the challenges of August.

Thomas offered great support. Sitting in the living room one early August evening, he leafed through a thick catalogue. "Course listings and locations are in this booklet," he said, holding it up. I peered over his shoulder. Numerous course listings ran through pages and pages on every imagined subject offered at Volkshochschule, "the people's university." I registered for a course from September 2013 to January 2014. Classes ran from 9:00 A.M. to 1:15 P.M. Mondays to Thursdays, leaving Fridays free.

Thumbing through the book, Thomas said, "You'll have two female instructors, Antje Becker and Konstanze Friedmann. They'll have you speaking German in no time." I conjured up *Frauen* with self-assured, steady gazes.

"Yay! I can't wait to begin," I said.

In September, when classes started, I caught buses from Wildpark that wound through the built-up city area and crossed the Saar Bridge. After fifteen minutes, I got off on Stengelstraße. My destination was across the street in a bright, renovated room, part of a larger three-floor health and social services building. I met other German language course participants there four times a week for five months.

The Volkshochschule course handed me a lifetime of insights. I began adding to the little German acquired back in Halifax and on the month-long summer course. I had read and heard that German was a guttural language full of throat sounds, but I soon realized that was a sweeping statement. German used more parts of the mouth than I had given serious thought to: the tongue, lips, teeth, roof of the mouth, throat, and soft palate. These parts moved in wily ways to create sounds forced through the voice box. Distinct regional dialects, vocabulary, and inflections persist in an otherwise united nation. As Thomas noted, Saarländer spoke a softer, perhaps subtler-sounding German than he did, hailing from Northern Germany. And in cities like Hannover and Göttingen, arguably the clearest tones of German ring out.

In my opinion, many Germans speak with a sure-fire force and intensity, to the point of sometimes sounding strident. This does not of necessity produce more volume than Bajans or Canadians speaking English. Add to this the more expressive uses of the face and mouth. It appeared to Leandra that German women in general possessed deeper voices than Canadian women, although the same could be said for Black women. Saying *schwarz* (black) surely tested the elasticity of my lips while keeping them poised over the teeth, a challenge I've still not mastered. Sometimes I eavesdropped in pure fascination on conversations between Saarländer women, wonderstruck. Was the woman speaking going to take a breath, or was she going to go on until she collapsed into an apoplexy brought on by sheer expressive force? Leandra admitted this forceful delivery of speech by Germans, young and old alike, carried with it such a commanding air of confidence that she often found the speakers intimidating.

Above all, I tried to overcome the difficulty of learning and speaking the language. I kept asking myself why it was so hard for me, given that I'd heard a fair bit of German over my married life. The answer revealed a combination of things, including conventions of the language for speech and writing, pronunciation, and the inconsistencies and idiosyncrasies inherent in any language. For starters, idioms and aphorisms were hardly ever self-evident, often relying on metaphor and analogy. But it also had to do as much with myself as with the language. I told myself I needed to show more grit, the ability to double down in order to learn and use this foreign language. As a Barbadian growing up in a working-class household, I'd allowed family and friends too much say in my education rather than standing up against mockery and criticism. In my home, no one encouraged or made room for growth and development of a second language. More than anything else, I feared making inevitable mistakes, mispronouncing words, feeling foolish and failing. In introspective moments, I promised to be more patient of my high school students' efforts when I returned to Nova Scotia.

Even after six months in Germany, I found it difficult to understand the meaning of any given sentence. Verbs often arrived at the end of sentences. *Ich weiß, dass Zucker ungesund ist* literally translates into "I know that sugar unhealthy is." That's fairly straightforward, but take this example: *Sagen Sie mir doch bitte, wie ich endlich meinen Zimmerschlüssel bekommen kann?* Direct translation of this diamond becomes: "Say you me yet something please, how I finally my room key get can?" The meaning of the sentence only becomes clear with the last few words, the nouns and verbs. By the time I'd followed such sentences to the end and figured out what needed to be delivered or acted upon, the meaning of the preceding series of words had evaporated. Perhaps Germans just have better memories.

When speaking of gender in German (or other languages), the right terms are masculine, feminine and neuter. So, examples are: masculine, *der Tisch* (table); feminine, *die Katze* (cat); and neuter, *das Paar* (pair)—except when nouns are in plural form and they take *die*, as in *die Taschen* (bags), the same article for feminine nouns. To remember the article differences appeared impossible for a late learner like me. After all, Germans have had a lifetime of learning and remembering. On top of gender, a foreigner is expected to learn the proper declensions of articles for four cases: nominative, genitive, dative, and accusative, each case, in my opinion, more difficult than its predecessor.

What attention to these grammatical details and structure meant was that every time I opened my mouth to speak, I was in danger of being wrong. Who wanted to be subjected to nonstop corrections? Right after I thought I could fly, my wings failed me. I couldn't pick up German the way I'd picked up English and Bajan dialect, learning from the womb. Bajan dialect is based on English as it was spoken by Irish and English field supervisors during the time of plantation slavery. I was born into a Bajan family of African ancestry. At school, it was all about the Queen's English, and then there were influences from attending church services and reading the King James Version of the Bible.

Applying myself to listening, speaking, reading, and writing German was beginning to resemble a life's work, the very thing I'd taken a deferred leave to avoid. I began to face the truth of my undertaking. I did not feel heroic, and I was in a race I could lose.

Possessing the right brain matter amounted to a flagrant assumption. As a woman in middle age, I began to have clear-headed second thoughts. My own limitations of memory, word processing, speech facility, exposure to spoken German, personality, and past experiences with foreign-language learning intruded upon my (in)ability to decipher the mysteries of German. I had inherited the broad-tongued drawl of my native Bajan dialect, overlaid with a kind of standardized English inflection copied from high school teachers and other professionals. I noted that German possessed a variety of subtle inflected nuances that were not part of English. I found the umlauts, *ä, ö, ü*, and the sound in German somewhere between an *a* and an *e*, absent from my repertoire. These were all tough confessions for me to own up to myself.

It's one thing to learn the meaning of a word or phrase and quite another to use it spot-on. How many times did I look up *sogar*, *sonst*, *kaum*, and *doch* only to be stumped by them again, even in the same day? It seemed that the more I pursued a word, the more it slipped away into the shadows. And then after forgetting about it and relaxing, sleeping even, it would surface like a flying fish breaking ocean waters. *Swoosh*. My mind had set the brain a task. Long after the request for the meaning of the German word for *stroll* had been set aside, an answer arrived: *bummeln*. How did that happen?

One of the most frustrating aspects in acquiring the language was how German prefixes changed the meanings of perfectly fine words. A few examples for the verb *legen* (to lay) illustrate the defeats prefixes often bestowed on German language debutants like me:

- *ab-legen*: literally, to take off (a coat)
- *an-legen*: to lay by/at, to attach something, to dock
- *auf-legen*: to lay up, to apply, to play (a vinyl record)

Here different prefixes make changes to the meaning of the root, just one example of dozens of verbs and prefixes that I found maddening. *What was I to do?* Should I yield to the temptation of more travel or keep trying to become a different, better person through more language learning?

And then there were the dreadful *trennbare Verben* (separable verbs). A warning must go out, as German has many such separable verbs, for example:

- *aus* (out, off), *ausgehen* (to go out), *ausmachen* (to switch off)
- *zurück* (back), *zurückgeben* (to give back), *zurückkommen* (to come back)

Trennbare verbs were disruptors of my peace. I refused to show stoic acceptance of their hazards. They were accompanied by cautionary words from our instructors. "What looks like a trennbar verb may not be a trennbar verb." Inseparable prefix verbs, having a fixed prefix, needed to be committed to memory so that they could be distinguished from the separable ones. The most common permanent prefixes found in German are *ver-*, *ge-*, and *be-*. The following words are examples:

- *brennen* (to burn, transitive); *verbrennen* (to burn, burn completely, transitive; to get burnt, intransitive)
- *raten* (to advise, to guess); *verraten* (to betray)
- *brauchen* (to need); *verbrauchen* (to consume or to use up)

Very confusing, hard to grasp and use.

As a rule, German sentence structure puts verbs in second or final place. For trennbar verbs, the prefix always appears in the final position. If a particular sentence structure puts the whole verb at the end of the sentence, then the prefix and root verb remain joined. If a sentence puts the verb in second place, then only the root verb will appear there. The separated prefix goes at the end of the sentence.

To recognize that a prefix can detach itself from its root verb and hang alone at the end of a sentence but, in reality, belongs to that verb in the second position is nothing less than miraculous. It seems to defy gravity. The first time I recognized this feature on my own and was able to decipher the meaning of a sentence so structured, I went to evening mass and lit a candle. Here is an example from a grammar book of how this oddity operates:

anfangen (to start)

1. Root verb in second place: *Ich fange mit der Arbeit an.* (I start the work.)
2. Root verb in final place: *Morgens trinke ich Schokolade, weil ich dann mit der Arbeit anfange.* (In the mornings I drink hot chocolate, because afterwards I begin work.)

As a lover of language, I had to admit, German worked in a mysterious yet beautiful way, but I didn't get it. If only I had another lifetime.

Leandra observed that many of her fellow summer course participants embraced learning German full-throttle. Some French chums displayed trouble nailing certain German sounds, often speaking with an adorable French inflection. For instance, the *h* or *q* sounds typically gave them a degree of trouble. Some Italians and Spaniards in the Volkshochschule shared similar difficulty. Served to show, even savvy European youths acquiring a second, third, or even fourth language expended much effort doing so. (This is something unilingual anglophones like myself ignore at our peril.) Leandra fared fine in Sarreguemines with French. In German classes, she learned what teachers taught her and struggled to apply it in conversations. It gave me solace to know that I was in respectable, younger company.

Thomas translated when I badgered him, but I think he thought I should open up my head, get rid of the concrete, and let the instructors pour in the language.

I never did learn to say the three letters in the German alphabet with umlauts, *ä*, *ö*, and *ü*, no matter how hard I practised. In fact, I wasn't sure I could hear the subtle difference of those sounds, although I pretended to. Words beginning with the *z* sound were tyrannical, requiring a firm *tz* articulation that could not be accomplished without spitting at the listener, whereas the true *z* sound was set aside for the letter *s. And all of this makes rational sense in language heaven?*

I considered everyday German to be a *höfliche und respektvolle* (polite and respectful) language. I learned too late that I should never go up to a complete stranger in Saarland wide-eyed and pop a direct question, saying for example, "Can you tell me where the train station is?" Or more rudely, "Where is the train station?" Politeness in German calls for an introduction, as in, "Excuse me (or please), can you tell me where the train station is?" as you would expect in any civilized part of the world. My consternation surfaced because I had on several prior occasions already done the impolite versions out of panic. See what living in a foreign country can reduce a polite person to? "Where is the supermarket?" "What time is it?" "Where is City Hall?" In future I promised never to approach German strangers in direct, abrupt ways.

After absorbing new language skills, I prefaced my questions to strangers with courtesy. I'd say, *"Sagen Sie mir doch bitte..."* (Tell me, please...), *"Darf ich fragen..."* (Allow me to ask...), *"Können Sie mir bitte sagen..."* (Can you tell me, please...), and *"Gibt es noch etwas..."* (There is still something...). I wondered why I had to travel all the way to Saarland to learn civil German. Couldn't I have acquired those phrases by staring long and hard at German language books?

No clear, systematic way beckoned me forward to negotiate this forest of noun genders, cases, prefixes, separable verbs, and fixed prefixes. Thus, I resorted to hiking solo, trying to figure out a labyrinth of trails to memorize.

14. The College Folks

I faced the Volkshochschule with a mix of eagerness and apprehension in September. It presented an opportunity for me to become better acquainted with Saarbrücken and the people in it. I wanted to meet people who lived there as citizens and migrants. In that bright Saarbrücken classroom, I met people from around the globe sharing a common desire. I was witnessing some of the effects of economic and political forces at work in Europe, the Middle East, and Africa in the early twenty-first century, shaping a small western corner of Germany.

At the classroom door on my first day, I swallowed hard as an eyelid twitched dreading to face the awkwardness I'd experienced back in the summer language course. Compelled by an inner force, I moved forward, faking confidence. Living in Germany with little knowledge of the language was akin to living in the shadowlands of a mighty fortress without a key to get inside. I felt lost and vulnerable without the language solution. I needed the key.

Among the others signed up for German A1 and A2 courses were people from Moldova, Romania, Spain, France, Russia, Portugal, Syria, Hungary, Poland, Liberia, Thailand, Vietnam, Iraq and Indonesia. Again, as earlier at the Ausländeramt—the foreigner office—I wondered why I had always presumed Germany was monocultural, or at least lacking in significant cultural and ethnic diversity.

Course participants, mostly new arrivals, came to a Germany that in 2012 was considered an European economic powerhouse, in contrast to some other European nations that during that time had been facing economic meltdowns, such as Greece and Italy. My course colleagues came as refugees from Africa or the Middle East, as seekers of educational and economic opportunity, or they followed loved ones attending university.

After two months in Saarland, I needed to move beyond interactions within my family. Thomas could meet and mingle with geographers and other like-minded, dishevelled academics. Leandra existed in the weird barrenness of a large high school absent of anyone yet to call a friend, but as painful as that was for her, it was still something daring with change at its core. Her every day took her beyond a narrow comfort zone toward personal growth. A social butterfly, in time Leandra would enjoy the challenges of study and a social life away from helicopter parents.

And what about me? Images of the professional life I'd left behind spun as I again landed on the wrong side of the teacher's desk. Was this experiment going to be liberating or humiliating?

When I converted prices for goods and services from Canadian dollars into euros, our expenses added up quickly. At €580 per semester, the course cost a good chunk. But for the number of instruction hours, it represented top value compared to the earlier Saarland University course. On day one, sixteen course participants introduced themselves to our instructor, Antje Becker. Slender with a twinkle in her blue eyes, she said she was a retired *Gymnasium* teacher. In the German school system, a *Gymnasium* is the most advanced and highest form of secondary school.

I introduced myself in baby German: "Ich bin Claudette Bouman. Ich komme aus Kanada mit meinem Mann und meiner Tochter für ein Jahr. Wir wohnen im Gästehaus der Saarland Universität beim Wildpark. Ich bin eine Lehrerin in Kanada." (I told them my name that I had come from Canada with my husband and daughter for a year, where I was living, and that I was a teacher.) With mixed feelings, I noticed that I was again the most senior in the group, barring the instructor. A Romanian man in a seat near the exit, perhaps signalling foreshadowing, may have been in his fifties too. After initial intense interest and participation, he disappeared from the course well before it ended.

Most of my new acquaintances planned to begin studies, seek employment, and settle in Saarland or some other German state. That meant beginning to select from the German language buffet table. Variation existed in their individual stories. Two women from nearby Lorraine, each with young children, had joined military husbands posted in Germany. Two young prospective university students needed to acquire at least B2 language skills before acceptance into any German university. Three foreign women were married to German partners. One student was a refugee claimant, while another worked as an au pair, testing the waters in Germany before taking a pivotal plunge.

For potential university students, the alternative to off-campus German meant a year of *Studienkolleg*, a university prep program. Arrivals from outside the European Union needed to meet residence requirements to get the much-coveted residence card. One of those requirements was knowledge of German.

A broad river of migrants was flowing into Germany. In 2012, arrivals reached one million as a direct result of the 1995 Schengen Agreement. Under that initial agreement, seven EU countries—Belgium, France, Germany, Luxemburg, Netherlands, Portugal, and Spain—abolished their internal border controls, harmonizing requirements and allowing their citizens holding visas to visit participating countries. Passports were only checked and stamped if people came from or went to a non-Schengen country. So, because internal borders within the EU had been erased in all but Bulgaria, Croatia, Cyprus, Ireland, Romania, and the United Kingdom, Europeans with necessary connections and funds could enter and begin seeking opportunities in Germany. They required places to live and livelihoods, as no country welcomes homeless people.

Two types of students emerged: those who enjoyed the challenges of the classroom and those who were being forced to tolerate it by some ruling or other pressures. The group crossed racial, social, and educational lines. It included people like me, holding a somewhat privileged position as a professional adult on a year's leave from work in Nova Scotia. With time and money on my side, I chose to pursue German courses. In the circle were a government-sponsored refugee and others less motivated who left the classes out of boredom or for financial or other reasons.

I found the group dynamics of course participants intriguing as I wore both my student and my teacher hats. Many actions and deeds resembled those I'd observed among adolescents at home. This confirmed the universality of human behaviour, even among a diverse group.

Andrea, a Portuguese student, had joined her partner in Saarland, she attending classes while he pursued a Ph.D. in science. A petite young woman in her early twenties, her light brown eyes lit up a pleasant, smooth face. Her personality was open and outgoing, exhibiting a spirit of independence in a frank, candid style. She was not embarrassed to admit she had little money to pay for anything, including course fees or textbooks; she held out on payments for as long as possible. She asked straight out in English, "Frau Becker, do I have to pay for any days I am absent?" This was discussed in detail during class time. *Aren't payments made at registration?* A few days later, Frau Becker came back with an answer: "Bring a doctor's note for missed days to have deductions." *Good, that's settled.*

Our room fitted five round tables seating four or five people each. I sat with three others, Anya, Estella, and Marlon, positioned mid-room and to the left, facing the instructor. Two tables were set ahead of us, one more was to the right, and another toward the back. I sat right behind Andrea's table. I noticed every time she latched on to her iPad to play Candy Crush.

In December, Andrea said to our table, "I applied for a job advertised online looking for kitchen help. I start this weekend." The workplace turned out to be at a modest *Imbiss*, a caravan-type food stand, on the bank of the Saar River. She worked for two evenings, then left, saying, "The amount of work the owner asked of me needed two people. He was rude and prejudiced against me because I speak little German." The two women at my table joined me in making sympathetic noises. I thought her employer was not unjustified in remarking on her lack of German. She seemed not to be paying attention in class or making any real effort to learn the language. No wonder she was having a hard time finding or keeping a job. Meanwhile, the only Indonesian in the group, a lean, tongue-tied young man, told us he worked at a local KFC from 3:00 P.M. until 1:00 A.M. After weeks of this schedule, he looked like a zombie with his exhausted, watery-red eyes.

Kareem, a teenager from Syria, was on his own in Saarland. A shock of thick, wavy, dark hair crowned his head. He was of medium height and build, with an amiable temper. With lucid responses and alert conduct, it was obvious that he interpreted and understood way more German than I did. He answered correctly when I and others faltered. Bit by bit he began losing drive as the course wore on and homesickness crept into his spirit. *If only he would exercise less frustration and more determination*, the teacher in me thought.

An uncle had taught him the German he knew before arriving in Saarland. Soon he became fixated on having German vocabulary and concepts he did not grasp right away, explained in English. This request drove one of our other instructors, Frau Konstanze Friedmann, wild. The purpose of the course emphasized German immersion, development of conversational German. "Why always effing English?" she exclaimed. Her reprimand meant: "Forget English, you're in German class now!"

Kareem stopped asking her for English words and started directing his questions at me. He said he was getting worried about losing his English by filling up his head with German words and grammar. When he asked me for English explanations or equivalents, I squirmed. I didn't want to ignore him. I'd wait for the moment Konstanze focused on the whiteboard and whisper, "*Bekommen* means to get, not to become."

"But it's not like English."

I'd nod, "I know." My table mates Anya from Moldova and Estella from France would smile and shake their heads. I felt like a kid in school, guilty of breaking the teacher's "no talking out of turn" rule.

In part, I shared Kareem's argument that some concepts required explanation in an understood language. But there was a problem: Konstanze did not speak Arabic, Kareem's native tongue. However, she did speak English, so what was the harm? But for most of the course participants, English was an additional language. Was the instructor supposed to provide words and explanations in every language known to participants? In our class alone, these were Romanian, Thai, Vietnamese, Spanish, Italian, Portuguese, Russian, French, Polish, Japanese, Indonesian, and Arabic. Surely no one could expect such accommodation.

I watched as the classroom negotiations swung first one way and then another until frustrations boiled over. Konstanze, a volatile type, took another swing at Kareem, who was pacing toward her with a laser-like aim. She yelled, "Enough already! Learn it in German!" Even the mature Romanian, now positioned away from his favoured spot by the door, jumped in, imploring Kareem in English, "Stop making comparisons between English and German. They are different languages. By prolonging the mistake, you are losing the time!" An awkward, shocked silence descended. At our table, we checked each other's startled faces with quick, covert glances. Our faces mirrored tight looks, gazing at nothing in particular.

Antje Becker, more patient than the impulsive Konstanze, wagged a finger at Kareem to "be aware of false friends," or false cognates. "Many similarities exist between German and English, but what looks like an equivalent is oftentimes different," she warned. I thought of German words that met Antje's description: *der Tag* means "the day" not "the tag," *die Wand* means "the wall" not "the wand," *die Tasten* means "keys" not "tastes." But of course, there are German words that are similar to English ones, and that is where the seduction has power.

Making meaning lay at the heart of our daily struggle with German versus English, Arabic, and other languages. For Kareem, something kept getting lost in translation. When I reflected on my circumstances, I saw I too faced a similar plight, for we two occupied the same boat in our daily language struggles. It was a contest we were in danger of failing without a hearty fight every day that we placed our vulnerability on display at the Volkshochschule. Without the heart to push back the boundaries of my comfort zone, I'd fall hard. Failing forward meant I'd have to learn how to rescue myself when lost in a sea of foreign words if I wanted to enjoy the cultural and linguistic benefits of the feast that was Germany.

In late October, a month into scheduled classes, a new student joined us. Anton, a Black man in his late twenties, originating from Liberia, was well built and sported a short haircut and a bold look. From the beginning, the seating arrangements with established groups of four or five gave him trouble. He made his mark at once with an abrasive, forceful style.

He struggled from the start to find a steady, cohesive group. Two female participants sharing his table shifted out of the room to a higher-level group. He sat by himself for a few days until joined by a mature student. Soon that fellow moved away to a different table of three young women, leaving Anton to try joining an established group of men and women, including Andrea and Kareem.

They did not warm up to Anton for I observed their body language leaning away. Perhaps they held stereotypes and racist attitudes, though no one among them showed any explicit, obvious dislike. Soon, he turned to our table and started "hitting on" Anya. Tall and slender, she had joined the course two weeks after it started with an attractive, petite acquaintance, Estella, from France with Spanish ancestry. These two women and I became chummy at the same table together with Marlon, a Spanish man who understood no English at all, just as I understood no Spanish.

One day, Anton made a brash declaration to the room during a class break. "I must make new friends," he said and began targeting Anya. He had already told the room something like, "I'm married with two children. I have an older child, with her mother in Africa, and a baby with my new wife in Saarland." After Anton left at break time, Estella turned to me and Anya and mocked him, saying, "Well, I guess we've made ourselves a new friend!" She and Anya laughed at Anton's clumsy attempts behind his back. Anya, uninterested in his antics, had joined her fiancé in Saarland. They had met at university in Romania. Married, Estella doted on two preteen daughters. She teased, "Anya, he's slobbering over you because, according to him, you're the youngest and prettiest of the women." Anya pretended to spit in disgust. I felt embarrassed for Anton. "Anya, ignore him to give a message of not interested. He'll get the point," I told her. *Unless in addition to being socially awkward, he's foolish too.* Soon enough, Anton did understand Anya's coolness toward him and retreated to regroup for a second chase.

I acted civil toward Anton, which gave him false confidence to start up his machismo act toward me within a few days. *Why doesn't this guy get it?* One day, he reached over and grabbed my notes to see what I'd written without so much as an excuse me. My head jerked up as I snatched it back. Anton had clued in that sitting beside Kareem was not going to help him learn German. He may have been thoughtless and lazy, but he wasn't stupid.

Before, I had tried being civil, helping Anton whenever I could. But he started triggering my nerves with his too-familiar ways and over-assertiveness, especially after the scribbler grab. Estella thought him downright rude, and I agreed. His actions were rash, without him meaning them to be, as contradictory as that seemed. I knew Bajan men like him; men who hadn't been taught to act in better ways. So, after the notebook incident, I cooled toward him, forcing him to absorb a lesson about social conduct the hard way. *Consideration for others is a must in groups when people are familiar strangers. Doesn't he get that?* I was fascinated by the dynamics that resulted from being forced to relate to the others. And we had to do this with English as the lingua franca.

Most students had little to do with Anton as the course progressed, avoiding eye contact and ignoring his behaviour. This deliberate social distancing peaked at a mid-December party held in our classroom. A warm, seasonal glow pervaded the gathering. We'd cobbled together cakes, tarts, pies, flans, cheeses, juices, and wine. One guy from Russia brought the most delicious torte made of layers of sponge cake, whipped cream, and quark, topped with glazed strawberries. It was beautiful to see, never mind the eating of it. I restrained myself to one helping, wondering why participants left three-quarters of the torte sitting on the table.

Anton thought it was time to confess. "There was a time when I chased many girls and had more than one girlfriend at a time." Marriage had changed him, he said. Silence reigned. Anya looked sideways, I stared past him, and Estella changed the subject to her older daughter now turning thirteen. *Did he think this made a path to friendship? Why couldn't he talk about something else?* This inept confession alienated him even more and at last, it began to hit home. When the group organized a diner as a final class event before Christmas break, no one expressed surprise when Anton, now an isolated figure, didn't join in.

When classes resumed in January, Anton was disengaged when he did attend. The instructor remarked on it, telling him, "You're so bored, you don't know what to do with yourself." With his feet up on a chair, Anton admitted, "I can't listen to anyone teaching, talking on and on." Alert for a minute, he declared, "That's not the way I learn." After that admission, he yawned, slouched deeper into his chair, and refused to answer any more of the instructor's questions. His actions reminded me of students acting out in Nova Scotia. Over the years, I've faced down some rough classes and tough students. I felt embarrassed for the instructor and for Anton.

I had learned something of Anton's past in early October. During a coffee break, he told me and Kareem about an encounter with the Saarland police. One day out walking his baby, he stumbled upon a semiconscious man sprawled out on the sidewalk, bleeding. Alarmed, he made a quick call to the police. Without any hesitation, he said, "I live in a shady neighbourhood with criminals." Two officers came, one male and one female. "The policeman asked me if I had anything to do with the injury. Can you imagine that? I asked him if he was nuts. Would I call the police if I had caused the injury?"

On the surface, it seemed a logical enough question for a policeman doing a tough job. Anton had smelled racism, which only a fool would be naive enough to ignore. He reacted by raising his voice and gesturing in anger at the officer's question. He could not be blamed for feeling defensive with the police, as he was trying to do the right thing. His anger caused the officer to overreact and threaten to arrest him causing Anton to explode. "I called the officer racist for mistreating Blacks. I told him, 'Arrest me and you will hear from my lawyer.'" The policewoman intervened to calm down an escalating situation by saying they were just doing their job and had no problem with Anton. To this, Anton said to me and Kareem, "I told her I had no problem with her, but I had a problem with her partner for treating me as if I committed a crime." In any case, the situation ended without Anton's arrest and with an ambulance arriving for the injured man. He was drunk, had fallen and hurt himself, and remained oblivious of the trouble caused by his condition.

Anton shared many Black men's deep hostility toward white police officers, especially male officers. Underneath that was perhaps a barely repressed resentment toward authority figures. His story reminded me similar situations in Canada and those relayed in American news reports. Anton had said, "White German policemen are often racist and tend to react too aggressively toward Black men for no good reason. The worst thing is for a Black man in Germany to have 'mus-kles.' Then he's really in danger because policemen feel physically threatened by ripped Black men." Unconscious bias operates as an intangible but nonetheless very real thing.

Fear, in Anton's opinion, prompts policemen to enforce total control and domination. My advice to him amounted to what I'd give to any Black man anywhere, relative or friend, even in Barbados with a Black police force: "Stay out of trouble and do your best to keep away from the police."

A naive piece of advice within the context of North American history might still be useful in Saarland

As for my best advice, when did a young, Black, invincible man ever heed the advice of a rational, older, Black woman? A string of factors other than gender came into play between us: age, education, experience, and culture. Anton shrugged, making no direct response. We turned back to the classroom.

Anton told me amusing stories, forthrightness being his strong point, even when in the wrong. He seemed by nature almost incapable of lying. He recounted an escapade from his time living in Cologne two years earlier. He'd been ordered to relocated under the refugee resettlement program after being involved in a fight. After that incident, the authorities gave him a dire warning: if he ever became entangled in another brawl, he'd be deported back to his birthplace. As a married man with family responsibilities, he wanted to stay out of strife. Learning German by attending language courses seemed a fair enough ground rule for residence status even if married to a German resident of Ghanaian origin. He said achieving an A1-level credit would help him to acquire permanent residence. Yet, he had little genuine desire to attend language classes and, as sympathetic as I felt toward him, it was plain to me how little he exerted himself in that regard.

15. A Language Barrier. Really?

In 2001, when Leandra was three, our family spent time in Northern Germany visiting with Thomas's relatives. For five straight days we rose, ate breakfast at leisure, and headed out in an old beat-up VW to Sehlendorf Beach, the coastline of Thomas's summertime childhood. Leandra frolicked in the sand, chasing and darting away from waves, as we lounged close by. Warm seas littered long stretches of the beach with huge, slippery jellyfish. Curious, Leandra took a stick to them, poking around at the opaque, slimy creatures, too squeamish to touch. A small girl, probably the same age as Leandra, played nearby. Abruptly, for no obvious reason, she took her plastic spade and struck out, catching Leandra on the side of the head.

What happened next was a near total collapse of character. Leandra wept long and hard, unusual at her age for such a little hurt. I cuddled her, offering soothing words. With a single act, she'd been sent back to near babyhood. I interpreted the breakdown as the result of rejection coupled with an inability to speak with the other child. Leandra, wanting a playmate, had inched like a magnet closer and closer, but that girl didn't want a new friend. Our daughter felt the frustration of the language barrier as a tangible thing. It wasn't the physical blow in itself; it was the foreignness of the entire experience. By striking out, the other child had triggered pain, homesickness, and defeat, all in one distressing moment.

Leandra's brother, Art, had displayed a similar meltdown in Germany some years earlier, at age six, when Leandra was three months old. Gathered around at a Christmas party in 1997, we, the Canadian visitors, shared the festive, fun atmosphere. A fireplace crackled nearby. The scent of grilled meats blew in from the kitchen. Ten people crowded a long wooden table set for dining. Seated in a restaurant, in a forest near Eutin, we chatted with Thomas's family, anticipating a fine meal of wild game. Mesmerized by the electric warming plates laid out on the table, Art fingered the heat conductors and received a shocking burn as a reward. It happened faster than anyone could say *stop*. Stunned by the pain, he yelped in surprise and then descended into a hearty crying spell. Thomas comforted, saying, "Yah, yah, it's good, Art. Must be homesickness and the new mixed in."

An overreaction to the strange or alien, so evident in a child's behaviour, resembles something of what an adult comes to bear under the weight of outsider status in a land full of new people, different cultural customs, and a foreign tongue. Unlike a three- or six-year-old, I was saved from wide-open defeat by the gifts of maturity, experience, and education. I held fast to the arc of my life story knowing that these challenges, born of the sometimes-uncomfortable present, would pass.

In Saarland, even without a command of German, life ticked on at a comfortable pace for me. I was well-travelled enough to know that I could not expect those passersby moving in and out of my vision to wish to practise conversational English with me at a moment's notice. I accessed all sorts of everyday things, as Saarland possessed wonderful infrastructure. Jumping on buses, I travelled across the city centre with ease. I negotiated purchases of various items from groceries to clothing to delicious baked goods from many bakeries. DM (Drogerie Markt) and Rossmann—offering cosmetics, health care items, household products, and health food—became favourite haunts. I bought bus tickets and passes from bus drivers. And the odd passersby, if politely asked directions in bad German, offered them if I lost orientation.

I ambled around the university, poking into campus spaces like the Mensa, the bookstore, cafés, and libraries, soaking up the promising ambience of student life. Students were remarkably well-dressed (no pyjamas or sweats as in Halifax). They sported a mix of trendy buzz cuts, man buns, long hair, slim jeans, T-shirts, tailored skirts, sweaters, and serious airs.

In and around the city, I inspected used bookshops and newspaper stands at the magnetic train station and other favourite spots, and visited the public library. I procured coffee, sandwiches, or hazelnut cakes at cafés where I sat, imbibed, and claimed Saarbrücken. With or without Leandra or Thomas, I journeyed back and forth on the Saarbrücken-Sarreguemines tram line without any glitches. But none of those activities required a real conversation.

In fact, the language barrier primed me to become an observant spectator of life in Germany. As an experienced teacher, I had arrived in Saarland well prepared in the art of observing and interpreting the actions of others.

My life in Germany centred around family. Thomas relished being back in Germany, and Leandra grew into her role as a student. I believe Leandra understood and could speak more and better German than I managed, although you wouldn't know it from a certain tongue-tied reluctance on her part. Her better grasp and comprehension of German showed up whenever she was addressed by her dad. Granted, I think most adults show a certain hesitancy in speaking a foreign tongue. Thomas made the comment that "English speakers even resist foreign pronunciations for names of people and places." It drove him crazy. Children, on the other hand, readily made mistakes, bold in learning and using a new language.

My perfectionism and pride as an English teacher stood in my way. German did not slip easily over my tongue and through my Bajan lips. To manoeuvre in this new environment, I depended on Thomas, and he grew into my mental crutch. Too often it was bare laziness on my part, not easy for me to confess. It's shameless, I know, but if all else failed, I expected some kind Saarländer to rescue me from dire circumstances by switching to English.

I didn't have regular German conversations, so I couldn't call up German words when I needed them. If someone assumed I spoke the language, any German words I knew took flight. Except that one time when a man asked me for the time and I miraculously sputtered "Viertel vor vier" (quarter to four). The need to use language skills on the spot resulted in a big failure for me. One day, I strolled at ease through a box store stocked with crafts, kitchen equipment, housewares, and fabrics and located somewhere between Fuchstälchen and the city. I examined the merchandise, passing time. Next to me, an agile, mature woman popped out an unexpected question in rapid-fire German. Stunned into silence, I had no sure way to understand her query except that she held out a bolt of fabric. *Is she asking about the cost, the fabric type, the colour, what? Where is Thomas when I most need him?* I could only manage a lame "Ich spreche kein Deutsch," thinking of escape. But it was the stranger who raised her eyebrows, turned, and sprinted away. In hindsight, I could have tried to understand the question. But how could I trust myself to phrase an answer in mid-flight while choking? In such moments, it was as if I stood on my brain.

In Sarreguemines, people, often older women, a few times posed questions about train schedules and things. If Leandra stood close by, she'd answer in French to salvage my uneasiness. But that was different, for that was in France, and Lord knows I couldn't be expected to know German *and* French. I would sometimes pretend that I hadn't heard the query and exit. At the Johanneskirche train station, if people asked for help with *Wabe*, train schedules, Thomas jumped in. (*Wabe* means "honeycomb" and is the word for the grid of different zones shown on city or regional transport maps.) Sometimes when I was alone, I thought to bus it back to the safety of our university guest house apartment surrounded by beech woods and never show my face again until it was time to hightail it back to Canada.

I learned and picked up dozens of words and phrases in German over time, but recalling them at the opportune moment and stringing them together into coherent sentences using that hard grammar consistently stumped me. Mark Twain had a dream in which "all bad foreigners went to German Heaven—couldn't talk and wished they had gone to the other place." I suspected my lot rested with the bad foreigners.

When Thomas and I met with Karl's wife, Julia, for weekly coffee and chats in January, it helped attune my ear for conversational German. Conversation flowed between Julia and Thomas, and often enough, I was able to follow ribbons in the stream. They both exercised huge patience, ever willing to switch up or translate if needed to uncover something hidden within the gush of words. Julia's diary, music, and poetry cropped up in her exchanges, while forestry and politics were Thomas's favourite topics. They shared remembrances of common university times. On occasion, I suppressed a mad desire to take off streaking down the pedestrian zone when the two continued to ignore my pleading eyes. Some of Twain's facetious, witty gems rubbed away the sting.

Language as identity was never so clear to me as in Saarland. Living among people who spoke a new language humbled me to the extent that I developed a genuine respect for foreign workers who spoke fluent German. Among them were the Nigerian waitress at a popular bistro, the Kenyan woman who worked at a meat-packing plant, and Romanians encountered in the woods near our apartment, digging mushrooms.

At a psychological level, below the shop purchases, bus rides, and lunch orders, language isolation made me feel alone within a crowd. Anna made a special effort to accommodate me by using English when we met for coffee (after greetings in German) to allow for meaningful conversations. What a lifesaver for my sense of self! But even she couldn't hide her irritation on learning that at the Volkshochschule, most students leaned heavily on English when socializing and on class breaks. That undermined steady progress in communicating in German, much to the exasperation of one of our instructors, Konstanze. Anna said, "It seems the chief purpose of the Volkshochschule is for foreigners in Germany to make friendships, as a priority over learning German." Yet being able to speak to other foreigners and understand what they encountered daily helped to reduce my feelings of isolation. And what about teenage Kareem, missing his language, friends, and home?

For many months, even the best students at the Volkshochschule scarcely understood the language spoken around them in random situations, say on buses or streets. Anya, the smart language learner, admitted that the first time she understood what someone said to someone else on a train occurred several months after arriving in Germany. This young woman spoke Romanian and English. At age twenty-eight, German would be her third language.

A similar light had sparked for our son, Art, in 2010 when he lived in Germany, first in Eutin and then Göttingen. It took from August, when he landed, until about April of the following year for him to begin to understand what people said in daily settings around him. By May, he could use the language well enough managing conversations in German with his visiting dad. Of course, age made a difference; Anya and Art had youth on their side.

Perhaps my brain was like an old mahogany tree, twisted and gnarled into alien shapes by Mistress Time. Whatever the case, fear of saying the wrong thing helped shut my mouth tight, like a green mahogany seed pod. It didn't help that I'd spent more than half my life marking errors of spelling, grammar, and sentence structure in my students' English essays.

Whatever language successes I'd produced in public amounted to a pitiable pile. In the Volkshochschule classroom, I managed small achievements, listening, answering basic questions, and participating in the A1-level course. I scored a small but proud victory by doing well in the first October language exam. But in the A2-level exam several weeks later, I bombed out, with dismal test results. My language track was a rocky path. As early as August 2013, I'd proudly spoken in German to a kind pharmacist for Thomas's medication only to struggle months later, in Saarbrücken, to ask a cashier at one of the small downtown stores about a lady's purse. I thought I knew the word for purse, *die Geldbörse*, but the checkout employee remained impassive at my botched articulation attempts. Thomas corrected my word usage later. "If you'd said *der Geldbeutel*, the money bag, she would have known."

With linguistic insight, Thomas concluded that one barrier to my ability to understand conversations of people around me had to do with the Saarländer accent. He acknowledged that he too found it sometimes difficult to figure out what locals talked about to each other. Anna clarified something of the Frankish cultural influences and distinguished between regional *Moselfränkisch* (Moselle Franconian) and *Rheinfränkisch* (Rhine Franconian). The term Frankish or Franconian is used by linguists to refer to many West Germanic dialects. North Americans who care to know will discover that Germany boasts surprisingly distinct regional differences in culture (including bread-making), customs, and dialects. It reminded me of my great-nephews talking to each other in Bajan dialect in Barbados several years prior, prompting a stunned Art to ask, "Mum, what are they saying? Are they speaking English?" Bajan accented "Pelt dah way or it gun sting yah!" (Throw that away or it's going to sting you!) meant nothing at all to him.

I couldn't identify the difference between one German dialect and another for a long time until I heard my husband's Northern German accent ringing out for the first time in a quiet room of a few dozen people. It happened at a presentation about energy alternatives held at a French cultural centre in tranquil, suburban Saarbrücken. His tones contrasted with the softer accents of Saarländer, and listeners eyed him keenly. At a reception afterwards, an older, pushy woman came up and addressed us. I couldn't understand her, but she refused to go away. Later, Thomas translated what she was brazen enough to tell him. She'd wondered how we were related, as I looked the older of the two. Rude! Perhaps she thought I claimed the fortune of being Thomas's mother, despite being only two years his senior.

I had an appetite for the German language but not the facility. This lack of communication led to a starvation of my spirit. I remained famished for much that could feed the mind and soul, but couldn't dine with passion. That inability incapacitated me, devouring me from the inside. I began to feel like those emaciated models traipsing down catwalks in confident façades; their too-thin bodies revealed their vulnerability, just as my lack of German language skills revealed mine. Like models denied hearty meals, I could only reach out and take light pickings from the nation's richest banquet. Much of its history, politics, music, and literature—conveyed through the vehicle of language—remained locked away, tantalizing behind sparkling glass. For sheer survival then, perhaps it was best for me to acquire an attitude of equilibrium, wearing it like haute couture, for fear of showing the real helplessness beneath.

Top left: Trail to Saarland University

Top right: Humboldt-guesthouse, our new residence among beech trees July 2013 to June 2014

Bottom: University of Saarland embedded in beech forest

Navigating public transit downtown Saarbrücken, Saarland

The tram for daily commute between Saarbrücken (Germany) and Sarreguemines (France)

The river Saar that connects Lorraine and Saarland

The Lycée Jean de Pange in Lorraine that Leandra attended 2013-14

A respite from school pressure for Leandra at the Wildpark across from the Humboldt-guesthouse

Summer 2013 visit of Anne Hathaway's Cottage in Stratford-upon-Avon, England

Summer 2013 visit of the 'The Roman Baths' in Bath, England

Train travels at high speed from Saarbrücken to Paris, Vienna and Budapest in fall 2013

Impression of the Kirkel forest (fall 2013): On the way to one of Thomas' research sites (top) and amazing carvings on tree trunks (bottom)

Two memorable impressions of the Schwarzenberg forest where we walked most days

Top: Wood harvesting in the Schwarzenberg forest

Bottom: A labelled tree trunk for monitoring of wood extraction

Winter 2014: Visit of Travemünde where Thomas was born

Visit of the village Benz where Thomas grew up

Top: Plaque in memory of four priests executed during Nazi rule, 'Herz Jesu' church, Lübeck

Bottom: WW II memorial in 'Marienkirche', Lübeck

Lasting impressions of German specialities: Marzipan cake delight in Lübeck (top), Spargel glut in Freiburg (middle), and Jugendherberge in Ingolstadt (bottom)

Memory lane, spring 2014: Thomas visiting his old student residence village in Göttingen (top) and bike parkade at the railway station in Göttingen (bottom)

Visit of the Großglockner region in mountainous Tyrol (Austria), spring 2014: Claudette fighting an uphill battle (top) and Thomas amazed by upfolded alpine geology (bottom).

Visit of the Großglockner region in mountainous Tyrol (Austria), spring 2014: Leandra above the clouds (top) and rural life on the edge (bottom).

Top: Visit of Ljubljana (Slovenia), a steep way up

Bottom: A view of a splendid landscape, May 2014

Visit of medieval Mont St. Michel, June 2014

The cloister on top of Mont St. Michel

PART IV

16. Being Black in Saarland

In the end, anti-black, anti-female, and all forms of discrimination are equivalent to the same thing: anti-humanism.
– Shirley Chisholm

What did it mean to be Black in Saarland? What experiences did I have there that would shed light on that question? Were they positive?

When I remarked that Saarland had very few Black people, Thomas retorted, "That's because Germany's not an African country!" His comment irritated me. By 2020, Germany had a population of about 83 million. Of that, an estimated 1 million inhabitants were Africans or of African descent. Germany does not encourage and screen immigration in the way that Canada does, but with modern trade and migration, cities like Frankfurt, Berlin, Munich, and Cologne have attracted an increasing number of Africans. The presence of Africans in Germany parallels migration patterns into Western Europe. Cities such as Hamburg and Frankfurt, former centres for occupation forces after the Second World War, have substantial *Schwarze* (Black) communities. More recent migrants are asylum seekers and economic refugees. Germany may indeed be considered a society attracting a multitude of nationalities.

Migrants and refugees always pose a challenge to integration and tolerance for any society. Germany had received over 600,000 refugees from Syria by 2020, and by 2022, over one million from the Ukraine. Canada welcomed 44,620 Syrian refugees between 2015 and October 2020. About 117,000 Ukrainian refugees have reached Canada as of November 2022.

The belief in Germany is that refugees will return home. Forced, illegal, and economic migration from the Middle East, Africa, and parts of Eastern Europe has encouraged the rise of anti-immigration sentiments and extremist political parties. A good illustration of this problem is the place of German Turks whose fathers were recruited decades ago to work in Germany and then stayed for good and invited their wives and families to join them. The integration of some three to seven million inhabitants of Turkish ancestry into German society remains often difficult due to language, religion, and politics (in both Germany and Turkey).

On the streets and buses of Saarland's cities, I stuck out as a member of a minority. I could not escape my racial identity and never wished to be reduced to a category. Like everyone, I am the sum total of all the experiences that have shaped and enriched my life. I grew up in a working-class household in Barbados, earned a university degree, became a teacher, immigrated to Canada, earned graduate degrees, married a German, and raised a family in Nova Scotia. I tend to be cautious but optimistic, value long-lasting friendships, and am a homebody, although I do love travel. Though I am non-religious, regular attendance at St. Barnabas Anglican Church as a child and teenager still influences my mindset. I am not shy but can be curiously lacking in confidence and sometimes solitary. It was from my unique perspective as a foreign, Black woman, wife, and mother that I thought about what it meant to live in Saarland.

I often felt a low-key uneasiness when out and about. Ancient, derogatory Christian/Judaeo biblical myths underpinned racist thought in European society. Eugenics, a scientific movement of the late nineteenth and early twentieth centuries, had been spread by scientists such as Francis Galton, Edward East, and Eugen Fischer. Their theories of "racial hygiene" predated and shaped many of Nazi Germany's persecutory policies.

My fellow student, Anton, and I fell into the category of Schwarze for Saarländer. While he felt he was racially profiled, I never did. The one time I was randomly asked to produce my tram ticket, so were a bunch of other people. And I never once had to show my ID card in Germany or in France. Talking to Anton was the closest I ever came to getting to know the life of a Black person (man) in Saarland. Hearing his story mattered, for it linked us together in a superficial notion of racial identity while defining our differences. It triggered questions about my own experiences living in a new geographical setting.

What did it mean to be Black in Saarland with foreigner status in Germany? Did I encounter racism? Racism is an emotional and behavioural response of discrimination due to someone's race or ethnicity. It shows up as prejudice and overt bias, stereotyping, racial profiling, and in subtler forms. Racist people may hurl insults at others, and employers or landlords may refuse people jobs or apartments because of their race. Subtle forms of racial discrimination can be detected by examining the circumstances. Racially profiling; not training, mentoring, or promoting racialized persons; subjecting them to heavy performance monitoring; and overstating their inability to get along with co-workers are examples of subtle racism. Racism exists at the societal level when we see institutional inequality connected to race or ethnicity.

I shared kinship with Anton as we happened to be the only two Black persons in the language course. This affinity surprised me, for we existed worlds apart in primary attributes (gender, age) and socially constructed ones (culture, language, education). I had no desire to be his best pal, but the affinity was real. This odd feeling is something people never know first-hand unless they have lived as members of a visible minority in a foreign or adopted land and been labelled as "other." People do not become friends because they share a common race or culture. Yet the reductionism and universality of racial division thrives. Stereotyping based on skin colour can define character for members of a group, forcing false kinship.

In her book *Caste*, Isabel Wilkerson tells an anecdote about Martin Luther King to illustrate deep-seated racial discrimination as a marker in American society, culture, and politics. On a 1959 visit by King to India, the principal of an "untouchables" high school introduced King as an "untouchable." At first shocked and upset by the depiction, King reflected on his reality as a Black man in America and accepted the label. The principal had used the untouchable rank to establish rapport with King. Wilkerson uses the notion of the caste system (based on ideas of heritability, divine will, and purity versus pollution) to analyze how the stigma caused by a rigid hierarchy of human rankings is alive today, even after significant civil rights gains and the election of an African American president. Black people in Europe and North America will grasp King's epiphany as I did.

In countries where most people are of African descent, as in Barbados or Nigeria, they may never come to see the insidious effects of the permanent stigma of race. They do not experience or think about racial inequality daily. In Black societies, people make distinctions about others based on actions, character, language, and social status (colourism is part of the equation, as it favours people with lighter skin over those with darker skin). Because most Black people see themselves in others around them, the struggle against life's unchangeable conditions is less of a burden.

But what about Anton? I could never accept his rough carelessness. Why couldn't he be a keener, looking cheerfully and with optimism toward his future in Germany? Perhaps he didn't have any supports paving his way toward bright prospects. Indeed, his demeanour and actions did not suggest any such privilege. Familiar as I was with similar behaviour by some Barbadians and Canadians, Anton's actions never surprised me, only embarrassed. In Canada, behaviour like his got linked to race, ethnicity, and location. In Barbados, a class-riddled society, unlikable actions are soon associated with a person's social and educational background. Barbadians criticize a person's character, manner, or a youth's lack of *broughtupsy* (good manners), not jumping right away to race.

Anton reacted with defensiveness and aggression to what may have been routine questions at a crime scene. Why did he rush to anger? Why did he not remain calm? An observer is inclined to blame Anton for not complying with the police. But why would he? Reasonable, ordinary white Germans trust police officers and may have little cause for fear in interactions with them. White policemen may be unaware of the fear and resentment a Black man like Anton holds for them. He resented a white police officer treating him as a suspect, rather than as a helpful passerby.

The impact of Anton's story forced me to think more broadly about racism. I limit my scope here, intending to explore the issue based on my lived experience in Saarland while referring to a wider societal context.

Thomas recounted stories for many years about historical invasions, migrations, and tribal and racial warfare in Europe. He made distinctions among various European tribes and religious discord stretching back to pre-Roman times. "Invasion" is a loaded word for North Americans, but Thomas used it to tell the conflict-ridden history of peoples and sovereign rulers of Europe. This is not to ignore persistent tribalism rife among continental Africans and the ridiculous degree of colourism among Caribbean peoples of African ancestry. Before Thomas's tales, I had never associated "races" with different peoples across Europe—tribes yes, races no.

Modern racism associated with New World plantation slavery showed us that insatiable imperial and capitalistic greed caused the subjugation and massacre of African peoples. The realization of the brutality experienced by my ancestors for centuries in Barbados helped me understand, in my university studies of "Western civilization," why Indigenous peoples and those with the darkest skins are positioned on the bottom rungs or margins of societies. Demands for the cheapest labour made "civilized" nations such as Britain, France, and Spain break all moral rules defining human dignity.

To pervert our innate human innocence and ability to love each other, lies were professed in religious scriptures, as in the sciences, starting in antiquity and continuing into our modern era. One only needs to read about the biblical "curse of Ham" justifying slavery, or "race segregation" at the height of the scientific eugenics movement. Ann Schmiesing's article "Blackness in the Grimms' Fairy Tales" reveals how pre-Christian and Christian colour symbolism, prevalent from ancient to early modern times, associated black almost exclusively with negative attributes or situations: punishment, wickedness, evil, the devil, and the menial.

After the First World War, racism reared up in the treatment of children born to mixed couples, German mothers and African men who were serving in the French army. They were branded *Rheinlandbastards*, and many were sterilized during the Nazi regime. *Destined to Witness* by Hans J. Massaquoi tells the author's story as the son of a German mother and an African father growing up in Nazi Germany. Massaquoi's account highlights the susceptibility of a young child to Hitler's vision. But it convinces readers that ordinary Germans did not always fall in line with Nazi racist ideology. He concluded that he fell through the "cracks of modern history" and was spared the fate of the other Black youth labelled Rheinlandbastards.

I think people of African descent are judged to be too far from the European ideals of beauty and civilization, ideals perpetuated in the media, literature, and culture, to be accepted and embraced in their full humanity. In the Volkshochschule, I experienced uncomfortable incidents among friendly acquaintances when classmates could not describe me. They avoided saying the most obvious things that characterized me as me, a Black woman with African features.

Participants engaged in a partner exercise using and naming colours to describe classmates. Anya, sitting beside me, partnered with Estella, leaving me and the Spanish guy at the other end hanging loose. At an instinctive level, I perceived their spontaneous reaction had to do with me being Black, though our differences in age likely factored in too. I had no problem talking about skin, hair, or eye colour, but my table chums couldn't do it for me. It seemed like a paralysis set in with them when it came to my physical description.

How should they name blackness, and what would doing so mean? Was it due to a lifetime of negative associations? What a revelation that people I sat and ate with, one of whom even visited our apartment, faced this awkward difficulty. It wasn't a fluke either, for it happened again the next day when course participants were asked to continue developing vocabulary for descriptions of people and their characteristics. To associate the word *black* with people just stuck in the throats of these polite, decent Europeans. In this bizarre exercise, I could fault no one. The only German in the room, the instructor, was a superb person. It amounted to clear avoidance, causing me a small injury. On the walk home among some of the same pleasant people, to my surprise, I felt vulnerable. It was only my gritty Bajan resilience that kept tears brimming at my eyelids from flowing.

In another classroom exercise, when participants described themselves, they copied each other. Even the darkest brunette, Andrea, the forthright Portuguese woman, described herself as blonde-haired and blue-eyed. And the dark-skinned Indonesian student, to my surprise, when talking about his future goals, hoped to marry a blonde-haired Muslim woman. Our Romanian said a sarcastic *good luck* to him that was ignored.

Another day, the South Korean student spent five minutes explaining to the class that Koreans have no eyelid fold like Chinese people. She even drew a sketch on the whiteboard. In oppressive air, we held a collective breath. Everyone, including Konstanze, looked on in silence, pretending not to know the student's meaning. It was the opposite end of a spectrum where no one dared volunteer to describe my physical appearance using racial markers, while another participant went to extremes to outline ethnic differences. I squirmed, convinced that had a Chinese student sat in the classroom, our Korean classmate would not have done that. She was likable, having gotten me excited about the Camino de Santiago de Compostela, or the Way of St. James, after she described her pilgrimage the previous summer through France to Spain. No doubt, I witnessed instances of racial and ethnic compulsion and psychological evasion in my multi-ethnic class at the Volkshochschule.

In Saarland, I encountered few Black people, even on the international university campus. Thomas told me about a Kenyan woman he'd met at a train stop on his way back from a research site. He said she spoke German well, had lived in Germany since the 1980s, tried to be an entrepreneur, and after that worked in a meat-packing plant for low wages. That morning she was on edge, for the tram managed to run late on the very day she had set out for a new job. Thomas expressed surprise that this energetic woman with effective German language skills worked in a meat-packing plant after thirty years in Germany. Chance meetings with people of African descent included fellow tenants in our university guest house, such as an aloof Senegalese professor well regarded by Émilie, the manager of our guesthouse.

I noticed a few random Black people step on and off trams and buses at hours that implied employment. On Mainzer Straße, a hole-in-the-wall computer store appeared to be operated by Ivorians. Once out shopping in Saarbrücken, we stumbled upon a Ghanaian woman working at Karstadt as a toilet attendant. A gregarious Nigerian waitress served patrons at the downtown Brasserie and was a familiar, jovial face when we became regulars.

In Saarbrücken, Black people appeared so few in number as to be judged insignificant. Even in Berlin, I did not see much of a Black presence, unlike in Paris and London. I concluded the Black people living in Saarland had arrived from Africa rather than from North America or the West Indies.

In public, it became amusing to observe others observing me. Thomas often said that social control, as in enforcement of social norms, is more explicit in Germany than in Canada. People often watched others with intention, especially foreigners. This happened to me on trains, buses, in grocery stores, and on streets. I had been tipped off about this by a Canadian friend, wife of a military officer, who lived in Hamburg two years before us. But scrutinising others is a Barbadian habit too, therefore I couldn't construe people inspecting me as a racist thing. Germans, like Barbadians, can oftentimes be caught minding other people's business. Canadians are politer, pretending to ignore what they cannot help but witness.

Anonymity breeds protection and concern at the same time. At home in Nova Scotia, our family bumped into people we recognized as neighbours, friends, current or past students, colleagues, and parents of our children's friends. Daily Saarland produced crowds of strangers who knew and needed nothing of us, altogether both a bane and a blessing. Sometimes I registered a strange loneliness in crowds.

As a newcomer and a woman, my fear of being the brunt of some random attack, a soft target of someone's anger or hatred on the street, stayed at a low-key, secret level. I never came close to feeling threatened during my stay. From the beginning, I thought the city safe when I glimpsed young women dragging suitcases through semi-dark residential streets at midnight. I wanted to explore and enjoy Saarbrücken, taking the city in my stride, and I did, holding on to the now, the here.

A person's fate is determined by multiple factors: social standing, race, gender, and chance. But regardless, life is to be lived. I'm so grateful for meeting Anton because he set me thinking about circumstances that supported the setting and meaning of my life in Saarland, a free life I enjoyed. My long-term residence status gave me a mix of joy and unease, not free of the pressures of being a foreigner. I knew the insecurity of sticking out, the inadequacy of proper conversational skills, and the alienation of loneliness in a crowd. I continued to risk discomfort and challenges, for they opened up paths to self-awareness, resilience, and learning.

In the Volkshochschule language course, I'd encountered experiences that forced me to question what it meant to be a Black woman in Saarland. My own resources and mettle, built up over years as a new Canadian immigrant in Saskatchewan and later living and working in Nova Scotia, handed me creative purchase. They gave me tools to accomplish an examination of my identity and what it meant to be a resident in Germany.

Without sufficient command of the language to participate in any meaningful conversations or impromptu dialogues, I continued to find it difficult to gauge subtle racism. I didn't look for it. I had heard and read that xenophobia and racism existed in Germany, but no one I met acted hateful or racist.

During our 2001 visit to Northern Germany, Thomas's relatives had warned us about anti-foreigner attitudes in the former East Germany. On a visit there in 2006, we ignored those warnings and visited the small Martin Luther town of Eisleben. A few people gawked at us as if we had just dropped from the sky, and once, a guy yelled something incoherent from a passing car. Those instances hinted that we'd tottered back into some weird past. An old-world quality marked East Germany's storefronts, structures, and streets. West Germany would pay a high price to integrate the former East Germany into a larger, wealthier, unified country, nevertheless, as tourists from the West, we felt safe.

When our eighteen-year-old son spent a year in Germany in 2009, he witnessed confrontations between neo-Nazis and anti-racism activists in Göttingen. Art described the bigotry on display in some demonstrations in Göttingen and other parts of Germany back then as "pretty intense and sick." As a mixed-race young man, being mistaken for someone of Arabic ancestry unnerved him. On the upside, he remembered spontaneous hugs from complete strangers when soccer star Oezil (of Turkish origin) scored a decisive goal for Germany, sealing the team's advancement in the 2010 World Cup.

Thomas had a level of cultural awareness I did not possess. A few incidents stood out, producing some unsettling questions during our time. Thomas wondered why people had glared so rudely at us at a restaurant in Kirkel where the waitress showing no intention of serving us forced us to leave. To him, it was like a scene from a movie about the US civil rights era. Another time, he asked, "Why don't the Saarland authorities close down that storefront on Mainzer Straße?" It displayed a repugnant name and logo in peaceful Saarbrücken. An avid follower of current affairs in Germany, Thomas told me the Society of the Old Order in charge of that storefront finally came under investigation by German authorities. Germany's federal and state governments began to acknowledge the extent and rise of criminal neo-Nazi activities. "What took authorities so long?" he asked. I answered with a vacant expression and a shrug.

Brow furrowed, he asked, "What happened to the slogan popular during my youth: '*Wehret den Anfängen*,' 'Resist the beginnings'?" He added that outdated neo-Nazi activities scattered around in former East and West Germany reminded him of age-old German qualms that made foreigners fear Germans. There's a saying, "Germans fear nothing more than their own *Angst*."

Living in a majority-white Saarland, I found in Pauli Murray, a Black American woman ahead of her time, a kind of inspiration. In 1960, Murray moved to Ghana to serve as senior lecturer at the Ghana School of Law in Accra. There, as in the United States, she spoke out against injustices, upsetting authorities so much she was almost deported. As she prepared to return to the States after sixteen months, she captured her complex feelings in an essay titled "What is Africa to Me?" She sought to come to terms with her African ancestry and the unique aspect of her African American background at the heart of her search. In *The Firebrand and the First Lady: Portrait of a Friendship* (2016), Patricia Bell-Scott quotes Murray as saying, "I am beginning to understand that I am the product of a new history which began on African shores but which has not been shared by Africans, a history accompanied by such radical changes in a new environment that over time it produced a new identity.... For me, the net gain in coming to Africa has been to reexperience imaginatively this break in continuity as well as to gain an appreciation for the peoples and cultures who remained on the African side of the historical divide."

Coming to terms with her "new identity" as a person of African descent meant Murray could never go back to the Africa of her ancestors. This reality brands all descendants of enslaved peoples in the Americas, including myself, who constitute the so-called African diaspora. Reading her words moved me. Finding her work crystalized something Thomas had mulled over for years and shared with me. He thought African Americans, forged by a long tradition of slavery, are "culturally new" while having roots in Africa.

Murray's acceptance of this new identity shaped the peace she found as a Black person, a woman, and a worker. She fought a brave fight against sexism her entire life and engaged in the struggle against racial injustice anywhere. She continued until the end to work, write, teach, and think, enriching her own life and attempting to be of service to others.

Murray's ideas and life proved instructive to me, even though I inhabit a different era and country. Historical and geographic divides on opposite sides of the Atlantic created large populations of untethered Black (and mixed-race) people in the United States, the Caribbean, South America, and Canada. These populations are captured in one large diaspora basket, sharing a single unique history and demonstrating many similarities. But they also exhibit important differences associated with various languages, cultures, national identities, and entry points into the diaspora. We must understand ourselves to share an existence derived from being tools of powerful imperial forces that profited from the Atlantic slave trade well after its abolition. The tradition of slavery left in its wake the continued subjugation of huge swaths of people for no other reason than economic imperatives. Although North American culture tries to relegate that history to the past, the effects still operate with force.

When I was growing up in Barbados, under a British colonial tradition, ordinary people judged each other based on wealth, gender, and appearance. But imperialism and racism had produced the very origins of our daily existence. In the island, the reality of the political situation ordained that the owners of the land held wealth, privilege, and political power that remained in the hands of descendants of British colonials and the lingering plantocracy long after Barbados achieved political independence in 1966. The vast majority of the landless poor comprised descendants of African slaves.

Moving to Canada planted racial aspects front and centre into my consciousness as my most significant primary feature. In public life, white Canadians tend to lump Black people of diverse backgrounds together.

I've heard it said white people see a Black person before they see their gender. Fair enough, but this was not of necessity so in Barbados, although a person could be mistaken about someone's gender. As I interacted with Africans from the continent in Canada, it became obvious to me that my own experiences as a Barbadian woman have shaped so much of my identity and outlook that the superficiality of skin colour often operated as a frustrating distraction in conversations about race, culture, and politics.

This harkens back to my German class experience, where people avoided acknowledging my racial traits. It confirmed that race is the lowest common denominator, a weird difference European youth found too scary to name and acknowledge. Hence, in Saarland, as in Canada, skin colour and race constituted the great common denominator for Germans and non-German migrants with no idea of who I was. This dumbing down to the lowest common denominator ensures Black people are held not only level as a group but also plumb in place.

17. Strolling the Pedestrian Zone

A mild late January wind swayed branches under grey skies. Leandra possessed a year-long student bus and tram pass for her daily commute to and from Sarreguemines and around town. Thomas and I had initially purchased monthly passes for tram and bus to accompany her but changed to passes for use only within city limits. With Leandra now used to travelling to Jean de Pange by herself, I felt good relinquishing that parental duty. On arrival we'd admired eight-year-olds daily riding the tram alone.

When we two needed to go beyond the city boundary by tram, for instance, to Riegelsberg or Heusweiler, we upgraded ticket fares after consulting a perplexing (though clear to German engineers) *Wabe* zone system at train stations. There, Thomas fed money into a ticket machine, sometimes messing up payment of additional charges and, on occasion, helping commuters in need. I thought the Wabe system tiresome, defying an easy fix, but perhaps Saarländer loved being tested.

After five minutes waiting at the Wildpark stop, the number 102 bus arrived. Thomas groaned.

"Why does it have to be 102? I prefer the 101. It's faster."

"But that avoids the Ilseplatz." I loved watching people moving about the neighbourhood square, at the bakery and in the restaurant locale. "How much faster than ten minutes do you want to be?"

"Three minutes," he answered cheekily. Here was a far cry from riding the bus in Dartmouth, where number 61 heading into Halifax lasted an hour. The three of us boarded, flashed passes, and were rewarded with a cursory nod.

During weekday peak hours, masses of university students squeezed onto the bus. Today, a Saturday, the half-empty, blue-and-white, square-faced bus swung out into traffic. It trundled down a dim, tree-lined street and halted at Waldhaus student residence stop before making a sharp left around Ilseplatz. I glanced inside the popular Barbarossa bakery, where customers lined up for fresh baked goods. An adjoining ice cream parlour was closed for the season. On the opposite side, a popular local pub welcomed customers on summer days to sit outdoors under bright umbrellas, sip frothy beer, and savour generous dinners. Those chairs and umbrellas had disappeared when late October days signalled fall.

As we passed familiar streets and plain, trim houses and apartments in pastel shades, the bus windows rattled, cars and vans rushed by. The occasional bus ran in the opposite direction. In the distance, a regional train whistled. I marked contrasts between the urban bustle of Saarbrücken, the tropical landscape and people of Barbados, and the natural and built-up world of Nova Scotia. Here, as in Nova Scotia, bus drivers slowed down for stops and waited for passengers alighting and boarding, unlike in Barbados where impatience, rush, and jerky bus journeys remained an old normal. What made for the differences in these three countries? I concluded: better training of bus drivers in Canada and Saarland, and in Barbados, shortages of buses and the nature of the buses themselves, which ran on jerky truck engines.

From our bus, most people departed at Johanneskirche to shop, jump onto a tram, hike to the train station, or take a connecting bus. Stores welcomed shoppers every day except Sunday. For people in the city, transport services excelled; however, late night and weekend buses scaled back to one per hour instead of four at peak hours. With public transport unavailable late nights, grabbing a taxi or walking were the next best options for city residents.

We made tracks for the pedestrian zone among a swarm of people. Among the German and French voices, we heard Russian and Eastern European languages. A few Africans dotted the crowds where women mingling in small clusters, wearing vivid cotton dresses. People of Middle

Eastern ancestry, mostly Syrians and Turks, hurried past, some wearing headscarves and a few in full-body burkas or niqabs. A significant number of Italians, Poles, and Romanians also live in Saarland.

We stopped at Nordsee, a popular restaurant chain whose specialty was seafood. Its doorway was jammed, but Thomas had no intention of accepting that. Already full, the restaurant seated twenty at a squeeze. Hungry patrons munched and sipped a combination of spuds, fried or grilled fish, vegetables, desserts, and beverages, including wine. Spying an opening, I inquired if it was free, but someone said, *"Es ist besetzt"* (It's taken). "Let's go," I said, turning to Thomas and Leandra, but our luck turned. A family of four stood up and Thomas flashed a signal: *There*. We zipped in just ahead of a couple seized by the same idea. At lunch hour in Nordsee, if you paused, you lost, and things were done with more assertiveness than in Canada. After fixing seats with our personal effects, we joined the queue at the smorgasbord.

Ahead of us, a French-speaking, animated Lebanese party made gallant attempts to place their orders in German to a long-suffering but on the mark server, likely of Polish origin. Thomas ordered crisp, breaded fish with *Bratkartoffeln* (fried potatoes with bacon and onions) for himself and Leandra. I directed the server's attention to plump salmon, mixed grilled vegetables, and a side order of mushrooms. For drinks, we requested *Apfelschorle* (apple spritzer), white wine, and *Sprudel* (sparkling water) before making the near-impossible squash back to our table.

It's funny how I often thought Barbadian food had little variety, but I was mistaken. It could compete with the spread at Nordsee.

For her own sanity, my mother used to stick to a meal plan. Sunday, she set out a big spread, and Monday she made soup (a full meal deal with chicken, beef or lamb, split peas, and ground provisions thrown in and fluffy dumplings floating on top). Twice a week she cooked rice and peas/beans with salted cod, fresh fish, or chicken. What we called "stew food," with macaroni, chicken or lamb, and Irish potatoes boiled to a thick mess, she served midweek. She prepared yams and steamed flying fish whenever it was plentiful. I remember my mother buying flying fish at twenty-five for a dollar from fish hawkers riding around on bicycles or motorcycles. On Saturdays, she'd cook breadfruit cou cou or prepare pudding and souse.

The pudding was made like sausage, with grated sweet potato, spiced with thyme, onions, and black pepper, stuffed into pig intestines and simmered. Souse was boiled pork marinated in cucumber, lime, onions, salt, and pepper. One of my favourite meals was okra soup made with bits of cod, salted beef, potatoes, okra, and a generous squeeze of lemon. I relished the slimy texture my younger sister hated. Cabbage, carrots, peas and beans, breadfruit, sweet potatoes, yams, and flying fish seemed plentiful. We added to these staples pumpkin fritters, boiled or fried plantain, and avocadoes.

If you say *conkies* to Bajans, you make them happy. By tradition cooked in a big pot on a wood fire in the backyard, they were a November treat. Made from coarse cornmeal mixed with sugar, shredded coconut, nutmeg, and raisins, they were delicious eaten warm after being steamed in banana leaves.

Now at Nordsee, I noticed that people in tight spaces tolerated slight bumps and knocks more so than back in Nova Scotia, where apologies ran rampant. Here no one cared. In fact, people expected small hits in populated spots. As long as a stranger did not intentionally touch or threaten me, I felt no danger of my personal space being invaded. That acceptance had long settled into my DNA, for in Barbados, people tended to be more comfortable with physical proximity than in Canada, which can be good and bad.

Having stumbled upon the Nordsee chain and its delicious seafood, Thomas enabled our indulgence after many a tough week. Sole, salmon, trout, cod, *Krabben* (tiny shrimp), and other fruits of the sea were on display, along with fried potatoes, mixed vegetables, fresh salads and their accompaniments. Side dishes and desserts of *Rote Grütze* (red berries) with vanilla sauce (a Northern German dessert) and *Quarkspeise* (curds with sweet or sour fruits) lined up for our selection. Leandra never objected to being dragged along to Nordsee.

While we ate, a skinny beggar woman, I think she was Romani, pushed into Nordsee with determination. Right away, an employee ushered her out with even greater determination. Looking down at my plate, I wondered, *Will she eat a meal today? Where and how does she live?* She might well have been treated the same way in Barbados and Nova Scotia, though perhaps with a softer touch. Thomas and Leandra witnessed the incident too, but we said nothing as we ate.

When we emerged from Nordsee, the crowd in the pedestrian zone was at its thickest.

"Wow, what a scene," I murmured.

"Yah, Yah, all part of city action," Thomas said. I started at a sudden tug on my sleeve. A tanned, dark-haired woman put out a stained palm for change and instinctively I reached to open my handbag when Thomas bellowed.

"*Unglaublich!* (Unbelievable!) I find that very aggressive!" he barked. The woman turned slowly away, unrepentant, zeroing in on another soft target.

"You remember what happened to Karl in Spain when he opened his wallet?" Thomas's friend had related a story to us two years earlier while we stood in this very spot. Karl, travelling in Spain some years ago, had been stopped by a panhandler. He'd reached into his pocket and drawn out his wallet. At the very moment he opened it to offer a few euros, the woman reached in with him and helped herself to three hundred! In a blink, she disappeared into the crowded streets, never to be spied again.

Karl's story topped the one Thomas had shared moments earlier with me, Leandra, Karl, and his wife, Julia. "We were en route to Saarbrücken from Northern Germany," Thomas told us. "I withdrew cash from the cash machine at the Cologne train station. Unaware I was a target, I flashed money while waiting to board." He laughed at his mistake.

"Two things happened that helped the thieves. I put my wallet into a side pocket without a button or zipper. Next, passengers had to switch trains at a station stop in Bonn. In the rush with reboarding, the pickpockets struck.

"I felt the swipe on the crowded platform but couldn't react fast enough as both my hands held baggage. I spun around and saw the two women working together. They threw me off, pointing out culprits down the platform.

"When I tried to insist, they played so innocent that a nearby German man hissed 'Asshole!' at me. Meanwhile, the suspects, having entered the train, slipped off again before it moved from the station. What could I do?

Jumping off and giving chase was not going to help. I got off a few stops later to report the theft to police authorities in Koblenz. They said dozens of similar thefts happened every day. They had no way of tracking down the thieves. Nothing could be done though I was never so angry."

With that, the big problem of pickpockets in Germany landed home for the first time. I blamed Thomas for his careless display. Leandra, rattled by the affair, defended her dad and shut me down, asking rightly, what was the sense of blaming a victim.

The incident was seared into my memory, for after the shock came a feeling of weakness. Thomas said the robbery made him feel naked. All the requirements for navigating the world of international travel had vanished: wallet, identity cards, credit cards, and money. Luckily, I had everything he had lost and ever since then, I doubled down on securing my valuables. Today on the Bahnhofstraße, I'd slipped up by not ignoring the pull at my sleeve.

Part of my Saarbrücken story was the panhandlers I watched. I wanted to see Saarland displayed in all its facets, the faces of rich and poor, the privileged and underprivileged. I wished to register how people acted toward each other. This direct observation put a genuine human face to life and taught me more about the real Saarland than government reports and statistical statements ever could. It told me about the energy and quality of human life and survival on the streets.

The beggars in Saarbrücken were stoic in expression, not vigorous in their soliciting. They acted like soldiers doing survival practice. I've found Canadian panhandlers to be the politest of anywhere I've lived, thanking people and saying "Have a good day" even when given nothing. Panhandlers in Saarbrücken operated in mute silence, even when receiving cash. Perhaps they spoke little German; I learned many were nomads, not citizens.

Nova Scotia panhandlers, most numerous in spring and summer, operate outside on the streets, at traffic lights, and at the doors of well-patronized establishments. Here people parked themselves on January streets holding out opened palms or cups. Nowhere in Canada or Barbados had I seen so many panhandlers in one spot, women outnumbering men. A man with a shrivelled leg, displayed for pity's sake, sat on the pavement, his face inert. In front of the Karstadt store, one woman dragged a bundle of clothes, blankets, and sleeping bags, tied together to make her bed. She wore multicoloured, ragged garments, and her head was shaved except for a long, skinny braid dangling down her back. She focused on her bundled concerns, carried in weather-worn, tattooed arms. She went about her business insensible to the clouds of surging humanity, and they appeared oblivious to her.

Some panhandlers resembled grandmothers, neat and silver-haired with kind, tanned faces. Others of Sinti and Romani ancestry escorted small, underfed children. Others looked young and able-bodied, asking for a few coins to buy bread or coffee. And still more individuals panhandled who, in Canada, would have been helped by a social or community agency. Many had crippled limbs like, in one case, a shrunken girl sitting in a wheelchair with a cup on her lap in front of C&A, a large department store. For ordinary passersby, panhandlers defined the backdrop.

I once witnessed a middle-aged, well-built woman with a colourful headscarf circle people waiting at the Rathaus bus stop, asking for spare change. A stern-faced, middle-aged Saabrückerin said angrily, "*Gar nichts!*" (Nothing at all!) looking the panhandler straight in the face. "*Das ist unglaublich! Es wird schlimmer und schlimmer!*" (This is unbelievable! It gets worse and worse!) Even as a newcomer, I understood what she meant. She was expressing intense frustration and resentment. I've never seen such a passionate response to a panhandler in Canada. I guessed it wasn't a worsening economy but the increase of bold panhandling in Germany. When European borders opened after the Schengen Agreement came into force in 1995, it caused a transformation in migration patterns. I imagined for one moment the effects of no checks for Canadian, American, and Mexican borders. More begging and bolder shows of it heightened emotions.

Mixed emotions arose in me when I faced those pedestrian zone dwellers. A few coins from a steady supply of passersby eased immediate hunger pangs, but how much more could any one individual do for the needy? Providing regular meals, shelter, and clothing for survival required more substantial and consistent help, especially for children. The superficiality of my interest did not escape me, knowing nothing of these people to whom most turned a blind eye.

Those forlorn-looking beggars on the pedestrian zone occupied my conscience. They slumped on the cold earth on thin blankets or bundles of grimy clothing in all weather. Why didn't a government agency or city council do more for them? How could people not notice? If they disappeared, who would care?

I witnessed a mentally ill woman habitually sleeping on the pavement right in front of the biggest department store in town throughout the winter. She carried her bedding and her few articles of clothing. Her presence shaped the setting as much as did the food stands and large stores surrounding the plaza. When that homeless woman disappeared, I wondered about her whereabouts. These human beings were real—they were part of the community, if only inhabiting the outskirts.

One day in front of Primark, a popular fast-fashion retailer, a skinny young boy sat on the ground holding a cardboard sign saying, *"Ich habe Hunger"* (I'm hungry). Thomas bought a pizza for him. I watched to see if the boy would eat or discard it, for money can be more of a valued commodity than food. Taking the pizza without a word, the small-faced figure with a tight, high-belted waist registered modest surprise. Then as if in a daze, he walked away, looking around for a somebody. Not seeing that person, he returned to his spot to hand the pizza over to a woman squatting nearby. Not even a flicker of momentary pleasure crossed an otherwise straight face. *Why didn't he eat it? Who was he looking for? Why didn't he give it to the woman beside him in the first place? Who was he and where did he live?*

I quizzed Thomas as we strolled. "Who are the people begging?"

"They are not Eastern Europeans—Poles, Hungarians, or Romanians who tend to find work in Germany."

"Then who are they?"

"They're people who prefer a nomadic life. Because Germany has a social safety net, if people register at City Hall and remain in the same place, they'll be given support like in Canada." He was convinced that an organized cartel ran the beggar business on the strip and exerted its presence as surely as established banks, stores, and other enterprises like Karstadt, Primark, and C&A.

The idea of a mafia-like cartel intrigued me. I never found good evidence of cartels running begging operations in pedestrian zones, but based on the number of children involved, some degree of social organization, hierarchy, and protection operated.

Linguistic evidence places the roots of the language of Romani or Roma people in the northwestern Indian states of Rajasthan and Punjab. Romani people are dispersed, but concentrated populations are in Europe, especially Central, Eastern, and Southern Europe, including Southern France and Turkey. Romani people in Germany are estimated at 170,000 to 300,000, constituting around 0.2 to 0.4 percent of the population. One-third of Germany's Romani belong to the Sinti group. The majority of Romani in Germany lack German citizenship, though many speak some German.

I found it hard to accept the nature of nomadic Romani reality. Without a stable home, how does anyone achieve a good quality of life? It was unfathomable even within the context of poverty. But I wasn't Roma, and that made all the difference. Living in caravans and begging sustained a basic shelter and survival. Beyond that, fundamental things like protection, security, and education of children appeared tenuous. The children looked so vulnerable. But the Romani people had survived a roaming life from about the eighth century CE, perhaps earlier. These customs and cultural ways would persist.

My classmate Anya gave me a pragmatic answer to the question of poverty and panhandling. "If you help these people, more will come. You can't help them all." She herself came from Moldova and showed little sympathy for Romani and Sinti people from Romania and other parts of Europe. "Why should I give them my money?" she asked. "We have to work hard for what we have, and they just stand there saying, 'Give me money.'"

I challenged her views: "That's the thing, isn't it? How can we as a society decide who gets to have their basic needs met? I think if people can do better, they do."

Her expression softened. "The only ones I feel sorry for are the children and the elderly." Moldova was categorized as one of the poorest countries in Europe. "Back home, people are leaving the country to the poor, the old, and the very young. The old are taking care of the children." Sadness tinged her voice.

"What about your family?"

"I left my family and friends behind, first for four years of university in Romania and then for a better life in Germany." Her voice was matter of fact.

Another day, I walked back from my language classes chatting with a cheerful Iraqi student, a mother of two. Arenata lived in our apartment building, and we often travelled to and from class together. A rail-thin, young Black man timidly approached us. Of African origin, he spoke in Arabic, wanting to know if any Somalians lived nearby. Arenata responded in Arabic, telling him we knew nothing of any such community. Desperate but not offensive, he asked for money for food, saying that he had arrived in Germany a few days before from Italy. Arenata offered him a few euros, and we moved on. She whispered, "I don't think he's doing the right thing."

We were both in more fortunate circumstances than the young man. I, a teacher from Canada, and Arenata accompanying her husband in a scholarship-supported Ph.D. program at Saarland University. I didn't ask her to say what the right thing to do was, but I thought she meant he should not have entered Germany illegally. I didn't know the reality of his circumstances and had no clear opinion. Pondering the stranger's uncertain fate, we continued on in silence for several moments. Random surprises came to us as passersby on the Saarbrücken pedestrian zone.

I couldn't bear to witness the consequences of the extreme poverty I saw there. It made me think of human castaways conjured in a poem by Jamaican poet Claude McKay:

But seated on the benches daubed with green
The castaways of life, a few asleep,
Some withered women desolate and mean,
And over all, life's shadows dark and deep.
Moaning I turn away, for misery
I have the strength to bear but not to see.

18. On Human Agency

One morning in spring, we planned a visit to Römerkastell, site of an old Roman fort built after 352 CE, close to a crossing point for the Metz-Mainz and Strasbourg-Trier highways. In today's cityscape, the archaeological monument was located in a small park on a street called *An der Römerbrücke* (at the Roman bridge), in the St. Johann district towards Sarreguemines.

"We'll get off five stops after we board. In Roman times, it belonged to the Roman province called Belgica," Thomas said, reading from a brochure.

"What did it look like?" I asked.

"It had six sides. Four round towers were on the side across from the river with a Roman bridge. It was built for security, but probably never finished."

"Whatever happened?"

"Says here, with the fall of Rome, it was abandoned and destroyed in the fifth century."

At the tram station, we waited in a lively city atmosphere among a bunch of commuters. I inhaled the gentle March air that rang with the rattling sounds of steady flowing traffic. Of late, when we walked in the forests, I imagined seeing the tree sap rising. On the streets, faces awake after a winter slumber glinted in substantial light. The city world had taken on more colour, becoming more physical and animated. Behind us appeared the famous brown-stone basilica; in front, two sets of light-rail tram lines ran in opposite directions. A Postbank (a retail branch of Deutsche Bank) dominated the corner opposite Ziegler bakery, a regular stop for Thomas and Leandra on Friday mornings.

A sudden ruckus behind us grabbed our attention when two women squared off, both scrawny under baggy clothes. One wore saggy black jeans, the other discoloured khakis. Stringy, dark hair hung down the side of the aggressor's face while an untidy ponytail held the other's light-coloured hair, pulled back from an anemic, pointy face. The dark-haired woman pushed the other in the chest, causing her to stagger back. Regaining her balance, the pushed one threw a fist, missing her opponent. They both reeled, lurching about, as a few unamused commuters looked on, puzzled or frowning, others ignoring the kerfuffle.

Before things intensified further, an associate, even more unsteady on his feet, stepped up to force the women apart using haranguing tones. It was all in German, so I could only guess at his words. Suddenly, the dark-haired, smaller woman began tackling the mediator. She gave him one on the chin, which he accepted with a small murmur. I guessed his interference was both uninvited and unappreciated, even if well-intentioned. In the middle of this commotion, another lightweight man tottered to his feet. Dishevelled, he rose from the bus stop seat he'd been occupying. Zig-zagging toward the tangle of bodies, he made perhaps three strides before tumbling forward in a crumpled heap. He remained still for a stunned moment, shaking his head in confusion. Another man from the assembly helped him up onto shaky legs.

I took in the scene, peering down the way toward the back of the church and its fenced yard near the curb. I saw scores of beer, wine, and liquor bottles lined up like soldiers on the verges. The numbers in this drinking party climbed from ten to fifty, depending on prevailing weather. Mild days drew them out like moths to the light, sparking eruptions like the one we'd just witnessed. They revelled in the company of like-minded buddies.

A joyful group, indulging in the occasional spat, they exhibited the tightness and enthusiasm any political party would envy. By mid-afternoon, the air reeked of alcohol, urine, and puke, products of excessive drinking. (Washrooms and toilets for the public seemed to me to be fewer and less accessible in Germany than in Canada.) I never felt any skittishness skirting this group, as members paid more attention to each other than to any ordinary passerby. But their antics incensed Thomas.

"Why don't the authorities clear them out?" he asked, knowing full well that this was as likely to happen as the removal of beggars from the pedestrian area. "It's disgusting."

In the past, he'd described how drunks had conquered and spoiled many a city pedestrian zone in Eutin, Göttingen, and Freising. Now he saw it happening in Saarbrücken and Dudweiler. Lovely, relaxing amenities and park-like spaces with benches were taken over by groups of alcoholics. It became so pervasive in Göttingen, where students in his time had enjoyed spilling from pubs into the open air, the municipality prohibited drinking in the pedestrian zone. Other town and city councils did the same. Thomas held robust opinions about capable people failing to act or work, giving up on the ability to be independent, resourceful agents of their own destiny.

Where did these people belong, if not in these public spaces? Who noticed them? How did the average Saarländer feel about them?

In Barbados, people called those who became intoxicated outside the gaudily painted rum shops "rummies." They either pulled themselves up with the aid of family or they dug down deeper, landing sometimes "in the gutter."

On a visit to Barbados in 2011, Thomas, Leandra, and I exited a public bus at the Fairchild Street terminal in humid, congested Bridgetown. Behind narrow, covered sidewalks stretched a line of glass counters supervised by a phalanx of boisterous women. They offered cheese, fishcakes, and ham cutters, coconut bread, and other local goodies for sale. Stepping down from the curb, I stumbled, almost landing on three men sprawled out on the sidewalk, oblivious to the chaos of the city around them. It was not yet noon. One woman remarked, "Look at these drunken idiots," adding an extra-long chupse, a sucking through her teeth. No one else missed a beat when Thomas and Leandra paused to take in this blot on the scene.

Who were the people shunted to the sidelines in Saarland? Citizenship and legal residency were not at issue for this drinking party. As citizens, they benefitted from shelter and food, provision of the basics.

To my mind, life goals, aspirations, and human agency were matters to be worked out at the individual level. It would be a mistake to lump together everybody who fell into vulnerable groups. But there was more than panhandling and drinking on the social margins of Saarbrücken.

What about the conspicuous brothel located beside a children's music school? What did that say about survival and human agency?

Thomas and I met Leandra at the smart Landwehr Platz tram stop late Wednesday afternoons prior to her music lesson. If she looked ragged at first when she hopped off the commuter rail, her eyes soon lit up. Several buildings, including a fire station, circled a generous public square decorated by oaks. A parking lot, a city-owned building that doubled as a music school, outdoor basketball courts, and an energy charging station stood nearby.

With insufficient time to make a dash home for dinner before her lesson, we grew into the habit of coasting to *Konditorei* Becker, a local confectionary and café, where the old city square met Mainzerstraβe, a cobblestoned street marketplace. A stir of efficient activity drew us across the threshold, where we were captured by the showcase full of the main characters—an assortment of *Obstkuchen* (fruit tarts), flans, *Torten*, and other mouth-watering pastries. Next door, a grocer balanced arrays of fresh, colourful fruits and vegetables on trays. Out front, red, white, and blue umbrellas shaded tables, trembling in light winds. We pushed toward the sensation of that first morsel of divine pastry.

At this café, we ordered coffee, tea, onion soup, *Schinken Käse* (ham and cheese) toast, toast Hawaii, or quiche. Toast Hawaii is an open sandwich of ham, cheese, and a pineapple slice with a maraschino cherry in the middle. It's broiled for the melted cheese effect. Portions of Obstkuchen or fruit Torten, baked with one or more of plums, sour cherries, berries, apples, or apricots and adorned or mixed with almonds or marzipan, arrived at our table, topped with whipped cream.

As a midweek pause, Wednesday evening gave Leandra's spirits a boost, rewarding her for enduring three long school days and encouraging her to push on for another two. Welcoming waitresses started expecting us, smiling and anticipating orders before our lips moved. I felt swell to be regarded as a regular. I hope they missed us when we disappeared from their landscape without a trace in July 2014.

The ugliest part of Saarbrücken flowered right out in the open across the street from the music school where a brothel stood open for business. And as if the red building with red lights and red hearts was not enough of an advertisement, three windows gaped wide. Out of these windows hung three to six "girls," resting their elbows on red velvet cushions. I observed as clients entered and women left their stations to meet them. I never heard of parents or music instructors objecting to this business thriving across from where children, as young as early elementary school age, practised piano, flute, harp, and clarinet.

One day, Leandra and I discussed the subject.

"I just don't get why a brothel house would be right there," I said.

"Nobody seems to pay any attention to it, Mum," she said, glancing over at the house.

"That's just it. It seems so normal. I'm not saying prostitution is absent everywhere else —" I tried to find the right words. After all, Halifax was a port city. In *Madam of the Maritimes* (2021), Blain Henshaw details the story of Ada McCallum, who ran one of the country's most notorious brothels in Halifax for four decades. McCallum faced prosecution for her business in the 1970s and 1980s, and eventual bankruptcy.

"But with it being so close and visible, it flags the attention of adults and children," I said. *Was visibility such a bad thing?* Some would argue it was safer for the sex workers than Internet or street prostitution. I didn't have the answers, although I did know I didn't like the whole business one bit, nor where it was located. What did parents say when their children asked about the flashy crimson house? Why did I burn against the out-in-the-open sex trade, the oldest profession?

My discomfort had to do chiefly with brothel keepers and pimps, who used the women, some of them very young, to make money for themselves by satisfying the sexual appetites of others. Those female and male sex workers had euro signs emblazoned on their foreheads, visible to greedy employers for whom the only question of any significance in this for-profit business was how much money their "girls" would earn on any given day. My concern was not so much the sex work itself, but rather the exploitation of workers.

Profit making is the objective of sales, banking, and commercial work where employees are under pressure to continually increase business and generate greater profits as a measure of success. I knew a few former bank employees in Nova Scotia who'd left promising banking careers because of demands to keep advancing new investment and loan opportunities to customers whose precarious household budgets needed careful stewardship rather than more debt. Yet, there remains something essentially different and ghastly about prostitution. Here the body itself, as opposed to jewellery, pizzas, or mortgages, was objectified to generate money.

Even when working girls claimed that they entered into the sex trade of their own free will, that assertion called for a critical look. The word "free" needed testing against available choices and sovereign long- or short-term decisions, given the constraints and precarious circumstances some people live under. True choices are attainable alternatives with associated and appreciated consequences. The matter of a person's dignity is at stake. Autonomy requires maturity and tangible pathways toward real life options. In the cases of many of the girls and women I observed, their ages, ethnic backgrounds, and resident status in Saarland screamed ambiguity.

Leandra and I talked about all that while the "girls" bent forward, showing off stylish hairstyles, deep cleavages, and heavily made-up, juvenile faces across from the music school. Leandra remained pensive after my many observations, later admitting she'd been more surprised than anything else that the bawdy house was located right there in the city centre. "It all seemed so commonplace," she added. Then she related a story her music teacher, Frau Schmidt, had told her. A young boy waited outside the music school for a parent after his violin lessons when three bigger boys came by and started bullying him. Two girls from the brothel rushed out confronted the bullies and shooed them off. It was a turn of events the music teacher, Leandra, and I all cheered.

Sometime later, Thomas pointed out that the *Saarbrücker Zeitung* newspaper reported on the struggle of the authorities to control prostitution and contain it to certain streets. It proved to be as heated a battle in Saarbrücken as anywhere else. The brothel and street prostitution disgusted Thomas. "There's an absence of respect for human dignity. People, men and women, give up their self-determination, their agency," he said.

What is the meaning of human agency? It's the freedom to turn our thoughts and ideas into real action. My ability to exercise agency sprang from chance and (lack of) fortune. My childhood circumstances had been disadvantaged by scarcity and alcoholism. My life could have ended up a train wreck. The support of my hard-working mother, the positive influence of teacher role models, the interventions of friends, and a certain stubborn perseverance carried me forward and helped me stay the course. A shared life meant I gave up some autonomy and control as a wife and mother, employee and friend. But I'm still activating sovereignty when I freely act to add to and extend generosity, knowledge, and awareness about the world for the benefit of myself and others.

I'd been seduced too, though not by the lure of money, sex, or alcohol. In fact, I'd exercised the freedom to give up a substantial salary for a year abroad without any replacement pay or employment. My seduction represented things I valued for their immaterial worth.

19. German Bread and Cake

This morning I lingered, summoned by the vision behind the window of Ziegler bakery. I was making my way across a wide-awake city to my Volkshochschule class. In Dudweiler, Thomas mixed with grad-school types and Leandra joined her French classmates. I stopped to salivate, for I was living in a *Brot* nation—a bread-lover's paradise. Crossing the threshold of any bakery offered a range of about ten different types of breads and rolls.

Vehicles' tires rumbled on streetways near and distant. A yellow four-car Saarbahn tram trundled behind me, one street away, heading out to Sarreguemines or Riegelsberg. A steady stream of pedestrians brushed past. Warm, grain-infused aromas escaped the bakeshop's doorway.

Big breads and little breads. Small white, round rolls and little sweet rolls. Raisin breads and nutty breads. Fat, oblong figures lay beside long, skinny crisp ones on wicker trays. Breads with sesame seeds, linseeds, sunflower seeds, and pumpkin seeds. Smooth-skinned breads sat squat beside rough, darker skins. I yearned to touch them. Grainy breads of pure wheat or rye rubbed shoulders with varying mixtures of oat, spelt, buckwheat, linseed, and millet, breads made with coarse and finely ground flour. Fermented sourdoughs of different mixtures claimed space beside yeast-inspired relations. Breads produced by various baking methods in various shapes, sizes, and seasonings of nuts, seeds, and spices crowded in. They commanded me to straighten up and inhale a feast for the nose and eyes, a spread of the warm and wonderful.

For Canadians, it's Germany's dark bread that seems unappetizing and engenders reluctance to sample. As with everything German, regional differences with *Brot* abound. As Thomas explained, "As you go farther north, you see more dark bread because of farming patterns." Called *Schwarzbrot*, this dark bread is characterized by malt, giving it a black colour and a slight sweetness. Prepared with presoaked and fermented whole grains and wheat flour, it contains rye and, like most German bread, is made with sourdough. Varieties include black, white, grey, and nutritious *Vollkornbrot* (whole grain bread), which is iconic across a regionalized Germany. Grey bread requires a mixture of rye flour and whole wheat, while white bread comes with raisins and over time became a sweet, traditional breakfast bread. There is a move toward organic ingredients and greater nutrition through whole grains and mixtures of different varieties of grains and other ingredients, such as sunflower and sesame seeds, walnuts, and raisins.

Perhaps pumpernickel is the best-known German bread worldwide. It's a heavy, dark sourdough bread made with rye flour and coarse rye meal. It's usually baked in long narrow pans with a lid and should not be confused with American pumpernickel, which does not undergo the extensive baking process. To achieve the dark colour of American bread, bakers add chocolate, coffee, or molasses. No artificial flavours or colouring agents are added to traditional German pumpernickel.

In addition to their devotion to a variety of *Brot*, Germans enjoy *Kuchen* (various coffee cakes made from sweet yeast dough) and *Torten*, rich, multilayered cakes filled with whipped cream, buttercream, mousse, jam, or fruit. These cakes are usually glazed or garnished. If the most famous German bread is pumpernickel, then the best-known tortes are the chocolate-laden *Kirschtorte* (cherry cake) or *Schwarzwälder* (Black Forest cake), with a taste of potent cherry spirit.

When I'd savoured enough of the breads, I turned my eyes toward competing spreads of pastries, pies, flans, Kuchen, and Torten. A brisk passerby obscured my vision for a split second, stepped across the threshold of the bakery, and landed beside a customer to make her order. Behind the counter, a wiry worker with speedy glances and brisk hands called, "*Der Nächste bitte*" (next, please).

I finally understood my husband's poppyseed-cake obsession. He knew what he'd been missing in Nova Scotia for too many years. Born and raised in Northern Germany, he grew up with his mother cooking meals for a family of eight. His was a region with its own specialties, including the poppyseed cake and German *Rote Grütze* (red groats or berries with vanilla sauce). What was all this to me and Leandra? Anticipation of good food, best exemplified by Germany's love affair with a head-spinning array of breads and cakes in every direction we looked.

Within a short time, Thomas's weekly custom dictated a twenty-minute amble along the nearby forest trail on Sunday afternoons. His internal compass pointed without fail to that local bakery and café door in Ilseplatz, barring hurricane-force winds. There, he ordered a slice of sour-cherry cake with whipped cream, a coffee, and a loaf of rye bread to bring home. He then sat there to delight in the mouth-watering treat as a reward for the start of another week. He had to be alert, for if he failed to make his Sunday visit before 4 P.M., bare shelves greeted him. His favourite poppyseed cake was often absent from Saarland bakeries. When available, it disappointed, not as tasty as up north in a place like Travemünde on the Baltic Sea.

We enjoyed our fair share of fresh breads and rolls at breakfast. The dark rye bread was eaten traditionally as evening bread in open sandwiches spread with butter, cheeses, thin slices of ham, sausages, or other cold cuts. With this heavy, dark bread, Thomas prepared sandwiches for himself and Leandra to take to school and his office. It had taken him ten years of living in Canada before he gave up on his attempts to find acceptable local breads.

I surrendered at once to my treat temptations, before long rubbing shoulders with dozens of patrons at a busy bakeshop. I marvelled at delivery workers fighting their way in through a crowd of customers. Pastries flew off the shelves as fast as they arrived in a flurry of lunchtime madness. "One *Ochsenauge,* please," I'd say, pointing at a delight resembling an ox's eye made of delectable shortbread, apricot jam in the middle, and a frill of thick marzipan circling the eye's periphery. Later, after I discovered the university campus convenience store, I joined the queue there to say, "One *Nussecke,* please." Called a "nut corner," a *Nussecke* is a sweet made with fragrant toasted hazelnuts, apricot jam, and chocolate glaze.

One day, I joined my husband for a Sunday afternoon date of cake and coffee at the local Barbarossa bakery. Ten customers waited. It was one of the rare places where people lined up with patience, unlike at bus or train stops. Thomas pointed. "How about sitting over there while I order?" A glass case showed off the pretty goods. Rows of fragrant breads lined the wall on racks. Three or four female attendants hustled about in a blur of activity, selecting, wrapping, and tallying, and sometimes slicing and serving cake and coffee. Thomas and I sat at one of three side tables along a length of white wall. Behind us, through a window, a quiet residential street separated the bakery from a shuttered ice cream parlour on the plaza. Sunday was a quiet pause in our school–office–German class habits. Today, two slices of *Bienenstich* (bee sting), a sponge cake layered with buttercream and coated with sliced almonds, sat on the table before us. Buses clattered along Ilseplatz.

When I forked the first piece of that bee sting into my mouth, I closed my eyes. It was my Marcel Proust moment. A shudder did run through me but not of dredged up memories. It was the pure, unvarnished pleasure of the here when buttercream mixed with sponge cake and almonds delivered a thrill to my palate.

Any moist, crispy, or cakey goodies with marzipan, nuts, or cream tempted me beyond my power to resist. Leandra craved the bready texture of soft pretzels, *Schnecken* (sweet buns), and raisin rolls.

"Life's tough, so after a hard-knock week, you do deserve a *Krapfen* with raspberry jam inside," I said a few days later, as her lips curled around the pastry, famously known as a Berliner. She nodded, satisfaction glazing her eyes while Thomas looked on approvingly. He couldn't feed us or himself enough indulgences. *It's so easy to grow fat in Germany.* Fruits of the land: Brot, Kuchen, Torten, and ice cream, careless of their effects, summoned us.

20. Wine, Beer, and Ice Cream Pacts

Ever since our arrival in July, Thomas and I had been seeing beer gardens and pubs as we bused into and out of the downtown. In mild and warm weather, across Saarbrücken, crowds gathered, tossing back some of the thousands of beer brands from as many as 1,300 breweries in Germany. I felt duty-bound to make my contribution.

"What's a real German pub like?" I asked Thomas one day in August.

"Not much to speak of." He liked beer only on hot days after an outdoor workout.

"Can we go over to Ilseplatz for a drink?"

"Yah, if we must. Next Saturday evening?"

I so wanted to soak up the homegrown pub air. I thought it would be the typical German experience I'd heard about from Thomas.

After a brief walk, we entered the small pub.

Red and yellow stained-glass lampshades hung low over pine tables, giving fair light in a dim room. Six rectangular tables lined a wall on the right; a bar half the room's length stood on the opposite wall. Male patrons in parties of two or three regarded us as we sat down. A curt waitress greeted us and gave menus. A long span of shelved glasses and spirits spread behind the bartender.

Thomas chose a *Bruch*. "Why Bruch?" I asked.

"It's Saarland's best, a Pilsner or pale lager—a light-golden beer."

"I'll join you in that." The efficient waitress fast-tracked our orders.

"Cheers!" We clinked glasses, then sipped our cold delights, taking a pass on more substantial fare: Bratwurst, pan-fried and cooked in beer with potatoes and *Rotkohl* (red cabbage). We spoke to no one but the waitress chipping fast back and forth. Locals chit-chatted in muted tones. After an hour in this quiet, amiable scene, we walked home. So, that was what a local German pub was like. Perhaps the food was the unique thing.

It had been a different atmosphere when Thomas, Leandra, and I ventured into the *Hofbräuhaus am Platzl* in summer 2011. Hofbräuhaus (the court's brewery house) am Platzl is a beer hall, restaurant, and popular tourist attraction in Munich, Bavaria. A heritage monument, it's a mix of the old and the new, having been first built in the late sixteenth century and remodelled three hundred years later. All the rooms except for the beer hall were destroyed by bombings in the Second World War. Rebuilt, it reopened in 1958. Multiple famous buildings such as the Hofbräuhaus theatre surround a cobblestoned plaza, making this public square a leading entertainment centre.

When we stepped inside, a cavernous room about thirty metres long and almost as wide opened up, lined with a crunch of tables and benches, each table seating eight to twelve people. It was the big, lively, main taproom on the main floor. A decorated ceiling soared overhead, featuring elaborate frescoes in baroque style. Friendly, red-faced servers burdened with food and beer squeezed between tables. Today, the place crammed in what seemed like hundreds of patrons, all screaming to be heard by people sitting next to them or across the table on benches. The almighty din knocked me off kilter.

We slid onto a bench at a table occupied by two young men, nodding hellos. Shared seating being the norm, there was no awkwardness in rubbing shoulders with strangers.

"Are you up for the *Schenscher* dish, Claudette?" A glint sparkled in Thomas's eyes and a mischievous grin crossed his lips. Not knowing what I was in for, I said yes.

"And you Leandra?"

"Nope. I'm having Schnitzel with Bratkartoffeln."

After half an hour, we attracted a harassed waiter's attention. It was mid-evening, and the man looked wiped out. I scanned the roaring Hofbräuhaus but saw no heavy-busted women in dirndl carrying nine or twelve steins of foam-topped beer.

"We'll have a glass of Apfelschorle, two mugs, one *Schweinshaxe* (ham hock), two Schnitzels and Bratkartoffeln." The serious-faced waiter nodded and moved off full of go, no time for chatting. Thomas passed on the Schweinshaxe. That should have warned me.

"Hello," one of the young men said. His face was blush-red as if sunburned. Perhaps it was the beer. His shoulder-length blond hair fell behind from an untidy ponytail. Jovial, he mischievously tried to get Thomas to pay for his drinks. "All professors are rich, aren't they?" he said when he learned what Thomas did for a living. His dark-haired friend, though quieter, laughed at his partner's antics. They told us they were Dutch students on holiday in Germany.

"Oh, my!" I gasped at the size of an upright Schweinshaxe coming toward me. Leandra's eyes widened while Thomas smirked. By the time the waiter plunked the ham hock down in front of me, I had almost filled up on the litre of Hofbräu Original lager he'd set down earlier. I thought it amusing that many regular patrons stored their mugs in small lockers at the Hofbräuhaus.

"It's the lower leg or knuckle of a young pig, roasted slowly at low heat and served with fried potatoes and sauerkraut," Thomas explained. "You don't have to finish it all."

"To do that, you'd need an extra stomach," Leandra joked.

"So true, wish I did."

It looked and tasted savoury, the tender pork falling off the bone and dissolving in my mouth. Both Thomas and Leandra demurred when I offered tasters. I left most of it unfinished when we rose to leave the ruckus, bidding *au revoir* to our Dutch acquaintances.

"*That* was not a local pub experience. Most people sitting in there are tourists—both German and visitors," Thomas said.

"But what an experience," I replied. The massive, crowded, noisy place where I had to scream to be heard gave me a headache, but the crowd, the surprising food, the size of the beer (at one litre each), and the cramped seating, sharing benches with total strangers, thrilled me. Although touristy and beyond anything I would experience later in Saarland, the Munich Hofbräuhaus was a unique social event with a mood not easily replicated anywhere else, well worth the experience.

In my mind, our patronage of Italian ice cream parlours in Saarbrücken amounted to a family sport. "Who's the biggest ice cream lover in our household?" I asked Leandra.

"You are," she answered without twitching an eyelid.

"That's not true." My face registered mock shock, for I was sure she'd say Dad.

"Mum, you cannot resist an ice cream invitation. You know that, so admit it."

I refused to concede. In Saarland, Thomas was the one luring us to the parlours and never missing coffee and cake hour on Sundays, even when I pulled back for blood glucose reasons. His was the sweet tooth in our family, and what was ice cream if not sweet? I ran a close second. Leandra sometimes loved ice cream and sometimes passed. Neither she nor I relished chocolate as much as Thomas did.

From our first family vacation visits to Germany, I discovered that ordering an ice cream sundae held the same weight as ordering a full-course meal. If we desired a cone, we didn't crowd the seating area but moved along after being served. Italian ice cream inspires overindulgence, and we devoted ourselves to it in Saarland throughout the summer and fall. Ice cream season in Germany ran from Easter to fall, closing for winter. Thomas and I fancied any style of ice cream anywhere. In Nova Scotia, an ice cream cone was a summer treat, but the sheer variety of the offerings and the parlour atmosphere in Saarland turned me into an ice cream fool.

Since the 1920s, Germans have encouraged Italians or Italian-Germans to feed them gallons of *Eis* at parlours, with no sign so far of asking them to stop. *Spaghettieis* originated with a Mannheim German who had Italian roots. It transformed into a German specialty after the 1960s. Pressing vanilla ice cream through a potato ricer to create "noodles" that are then piled over a heap of whipped cream was a brilliant idea. Strawberry pulp could be mistaken for tomato sauce and white chocolate shavings for parmesan cheese. An irresistible sundae combo, it's reputed to bring out the kid in everyone.

In the cobblestoned market square, surrounded by shoppers, we eyed the displays, even some with vegetables and grains as ingredients. Piled high to satisfy the eye and taste, they beckoned, secure behind shining cases. The lavish diversity and shameless way they arrived at adjoining tables seduced me. "These dishes come in glassware or on silver platters," Thomas pointed out. "Now that's service." The many flavours would require months to sample. Cream blended with nuts, chocolate, coffee, liqueur, waffles, brittle, coconut, sprinkles, cakes, and cookies and concealed under whipped cream, drizzles of chocolate, caramel, and fruity sauces, they enticed the eyes, the nose, and the tongue. My fingertips moved over the bright-coloured menus and pointed at Spaghettieis, my all-time favourite.

"I'm not going to order spaghetti ice cream today," Leandra said. "I'll have a fruit bowl topped with strawberry ice cream, whipped cream, and vanilla sauce." Other times, a dish of hazelnut ice cream loaded with banana or pineapple chunks delighted her most, especially when dripped with strawberry or raspberry sauce.

"Yum. What about you, Dad?"

"I'll have this." He pointed at a large coffee ice cream fruit bowl covered in whipped cream and strawberry sauce and topped with a chocolate wafer.

The young female server set down our orders with a solemn air under sweltering summer heat.

"How's yours, Leandra?" I asked.

"Mmm, delish," she said, eyes out of focused.

Ice cream lovers chilled beneath a barrage of bright umbrellas. Crowds hovered around the old fountain or flowed by, lost in thought or talk.

Our shared family rituals and, simple pleasures and indulgences were special moments. We had travelled to Europe and Barbados years before and camped in France with our young children. We couldn't take this time together with Leandra for granted, Art had already left home and in a few years, she too would begin making a life for herself away from us. For now, we kept her close; living in Saarland was different from living in Nova Scotia, where Thomas worked hundreds of kilometres away. In Saarland, we faced the security and challenges of living together every day, testing and strengthening family bonds.

21. Christmas and New Year's Eve

Small red cabins started populating the Bahnhofstraße in early November. They cast new colour amid an assortment of people and objects crowding a thoroughfare already alive with shoppers, beggars, snack shops, city vehicles, and construction. *Weihnachtsmarkt* (Christmas market) had started. I passed these temporary pavilions on my way to and from my German language classes.

A jolly atmosphere of Christmas brought me and my family to market booths on Saturdays when we checked out wreaths, ceramic and woodwork nativity scenes, handicrafts, and knitted items. Amidst the flurry and noise of scraping feet and mingled voices, we took in the nutty potato aroma of roasted *Maronen* (chestnuts), the fragrance of warm cinnamon rolls, and the chocolatey hazelnut scent of Nutella crepes. I paused at stalls of chocolate-covered fruits and the Saarland specialty *Dibbelabbes* (fried or oven-baked hash, made from grated potato, bacon, and leek, served with apple sauce). I acquired a taste for roasted chestnuts.

From childhood, I had loved Christmas time with its bustle of getting ready for something big. The household hurried, floors and furniture got new varnish, and mother hung new curtains, prepped fruit cakes steeped in rum, and bought gifts. Then Christmas Day passed as the most serene day ever, with everyone eating ridiculous amounts after an early promenade in Queen's Park, Bridgetown.

The Christmas Day spread in Barbados was Sunday meals quadrupled. A crispy leg of baked ham poked with cloves loaded down the dining table alongside stuffed, roasted chicken macaroni pie, and jug-jug (a traditional dish of pigeon peas, barley, and pork or beef combined into a moist deliciousness). Barbadian desserts were not plentiful, but fruit and pound cake were served with scoops of ice cream or dashes of rum. And Christmas wouldn't have been the same without freshly baked coconut bread. We parked sorrel saturated with cane sugar next to fruit punches and fruit cocktails, falernum syrup, mauby, and pop drinks, a Bajan feast.

In Nova Scotia, Christmas was a much-needed pause after the hectic fall reboot. Thomas and I'd come home lopsided from rounds of Christmas and grocery shopping, toting an incredible Christmas tree. We'd fuss and decorate it with small tokens, homemade or purchased, and set it blinking in the living room. I'd catch a break soaking up family time with everyone at home for two straight weeks, sipping drinks while warming my toes in front of a flickering wood stove, the children playing nearby. If we were lucky, snow blanketed the landscape. Each year's Christmas was a little different—we chose the tempo, as busy or slow as we wished. Since we had no extended family in Canada, we made a point of inviting friends for dinner over the holiday season. Even as Christmas in Saarland felt different, a Christmas tree was a must to liven up our Christmas festivities.

In Saarland, the last Saturday in November was comfortably mild, Saint Johann's Square was packed with people, and expectancy filled the air. Faces of adults, youths, and children beamed in the crush.

"I've never seen so many people in one spot," I said to Thomas and Leandra. In truth, I'd seen more in Barbados during Crop Over, an annual summer festival and the closest Canadian experience I could compare it to was at the Canada Day fireworks on Parliament Hill in 2009. "Stay close, Leandra," I whispered, but she was in little danger of getting lost.

I'd arranged to meet Estella and Anya from the German course downtown to see the flying Santa Claus and angel. A special Saarland attraction, Santa Claus in his reindeer sleigh, accompanied by a Christmas angel in a cloud, floated over the market.

Pushing through the throngs, we arrived minutes before the start of the fifteen-minute, gravity-defying event. Estella had planned to come with her husband and two girls, Anya with her fiancé, and I with Thomas and Leandra. We thought to meet at the landmark fountain in the old city, a good idea at the time. The plaza now ruptured at its seams with humanity, and still more poured in.

I needed a tiny miracle and got it when Estella spotted me—one of three Black people in a throng of thousands. Our luck ended right there, because Anya remained lost in the crowds all night. Estella had convinced her eight-year-old to join her, but her twelve-year-old had grander plans for the evening. Thomas hit it off with Estella's gregarious husband, and our little group settled in for fun, crowd-bathing, drinking *Glühwein* (mulled wine), and eating *Weisswurst* (white sausage) and marzipan balls.

Being in that crowd made for an amazing night after the *oohs* and *aahs* of the Santa, reindeer, and angel high-wire act. We had little wiggle room in most spots, especially around food stalls, making for an exceptional Christmas market experience, Leandra's and my first. Estella chatted with Leandra about her Saarbrücken and Sarreguemines school experiences in French. Like many people our daughter met in Saarland, Estella expressed amazement about Leandra's assured French and her attendance at French school in Canada. Eventually, zapped by the demands of the surging crowd, and markets sights and sounds, our families parted ways for quieter spaces at home.

Thomas played secret Saint Nicholas on December 6, placing goodie bags with chocolates, mandarins, and cookies on doorknobs for children in our apartment building. His good neighbourliness was rewarded when he awoke one morning to find two bottles of cold-pressed olive oil, gifts from the Italian couple across the hall, glinting in the pale morning light. The couple were parents to Leonardo, an adorable, four-year-old dynamo. A few days later, Arenata, one floor below, surprised us by knocking at our door bearing a platter of shortbread, almond, and chocolate cookies, and staying for a fun visit.

Christmas was the time I missed home, family, and friends. I'd kept in touch with my younger sister in the USA, who had wanted to visit us in 2014. Even after I encouraged it, detailing how to take the connector train from Frankfurt airport to Saarbrücken, she chickened out and decided against it when I pointed out we couldn't meet her at the airport.

I communicated by email with two colleagues and a few friends, one very encouraging of my beginner's German phrases and another telling me to enjoy every moment abroad and not think about school things waiting for my return. Another friend who had lived in Germany identified with Leandra's plight, as her children had attended school in Germany, calling Leandra a fighter. Those connections helped to anchor me throughout the year.

As Christmas Day drew nearer, a curious sentiment winged its way into our living spaces and settled in my heart where nostalgia bred homesickness. Even with Thomas and Leandra for company, Christmastime outside Nova Scotia seemed weird and lonely. Not even a thumbnail of snow graced the outdoors, and I didn't know whether to laugh or howl in disappointment. Saarland can receive plenty of snow, as it did the year after we left.

Leandra looked dejected, saying: "I miss my friends."

As Christmas came closer, Thomas was buoyant, striving to remain chirpy, though he absorbed some of our sadness.

"Let's get a Christmas tree and decorate it together. How'd you like that?" he said to Leandra a week before Christmas.

"Sure, Dad." She voiced little enthusiasm.

One Friday afternoon, after making our regular round through the Schwarzenberg Forest, Thomas and I stopped at the yard of the local forester to purchase a tree. We picked a medium-sized one, and Thomas hoisted it onto his shoulders. We then hiked for another twenty minutes uphill on the wooded trail and up the fifty-six steps to our apartment. All seemed fine until the next day when Thomas lay in bed, knocked flat by pain. "My back, the ache is unbelievable. Do we have anything for this backache?", he asked, wincing.

"I'm looking." I scrambled through a few drawers, knowing we had nothing before deciding to hasten over to the Apotheke for a tube of muscle relief medication.

"Leandra, you coming?" I called. She hopped out of her bedroom door in a flash.

It was midday Saturday, and she joined me for a jaunt into town with the promise of a stop at Netto grocery on the way back. I spoke to a sympathetic pharmacist in deplorable Bajan-accented German to obtain what I needed.

Leandra looked on, correcting me later by saying, "Mum, you used the informal 'you,' not the formal."

I nodded, silently noting she could be such an annoying perfectionist sometimes. I said, "But you must admit, the pharmacist understood my German."

"True." She tapped my shoulder, still not convinced I'd tried hard enough.

After the Netto stop, our bags bulged with weekend goodies: peanut flips, cashews, chocolates, Hanuta wafers, pretzels, yoghourt, quark, fruits, vegetables, and Gouda, Géramont, and Caprice des Dieux cheeses.

Back home, I applied the penetrating heat cream, the German version of a RUB-A535 balm, to Thomas's back, giving rapid relief.

"Thanks. I'm so embarrassed about this back pain after so small a job hauling a silver fir. Old age will get us all in the end."

"Yep, but I'd rather not think of the alternative," I said, relieved.

We surveyed our brave Christmas tree decorated with glitzy, store-bought gold and silver balls, tinsel, cotton wool, and a too-large gold star, purchased from stores in Dudweiler. We'd limited ourselves to buying practical gifts and festive treats, not wanting bulky items we'd have to haul back to Canada, which we wrapped with as much care, attention, and cheer as we could muster.

Leandra spent quiet hours reading in her room until near suppertime on Christmas Eve. Her classes had ended December 20 and would resume January 5 after a two-week break. Thomas and I busied ourselves cooking small potatoes and Brussels sprouts, frying beef Rouladen, bought from a Dudweiler butcher shop, and then simmering it in a thick gravy. Divine aromas erupted from our kitchen, lifting my spirit.

In German tradition, we unwrapped our gifts after supper on December 24: sturdy hiking boots, cashmere sweaters, winter coats, boxes of marzipan chocolates, and German Christmas cookies. Leandra had bought us a surprise gift, a lovely fire-engine red tablecloth, so fitting for the season, I laid it out right away. After supper, we stuffed ourselves with fine chocolates and munched gourmet cookies. The mood grew into a cozy, family-warm atmosphere with splashes of nostalgia when we contrasted what we loved about Christmas, both in Germany and at home. Art, far away in Canada, was the only absent member of our immediate family. We missed him, our friends in Nova Scotia with whom we usually shared the holidays, and our wood stove, but Christmas market in German was a big hit

Thomas reminded us the next day we were invited to Hermann's, an acquaintance he knew from his university days.

"It'll be good to see how a local family spends Christmas Day," I said, sipping wine.

"Where's this exactly?" Leandra asked, her gaze on the magazine she was flipping through.

"Oh, out toward Riegelsberg. Not far by tram."

Christmas holidays and invitations proved a welcome break for Thomas too. He'd completed fieldwork in Kirkel, Sankt Ingbert, Ormesheim, and Saarbrücken forests, had wrestled his data into smart tables and charts, and now struggled to compose a scientific paper for journal submission about plasticity of beech trees in Saarland.

Next evening, an unusual quiet shrouded a just-about-deserted city. We boarded a tram at Johannes Station, empty but for three silent passengers, riding for fifteen minutes out toward an old miners' settlement. Getting off at Riegelsberg, we strode for ten minutes under a dark, moonless sky. Bordered partway by trees and shrubs on both sides, the village road was in time lit by muted electric glows escaping a few still houses. Our footfalls echoed in a silence that approached the mysterious.

We stopped in front of an attractive two-storey house of stone with a red door and trim. "I think this is it. This used to be a schoolhouse," Thomas said. At the sound of the doorbell, a pleasant, fit middle-aged man appeared in the doorway.

"Hallo, Thomas. Wonderful to see you. Come in, come in."

Thomas's friend, balding and slight in built, was animated. Standing beside him, his wife, Clara, was half a head shorter. Neat and trim, too, she held a cigarette between her fingers. For some reason, her white, spiky haircut and red-rimmed glasses gave her an air of being more French than German.

"How's your German coming along?" The husband asked me as we sat down.

"*Ein bißchen,* (a little)," I answered, laughing nervously.

"We won't torture you tonight, then." Our host laughed too.

"It's too soon to know much German—you've been here how long?" Clara asked.

"About six months. We got here in early July."

Our conversations lurched from English to German to French and then back again. The couple had lived in Benin, West Africa, for a few years. Sometimes Thomas or our hosts translated for me and Leandra. Having lived overseas in francophone West Africa, they knew what it was like to be away from home.

Their wire-haired dachshund, a *Dackel* in Germany and a badger or sausage dog in other places, put on a spirited show. He yowled non-stop as we sat around chit-chatting, pleading for someone to throw him the red ball, which he scampered after as if dashing to the edge of the earth. Our hosts tossed it deep into the backyard. After retrieving it, he yowled to have someone do it again, never getting tired. It helped me understand the dog's behaviour when I learned that this short-legged, long-bodied, hound-type breed was developed to scent, chase, and flush out badgers and other burrow-dwelling animals.

We dined on wonderful roasted chestnut soup, rice and beans, cuts of succulent beef, and ice cream with apple preserves from our hosts' garden. The open-concept sitting room spilled into a comfortable dining area dominated by a table with red and green festive settings for five. Plush rugs covered areas of the grey slate floor. A wood stove tiled in baby blue acted as a partial room separator, the cream-coloured walls contrasting with the stove's hue. That stove was so well engineered, it needed only one load of wood a day to keep the two-storey house warm for twelve hours. Leaning back against its warm tiles took me close to heaven.

"What are you taking at school, young lady?" Our host turned his twinkling blue eyes toward Leandra.

"French, English, chemistry, maths, Latin —"

"Latin, now that's a waste of time."

Leandra halted, dropping her eyes to the table.

"Oh, why so?" Thomas asked, engaging Hermann.

"I was forced to learn Latin in school, and it was a waste." His fingertips tapped the table.

Leandra spoke softly, fiddling with a table napkin. "But I chose —"

"Latin is a dead language. Now Italian, there's a language that's useful," Hermann said, interrupting her.

"Why's that?" I asked, curious about his reasons. I had given Leandra a Harry Potter novel in Latin after she'd said she wanted to learn the language.

"Italian is a modern, spoken language that helps you with all other Latin-based languages. You learn Italian, you can understand French, Spanish, Portuguese, and other Romance languages like Romanian." Hermann's face looked intense but not unkind.

Leandra kept quiet, intimidated by Hermann's outspoken directness.

"I've always regretted not learning Latin when I did a forestry degree and had to learn hundreds of botanical terms," Thomas said. Our host held fast to his view while Leandra kept silent.

We switched to talking about the couple's twenty-year-old son who had struggled to finish secondary school, complete his final year college-prep exams, and figure out his next move. He was now visiting Berlin. It sounded so familiar, making me think of Art, who had fought to stay motivated during four years at Cape Breton University.

"Would you like to see our backyard?" Clara offered, rising.

"For sure," I said. Joined by Leandra, the men behind, Clara showed off a large backyard of mixed fruit trees and vegetable garden beds, although the yard's full glory could best be appreciated in summer. Outside, the cool, late December air chilled my face as we toured, walking beneath a long arrangement of yellow lanterns on poles lighting up the darkness. Slate paving stones marked a twisting path through fruit trees and remnants of vines, shrubs, and raised garden beds. "We harvest lots of apples and peaches by late summer," Clara said. "And over here, we get green beans, kale, lettuce, carrots, and tomatoes, now under burlap," she pointed.

By the back door, a covered nook sheltered cushioned benches and a vintage wooden table. A *Schwenker Grill*, a specialty of the Saarland, hung from a tripod by a chain. The next summer, we would sit there to enjoy the griller that swung a meat-covered rack over flames, keeping it in constant motion as it cooked wild boar meat, beef cuts, hamburgers, and white sausages.

"Well, I guess we should be getting back," Thomas said after midnight.

"I'll drive you up to the station," Hermann said, grabbing his jacket and car keys. Riding back, the Saarbahn and streets seemed darker and emptier than ever. We'd missed the last bus to our apartment and hailed a taxi.

It had turned out to be a great evening, distracting me from the longings lodged in my heart. Leandra had enjoyed the distraction too, even though Hermann had shot her down after the first question he asked her. She'd been drawn back into the evening's diversion in the backyard. And as for Thomas, he'd been in his element, reminiscing with an old friend in his native tongue.

"He was really opinionated," Leandra said to me on the way back.

"Yep, he dismissed you out of hand." Sometimes our German acquaintances projected that they held on to some kind of high ground by being very serious about something minor. Leandra tended to be quiet and tactful, especially with adults and people she hardly knew. But she could be contrary too. I thought Hermann too blunt and dogmatic, not engaging and listening to a shy teen so different from how we interacted with her. With us, on many issues, she held on to her own opinions, confident in expressing them. At home, weary, we hit the sack, ending our first ever Christmas Day in Saarland.

A second holiday invitation took us to my friend Anna, who lived in an idyllic village near Heusweiler, surrounded by mixed woods, manicured lawns, and charming neighbourhood gardens. From her backyard, we looked across a scenic, undulating landscape into Saarland heartland. It would be our second visit to her home.

Our first visit remained fixed in my memory. On a cool and cloudy Saturday afternoon back in October, Thomas, Leandra, and I had set out. At Johannes Station, annoying drunks occupied the shelters and ruled the church wall, the air around them rank. We were travelling outside the hexagon of the *Wabe*, so we had to figure out the route. "Here it comes," Thomas said, nervous and wired. The tram emptied out at our stop so that Leandra and I had a full choice of seats, sitting together, swaying gently with the tram as it moved.

"Who is Anna again?" Leandra asked, tilting her head toward me.

"I told you, a woman I met at the university back in September. She's a retired teacher."

"Oh, that's why you like her." Leandra hadn't objected to joining us—she enjoyed meeting new people and discovering new places—but she hadn't been excited about it either.

"That's not the only reason. She's very outgoing. You'll see." The tram slowed and twisted, scraping by so close to plain, rebuilt houses of the 1950s era, we could reach out and touch them. When we reached Riegelsberg, we were among the few left on board.

We disembarked and stood waiting, uncertain, looking for a fiery red station wagon across the way in the parking lot. I'd expected Anna to collect us here, as she resided yet a good distance off.

"Did I make a mistake?" I wondered aloud.

"Let's give it a few minutes," Thomas replied. "Perhaps she's just late." He could be patient when it mattered.

I caught sight of a woman dressed in a black jacket and a flowy beige dress hurrying toward us. Her dark brown hair was swept back from a pleasant, friendly face that bore a striking resemblance to Anna.

"Are you Claudette? You must be here to meet Anna," she said, flustered.

"Uh-oh, yes." *Was something wrong*?

"Anna asked me to meet you. I'm her sister, Clair—I'm afraid she's had an accident."

"Oh no!"

"Luckily, she's all right, but her car isn't. She's just down the road from here. Come." Clair led the way, and we followed, my mind twirled dreading the worst, not sure what to expect.

We rounded a curve, and I spotted Anna, gesticulating and talking to two police officers. Nearby, her red car teetered against a tram pole. She looked anxious but unhurt.

"Hallo, Anna," I greeted.

"Hallo." As she turned back to the officers, we stood aside, waiting, wondering if it would be better to turn around and head back to Saarbrücken.

"Anna, we can come back another—"

"Oh, no," she said, waving, insisting we go on as planned.

We waited, listening. The police officers left, the car was towed away, and Clair drove us to Anna's house for a visit and tea. A knob of guilt nagged at me throughout the evening.

"Anna, I feel bad, the accident happened when you drove out to get us."

But she wasn't having any of it. "Shit happens!" she said.

The evening had been spoiled, in the end we travelled back in a subdued mood.

In two weeks, Anna had settled the finances and had her vehicle back in working order. The repairs had cost her insurance twelve thousand euros. If she had written off the damaged car, she would have had to pay eight thousand euros out of pocket, the difference between the cost of a new car and what the insurance was willing to pay.

"Okay, that's it," Thomas said, "any time we take up Anna or anyone else on an invitation to visit them, we get there on our own steam." I agreed. "After all, we're seasoned travellers." It wasn't our fault Anna had crashed her car, but she'd said that being late, she'd rushed to meet us.

So, for our second visit out to Anna's, on New Year's Eve, we took the train, going beyond Riegelsberg to Heusweiler, getting off at a large shopping complex, and catching a waiting bus. Oftentimes things worked so seamlessly in Germany I wanted to give a shout out to the universe. But on this trip, we observed curious and abject human conditions on the Saarbahn ride.

Teenagers climbed on board, giddy with the excitement of New Year's Eve, raising beer bottles, and in some cases carrying them stuffed in their pockets.

"Can you imagine that going on in Nova Scotia?" I said, nudging Leandra.

"Boy, drinking is different here," she replied, having already seen it at the wine tasting in August and later at the language-class party. None of this was surprising to Thomas, who looked on with disapproval.

"I hope they don't get too obnoxious," he said, eyes glancing around the car as he pulled his tweed coat tighter.

Their behaviour was not the problem, it was their smell—a rancid stench of alcoholic breaths permeating the air to the point where I was in danger of losing my lunch. I had experienced a similar air on the bus to Fuchstälchen, rammed full of a jovial university set one Friday after midnight; the air had stood thick with the stench of beer, sweat, and pickles. I barely held on to consciousness in that battle, running from the bus when I left the sweetish reek.

Behind the teens came a washed-out rummy, raggedy and accompanied by stale whiffs. His hair streaked to his shoulders, and a baggy shirt swallowed his skinny frame. He high-stepped gingerly onto the tram, holding two large grocery bags brimming with empty bottles. His bags dripped out the final remnants of their contents. He could hardly be expected to manage his load as well as use fancy footwork to balance himself on a full tram. No one offered him a seat. Before long, his consignment crashed to the floor, clattering and splattering along the way.

I made a mental note: *When travelling on the tram or bus, sit at the edge of a two-seater so that the inside seat is blocked. If a determined person persists in claiming it, my escape route is clear.* Leandra had learned this uncharitable strategy after a short time into her trips to school. She'd watch fragrant, meticulously dressed young women block seats on trains and buses and show real scorn even when clean, polite passengers insisted on sharing. Leandra now understood why this behaviour persisted in public spaces as she looked on, holding her nose on the sly.

"This is unbelievable." Shifting his legs, Thomas could barely contain his annoyance.

But on this night, a few kind passengers stooped to help the happy fellow gather up his treasure for recycling. Helping him to refill his bags ensured he'd make enough spare change to buy more alcohol. Unlike in Canada, in Saarbrücken, and perhaps all of Germany, wine and beer were almost as inexpensive and accessible as water, and on this night in particular, alcohol splashed in public places. In Germany, New Year's Eve is called *Silvester* and is a lively and popular festival named after Pope Silvester, who headed the Roman Catholic Church from 314 to 335 CE.

The connector bus to Anna's passed through scenic, rolling landscape and edges of residential areas, then deposited us at our stop. In semidarkness, we followed a tangle of deserted, meandering residential streets with names of flowers, shrubs, and trees. When Thomas asked a group of teens for directions, one pointed and mumbled. He next asked a mysterious, overdressed person with no better results. Finally, he approached a skittish older woman who eyed us with distrust, later warming to us. She must have been relieved we meant to play no tricks on her this night of fireworks.

"Did you have trouble finding my place?" Anna asked on arrival.

"Nope," I lied. "Easy-peasy."

We entered the white, roughcast house with brown window trimmings from a side entrance next to a garage. Framed wall photographs, plants, and paintings decorated the bright walk-out basement. It displayed precious memorabilia: souvenirs, art pieces, and crafts collected over decades of life and travels. Anna's son's old room now waited for his infrequent visits and stayover guests. Up a flight of stairs, we landed in an open room of cream and baby blue walls. In the centre, the dining table was set for a seasonal holiday dinner. A white tablecloth lay under red-and-white laced table mats. A holly berry garland circled a crystal vase overflowing with a red and green poinsettia. Anna had arranged five table settings of gleaming cutlery and sparkling glasses. On a side table, Christmas goodies added to the colour and festive feeling: *Stollen* (a spicy fruit bread), *Lebkuchen* ("life cakes"—soft, gingery cookies), and *Spekulatius* (traditional Christmas spice cookies). A sitting room and kitchen led off in opposite angles. The backyard deck overlooked a variety of raised garden beds and shrubs. In the distance lay a darkened landscape, relieved by pinpricks of light.

Clair advanced, smiling in the dining room, welcoming us in as we exchanged season's greetings. "Make yourselves comfortable. Red or white wine?" Anna beamed, moving around the table to the kitchen. We took red wine while Leandra favoured sparkling water

"Okay, make yourselves comfortable," Anna repeated, "because we're going to enjoy a German tradition first." Clair turned on the TV and we watched the tongue-in-cheek "Dinner for One," with James, the butler, serving Miss Sophie in the same procedure as before, as every year. It's a two-hander comedy sketch, recorded by the BBC in 1962. With the traditional viewing on New Year's Eve in Europe, in 1995, it was declared the most frequently repeated television program of all time in Germany.

Over glasses of red wine, we enjoyed a meal of creamy pumpkin soup, leek pie, potatoes, and Spezzatino, an Italian beef stew. Anna and Clair gently hushed all my offers to help with serving, insisting I sit and enjoy the evening.

"Ahh! Stollen," Thomas said, loving the traditional bread containing dried fruit, nuts, and marzipan. "Now this is a Christmas season specialty."

"And then there's more, *Aprikosen-mandel-zopf* and Italian ice cream," Clair said, referring to a braided bread with apricot and almond, launching my husband into dessert heaven.

At supper, Anna played Spanish guitar music and offered up a steady supply of wine. It was a marvellous New Year's Eve celebration, thanks to the generosity of these wonderful women. Anna shared stories of travels to Italy, Spain, England, France, and Luxembourg. Her love of languages matched a lifelong desire to know about how people lived across the world. She probed me for stories about Barbados and asked Leandra to tell stories about her French school experiences. It was a special evening.

By 11:00 P.M., Leandra looked bushed, and the wine had done its work on the adults. Anna wanted us to stay over saying something about Silvester night madness and that we did not want to be on a tram heading back into town. Thomas declined the invitation and made excuses to avoid staying overnight and I backed him up as we had not intended to stay the night. We made several attempts to phone a taxi company to take us to Saarbrücken before finally booking one. Buses did not run into the city at such a late hour.

After a thirty-minute delay, the taxi arrived. We hugged Anna and Clair, thanked them, and wished them a happy new year. The taxi driver gave us nervous looks, almost breathless. On the way, he and Thomas talked loudly in front. We learned the driver wanted nothing more than to be in and out of the city before the clock struck midnight when Thomas translated his anxiety. That should have been enough of a warning to us in our naïveté.

"What's that?" Leandra asked, leaning closer.

"Oh, the driver doesn't like driving on Silvester night." I kept my tone ordinary.

Anna's words echoed in my head when she'd pressed us to spend the night at her place, stressing not to take the tram: "You don't want to do that!" Also, at the Volkshochschule, Frau Becker had talked vaguely about an experience when she'd been in the path of youths tossing fireworks on Silvester night years ago. But I had wanted the experience of a German

Silvester night too badly, too innocent to heed good advice plus, some nuances had been lost in translation.

At present, hitting the highway like a man possessed, the taxi driver's singular focus was getting in and out of the city with one more fare before midnight. On the way, he disclosed that the insurance for his company did not cover any damage to vehicles after that time, standard practice for New Year's Eve.

"What's all the excitement about? I don't get it," Leandra said.

"I don't either," Thomas replied, only by then I held troubling suspicions. Deposited in downtown Saarbrücken at 11:50 P.M., we strolled along main streets surrounded by lit up city buildings before coming to stand on the Saar Bridge, watching what we thought were a few preliminary fireworks way off down the river. Waiting for the main event, we saw happy-go-lucky youths strolling past in clusters. The streets were nearly empty of vehicle traffic except for the occasional car and accelerated taxi.

Beside us stood a middle-aged, amiable couple lolling over the bridge guardrail. I thought I saw in the distance the beginnings of what would be a buildup to a grand finale and dazzling display. Thomas approached the couple. "Excuse me, is this a good location to see the fireworks display?" The man replied that fireworks would be going off all around the city, all night.

"So where do we see the city fireworks?" Thomas continued, still not getting it.

"The city doesn't have fireworks—it's a time when everyone can set off fireworks as they choose."

"Oh, I see." The truth was coming home. Unlike Halifax and other cities in Canada, the Saarbrücken City Council did not waste money on rockets, bangers, firecrackers, and sparklers. Silvester night allowed anyone who had the money to buy fireworks and set them off at random every which way. Leandra was not the only one looking startled at this revelation.

Minutes before, as we stepped from the taxi, someone had thrown a firecracker in our direction, making Leandra and I jump out of the way. As we stood wondering what to do, a father with two toddlers lit rockets from the trunk of his car packed with pyrotechnics, right on the sidewalk. Others tried the middle of the road, seizing the opportunity to reclaim the streets for one night free of traffic. People passed by us, lighting and throwing things, letting out chortles when explosions followed. Jumpy, I looked around and saw a group of teens with beer bottles and fireworks approaching, getting too close for comfort.

"Let's go," Thomas muttered, relief marking his face when a bus pulled up. It was an escape hatch from a growing menace, and he hailed it.

"Quick, let's jump aboard this Dudweiler bus and head home."

The driver yelled something. "What'd he say?" I asked.

Thomas translated: "Buses are yanked off routes for the next hour or so." I paid close attention to the phrase "or so." With no buses available, nervous taxi drivers gone, and our anxiety growing, we chose to race home on foot. It was as if we acted with one mind, beating a hasty retreat from the mounting chaos of an unpredictable New Year's Eve.

"But this is *Germany*. How can this be happening?" I asked. The control, order, and good sense I expected were missing.

"Not sure what's going on here and I'm not waiting to find out," Thomas replied. Leandra's swift steps matched ours.

As we quickened our pace through semi-dark, deserted city streets, we paused at a lively corner pub where ten or more customers laughed and gesticulated outside, a few setting off bangers. Some people hung out upper storey apartment windows, taking in the scope of pyrotechnics raging across the night sky, noises building to a crescendo. The air rang with the racket bouncing off stone and brick, exhilarating and unnerving me at the same time.

Some people appeared to enjoy blasting fireworks at other people. No wonder that woman we had approached earlier near Anna's house had been uneasy. *Will the next person we encounter have a cracker or a rocket up their sleeve to let fly at our heels?*

After twenty minutes at a brisk scurry, we had left the city and most of its noises behind. Hardly talking, we sped up the now familiar dark, tree-fringed driveway, not breaking our strides until we reached the door. Any remaining threat would be wild boar that rummaged in the woods. I guessed with the unusual Silvester night ruckus, the wild boars had hidden themselves well within the secluding bosom of comforting forests.

It was 12:50 A.M. on January 1, 2014, when we set foot inside the bright silence of our apartment.

"Boy, what a relief to be inside," I said, flopping down and pulling off my shoes.

"Anna was right. That was madness. I don't remember that in Northern Germany or Göttingen."

"Things have probably changed since you left Germany, Dad." Leandra pulled back her hair and shrugged off her jacket.

"Obviously, and not for the better. Good night," Thomas added, his brow knitted.

I could still hear distant pops and claps well after diving into bed.

Next morning, we learned more about the fruits of New Year's Eve celebrations. Mopping the stairs, Émilie stopped to tell Thomas that Silvester was turning into a free-for-all. A small fringe used it to create confusion through damage. Many participated in the fun, some looked on with approval or disapproval, and others hunkered down indoors, avoiding what was coming to be regarded as growing lawlessness.

As proof of Émilie's words, the local Saarbrücker Zeitung reported a busy night for police. Several small fires had been started and four cars were burned out in Forbach, eleven kilometres away. It sure was different from the cheery New Year's Eve music and party madness in the Grand Parade square in front of Halifax City Hall. Silvester night had shades of a crazy Halloween night.

I'd been told many times by Thomas that in Germany, there was a clear right and wrong way to do almost everything. Those who disregarded the rules could expect to be corrected by others, even by total strangers in public. The reality of our Silvester night experience contradicted my image of what to expect in Saarland. Nevertheless, it turned into another moment of our family coming together and connecting over the unfamiliar—an unexpected night in Saarland.

22. Money Matters

Dirty clothing spilled over the wicker baskets onto the bedroom floor, calling me to action. Living on the third floor without an elevator required the steadfastness of a bullock to produce a steady supply of crisp, clean household laundry. It also required the display of a certain social acuity, as certain unwritten regulations about household duties prevailed in the Humboldt building. To avoid all-out laundry wars, brandishing detergent, stain removers, and baskets, I practised cautionary surveillance. For two weeks after arrival, I scouted the laundry room at odd times for quiet non-activity, only to hear the low, heavy roll of machines going full-tilt. Eventually, I figured out the system without the need for divine intervention.

In our university guest house, people had set days and times for washing. Émilie needed mornings until noonish, Monday through Thursday, to finish all her work, wash included; all tenants (mostly mothers) needed to leave her in peace to do that. New tenants sought out free times in between uses by others. I settled into a pattern of doing my laundry in the afternoon of Wednesday or Thursday, usually before my husband and daughter came home. My pattern streamlined into an amiable arrangement, except that one time when I ran down fifty-six steps to find my dry laundry exposed on top of one of the large pine tables. I cursed the person who had dared touch my clothing and, happily, it never happened again.

Laundry day developed into a trial, exceeded only by two previous experiences. When I was a child and teenager in Barbados, my mother would sometimes leave me, one of five children, to wet the white clothes left to bleach under a tropical sun, spread out on a grass patch between our house and the neighbour's. Bleaching and wetting this way made whites super white, mysteriously of the utmost importance to Barbadian women. To have your white dress or shirt referred to as *dingy* was one of the biggest Bajan insults imaginable. Indolent children often received a well-deserved cuff about the ears for forgetfulness of this domestic burden.

Another laundry test dated back to my days as a student at UBC in Vancouver, where I shared lodgings with a mother of two with little means. As we had no washing machine, short of washing our clothes in a bathtub and hanging up wet things to drape like flags (which the mother often did), the only option was to bundle dirty laundry into a travel bag and tow it to the nearest laundromat by bus. My lack of enthusiasm for Sundays in Vancouver was due to it being established as washing day.

But my most unforgettable laundry incident occurred in Saarbrücken and triggered the summoning of a locksmith. I was minding my own business on a predictable Thursday afternoon, getting on with my household duty somewhat later than usual. By now, this repetitive work meant I had mastered the intricacies of operating German washing and drying machines. At first, their operation was complicated enough to require the input of two people with advanced degrees. Of a smaller type than our Whirlpools in Nova Scotia, the machines did not run at hot enough temperatures and therefore ran longer.

Having descended to the quiet, just-short-of-being-creepy laundry room and succeeding in my battles with the mysterious workings of those sophisticated machines, I ascended the workout stairs. Thomas was home, and I settled in for a long wait while he relaxed, watching the early edition of *Tagesschau* TV news. An hour later, approximating the end of a dryer cycle, I grabbed the set of keys near the door to head down to the laundry room.

"I'll help," Thomas offered, jumping up.

I should have said, "No, stay where you are," but didn't.

"Got the keys?" he asked.

"Yep. Let's go."

The door gave a reassuring, decisive click behind us. In Germany, doors usually lock automatically unless fixed otherwise, unlike in Canada or Barbados. A locked door here was the default position. Germans believe in locking doors, and keys and locks are important—and expensive. Downstairs, we bundled the clothing basket and bags of detergent for the haul upwards. At the door to our apartment, I fished the keys out of my pocket, but the key wouldn't turn in the lock. I stared at the door, at the keys, and then at the door again. Was I trying to get into the wrong apartment? That had happened to me more than once.

"Okay, you try." I handed over the keys. One look at the bundle in his hand, and dismay coloured Thomas's face.

"These are my office keys. You left the apartment keys inside."

"Oh no!" I threw my arms up in exasperation.

As in any country, doors are locked in Germany for good reasons. One day, Estella had arrived at language class, eyes red and swollen from crying. She'd suffered a robbery while in class the previous day when thieves broke into her apartment, stealing treasured jewellery items.

"Damn! And Leandra's out with her buddy tonight. What do we do now?" An authentic Bajan would at this time exclaim, "But look at my crosses though nah here today!" because Bajans shoulder more burdens than any other people on the planet. Many of my fellow Bajans turn vexed and grumpy when something inconvenient happens.

"Why did you have to come down with me? I always do this by myself!" I shouted.

"I only wanted to help. Anyway, you said you had the keys. But what's the use of being angry and blaming?"

Our frustrations boiled over. We needed a locksmith quick. A knock on the door across the hall yielded the friendly Italian woman and then her husband looking out from behind. Our anxious faces, a basket of clean laundry at our feet, and a key bundle that didn't work told everything in a glance.

Thomas spoke in English. "Hi, I'm Thomas. This is my wife, Claudette. Sorry to bother you, but we need a phone."

"Come in, come in. Of course, yes, you can use our phone." The wife was a tiny woman with a lively manner, shoulder length straight brown hair, with blonde highlights. Her husband stood taller, with a mop of dark curly hair and deep-set, golden-brown eyes. Thomas made a quick call to locate a locksmith who said he'd arrive in half an hour. Our genial neighbours broke out wine, glasses, and peanut snacks, creating an inviting air as a segue into small talk. Soon Thomas dashed downstairs to meet the locksmith, returning with a tradesman who looked like an engineer.

In less than five minutes, the athletic handyman had the door open. He did it by sliding a hard piece of flat plastic back and forth a few times in the door crack. We gathered around, curious about the *how* of his work. I let out a sigh of relief when the lock clicked, moved, and our door creaked open. The locksmith stressed that by law, he was not allowed to let people into apartments without proof of identification. We could provide none, but he took a risk because we were already inside the building. Had it been the exterior door, the police would have had to be notified, making things much pricier. *Much pricier, the knave!* He charged us €150, about $225 CAD. I thought it highway robbery, calculating the cost of a locksmith call in our hometown in Canada to be closer to $50 for five minutes of work. It was a costly lesson on an ordinary laundry day. Thomas thanked him and asked for a ride to the nearest bank for the cash. I lifted the laundry basket into our apartment after thanking our neighbours.

To allay my vexation, I reminded myself of the luck, financial privilege, and time-fortune afforded me and my husband by professional careers. *How many of my colleagues could give themselves the gift of a year abroad in Germany?* A flashback nudged me into reflective memory of my teenage years and tougher financial times in Barbados.

On a sun-filled Monday in September 1974, a sprawling old mahogany tree lent its shade in the swelling heat of a tropical morning. A few wooden benches, bent on shedding their tongues of laughing green paint, circled the stout, rugged tree trunk in a half-hearted embrace. We excited teenagers waited near the front entrance to the Barbados Community College (BCC) on the left side of a once stately white colonial house. It was now converted into offices and classrooms for post-secondary learning. This spot would become my group's familiar stomping ground over the next two years. The grassy pitch beneath our feet would be worn bare by our excessive, sometimes animated trampling.

The college building appeared a tad shabby. Situated in Sherburne, Two Mile Hill, it had been built back in the 1770s at the height of British colonial rule for a high-ranking British army officer. Today it contrasts poorly with the current modern, sprawling college complex constructed more than two hundred years later in the 1980s, a kilometre away at Eyrie on Howell's Cross Road. The story of change did not end there. In 2002, the old house and stables at Sherburne were demolished, making way for a new, high-tech Prime Minister Management Centre.

We were a group of about ten chattering young people, hearts thumping in anticipation. The previous June, the members of our fearless band had finished secondary education. We girls had attended the same school. September marked the thrill of a new beginning, hanging low like ripe breadfruit ready to be picked. Today was an important day, its significance lost on none of us.

I had opened my eyes at seven o'clock that morning amid the commotion of my parents rising for work and two sleepy younger siblings readying themselves for school. By the time I finally rolled out of bed, my mother had departed for work. Adella had to walk three miles and arrive at her domestic job in Rendezvous at eight o'clock. My father had disappeared too, leaving on his trusty Triumph bicycle for work in Bridgetown as a warehouse porter. After my brother Mackie and sister Katie slammed the door and yelled their goodbyes, I began to get ready. From the standpipe in the backyard, I drew buckets of water to fill up the big aluminum tub and bathed in the makeshift bathroom in the yard beside the outhouse.

My two older siblings lived elsewhere, allowing for a bit more room and privacy in the rustic shack I called home. Cheryl already bounced a two-year-old son on her knee on the outskirts of Bridgetown, residing with her boyfriend. Theo had bought a small house, a rickety hovel really, near our neighbourhood that in no time at all, he'd shoved down and then pushed just as hard to build up a new place, proper foundation and all. His vision was a lovely, spacious wooden bungalow, with three roomy bedrooms, a bright sitting room, dining area, kitchen, and front-facing, airy veranda. An interior water closet and bathroom hovered in the shadows, but he decided they would have to wait for now. He used his lucrative pay from seasonal work as a seaman to afford the brand-new construction. Everyone knew he owned good fortune, blessed with a sharp shrewdness when it came to securing and managing money.

Theo's rush to build had an exterior drive motivated by the dislike he and his stepfather had for each other. As he developed into an older teen, the hatred grew, the air crackling with tension whenever they sat in the same room. It was just as well that Theo now lived independently, away from Andy, my father. A year earlier, Theo had been put out of the house after a terrible quarrel that nearly ended up with bashed-in heads. As a consequence, Theo was never to set foot inside the family house again, an order he happily defied when the old man was absent.

Thus, the changed living arrangements afterwards accommodated five people at home—the two adults and their biological offspring: me, Mackie, and Katie.

I fought to suppress a mix of emotions. Before departing for college, I secured the faulty front door, paned-glass windows, and shuttered side windows, exiting the house by its back door. This door was made of two heavy pine panels, a hinged, four-foot bottom part that opened wide from left to right, and a hinged, flap-down top piece usually propped open by a sturdy stick, sometimes used for hitting. The bottom part of the pine door was shut and bolted when the house was vacant, but the top part was brought down and commonly left unbolted for easy entry on return. Really, any stranger tall enough could enter the backyard and the empty house once they had accessed the back gate. They could open the door by standing on tippytoes and reaching over to unlatch the top. In fact, years earlier, when I attended elementary school, someone had grabbed a young girl who'd been caught clambering over the paling into our backyard. The brazen ten-year-old was probably just looking for a few pennies to steal and would have found some if she'd only known where to look. My father kept a fat jar full of small change in the backyard, near his man-cave, hidden in plain sight.

People in St. Barnabas and similar garden villages around the island often left doors and windows unsecured when venturing out, gallivanting or otherwise. In the case of the Gittens, our home beckoned no robbers for a more intimate look as it held no real treasures. Without electric power, no valuable electronic merchandise such as a cool television set, boom box, or pricey kitchen equipment, resided inside and definitely no fine-quality jewellery rested within.

I took the quickest route to the Sherburne community college via the neighbourhood's narrow, paved roads. Our village lay beyond the eastern reaches of Bridgetown. Tamarind trees, khus-khus grass, and acacia trees bordered paths baked to marl-like dust in dry weather. No mystic white fairyland houses lined these streets in a housing area that was clearly transitioning. It bore a blend of tottering, blackened chattel houses huddled close like frightened sheep among prosperous, sometimes brightly painted homes of concrete or wood. Occasionally, a home tilted inwards in a state of leaning construction, a hallmark of the transition.

A tired looking wooden house in the neighbourhood might remain defiant though almost encased in concrete walls that locked it in a gradual embrace—a Bajan way of building. Starting at the back, a homeowner would put in indoor plumbing and kitchen facilities, building forward. This kind of home improvement never failed to draw attention. Someone, a seaman, a government worker, someone with a good, steady-paying job, or perhaps a combination of family members, worked to improve their living conditions. Often the process took years, even a generation, for that cuddled wooden house to give up and accept its final demise. Other times, it happened in a desperate hurry. Some fortunate families co-operated and progressed together.

My powerful strides on this first day of college took me deeper into the village, past the assorted residences, past the age-grey Anglican church guarding its buried dead, and away from the main road where the bus serving the area rumbled by. I went directly toward a winding shortcut between a pink-walled bungalow and a neat convenience store. At Nita's, neighbours bought flour, sugar, soda biscuits, Anchor cheese, macaroni, Canadian tinned salmon, and all manner of food items when they ran out of the basics before another week's grocery shopping trek into Bridgetown.

The shortcut led through a jumbled shroud of overgrown shrubbery on both sides, banana plants, avocado trees, coconut fronds, and tall bamboo grasses. A thin trail suddenly opened up for me to arrive on the college grounds. After a fifteen-minute walk, I surveyed the scene, keyed up and nervous seeing on the left "the stables," neglected sheds. I faced the back portion of a wraparound courtyard surrounding the core, two-storey, wooden building with roomy, covered decks on opposite ends.

Back under British rule, when this property served as a great house, the stables had been actual horse stables. In 1968, the community college came into existence and the buildings and environs were repurposed for tertiary education. The government of the day extended post-secondary education to all qualifying citizens. At first, the college's offerings were limited to liberal arts, science, and commerce, but later they expanded to include hospitality studies, health sciences, and technology at different locations on the island. Off to the right were two nondescript row buildings, each with four or five rooms, pleading for more light, that served as classrooms.

When I spied a group of friends and acquaintances, my heart hopped. I made out Francine, Charmaine, and others and made a beeline for the mahogany shade. They were recent graduates of my girls' school in Christ Church. In a sea of flutter, known faces, joined by those of a few unfamiliar teenage boys, turned my way.

"Hi, Francine," I squealed in high-pitched glee; I was so happy to see her.

"Girl you, I was looking for you for the last ten minutes."

"I just get here."

I tried to act casual, feeling awkward and unsure of what picture I cut. On pins and needles, I sported a big, airy afro, and had taken pains to contrast new jeans with a home-sewn, white cotton blouse. On my feet I wore leather Rasta toe sandals. Francine looked smashing in a blue cotton frock and black pumps. She wore a matching headband holding back unruly curls from a cheerful oval face. Charmaine's hair was freshly straightened and curled. She sported tight black jeans, a green T-shirt, and on her feet, black and white sneakers. All the girls in the bunch looked like they'd just stepped out of an *Ebony* magazine, some faces covered with too much pink makeup. They looked fresh, like newly peeled coconuts. A few of the boys looked razzy, on purpose. I wished I'd put on my floral blue A-line dress and three-inch clogs.

"You know what subjects you taking?" Francine asked fast, reining me into the circle.

"Yeah, English, history, and geography," I answered in a rush. In the previous weeks, new students had been arriving at the college for registration and to pick up information packages on courses and schedules. I'd preregistered back in August.

"I ain't taking no geography. That's too hard. I goin' to settle for English and Spanish," petite Charmaine butted in.

"For me, it's going to be English, history, and economics," Francine offered with crystal-clear decisiveness. Labelled as one of the brightest sparks coming through high school, she often moved with dynamic force. I guessed in two years she'd be fit for an island scholarship. To my surprise, she'd refused to even consider going straight on to university at Cave Hill Campus, even though she'd met the requirements. She could also have applied to attend Queen's College or Combermere High School, as both offered sixth form A-level programs in an atmosphere of old-style Barbadian grammar school cool. A student had to pass a minimum of seven externally marked Cambridge O-level certificates at one sitting, including mathematics and a foreign language, to qualify for university straight out of high school. Francine had earned eight subject passes, including Spanish and mathematics, with great grades.

Though Francine wouldn't admit it even on threat of being strangled, I believed it was her fear of the unknown, which we all shared, that held her back. None of us, whose mothers had reached only as far as a standard six education, knew what to do with the rest of our lives. Like Francine, I had no wish to leave the security of our buddies behind and assume a more independent path. This all played into our collective decision to continue school at the community college with friends in sociable, non-threatening companionship.

The descendants of enslaved people and of the working poor, our semi-literate parents weren't much help in shaping our lives—a group of young women in a small but mighty post-independence transition. We stood unsteady on the cusp of a new society. As fledglings, we embodied the first members of our families to enter college or university and relish the prospect of professional occupations and middle-class lives. Charged with the promise of as much pleasure as pain, security as danger, our futures lay wide open, fearfully exposed.

A tumbling muddle of life decisions awaited. Sometimes I could hardly bear to exhale. I didn't know it yet, but in two years' time, I would apply for a teaching position at one of the local secondary comprehensive schools, built in the '60s. Having already passed six O-level certificates myself out of high school, I would add to those two A-levels, English and history. But when the call came from the Ministry of Education in August '76 saying that I could start teaching at the Memorial School in September, I retreated. Sometimes I saw myself in the corner, small and frightened.

Thinking of facing a classroom full of scoffing students, in some cases barely two years younger than me, left me breathless. I thought myself too ridiculous and ill-prepared. My mother would beam with pride, running up and down the neighbourhood, making a nuisance of herself and telling any neighbour who stopped to listen about her daughter's successful college results and teaching application. In conversations that followed, my sister Cheryl offered a jealous, critical reaction. "Why should she get all her education paid for? She should start working and pay for it herself. She's going to start getting 'poor-great,' uppity, and eventually abandon the family, anyway." Luckily, the decision wasn't Cheryl's to make. Our mother had come through with her usual resolve, saying she would support any of her children as best she could if they wanted to further their education.

While my friends yapped, teased, and parried, I reached into my fob pocket and fingered around. My mother had put a hundred-dollar bill into my hand the night before to buy college books.

"Here you go, take this money to buy you' books tomorrow," Mummy said. She unfolded the hundred-dollar bill and placed it in my palm. "Take care you don't drop it. I know what it is to be without a' education." The weight of the moment settled on me, light but clad in cast iron. Six years earlier, she'd been unable to raise as small a sum as two dollars to pay for my newly acquired Form One class reader. Embarrassed to the core and with all the power I could muster, I'd rejected her maternal pleas to leave right away for school without the two dollars to pay for my reader. She was forced to cave in, run next door, and borrow the money from a kind neighbour who owned a market stall in Bridgetown.

A warm glow of appreciation washed over me at my mother's gesture. I hadn't dared ask about book money. I was too terrified—of what, exactly, I wasn't sure. Money always translated into problems in our household, as we never had enough of it. Instinct told me that my mother would find a way to help me with ongoing studies, but this amount of money exceeded anything I'd permitted myself to imagine.

In 1974, $100 BBD was equivalent to $50 US. Today, my mother's gift of $100 Barbadian dollars would be worth about $522 BBD. Barbadian women knew how to be thrifty. Adella ran a "meeting turn" with a group of women friends, where she collected a sum of money from each woman weekly and paid out the total sum collected each week to one of the women until everyone got her turn. They continued these turns for as long as verbal agreement lasted. A few hundred dollars came in handy for buying school uniforms, furniture, and other relatively expensive items. It gave women some measure of financial independence.

In most Barbadian households in 1974, a hundred dollars represented rich bounty. It transformed into a week's food supply for a family of five. Such a grand amount guaranteed a month's rent in the neighbourhood or several pairs of inexpensive shoes from the Bata store in Bridgetown. School uniforms and supplies could be provided with such a sizable sum. It was my mother's weekly pay as a domestic servant working five days a week for a white Closed Brethren family in Rendezvous, Christ Church. The husband in that family sometimes brought by piles of flying fish to our house for Mummy to scale, gut, and bone for a pittance. She had been hoarding this cache for the right moment.

"A college education don' come for free. You need them books." Her eyes were soft.

I clasped the money tight and mumbled a fast, self-conscious "thank you" before turning away, hiding tears brimming in my eyes. My father would not have handed over that kind of money. Set in his out-of-touch ways, he rebuffed ideas in favour of educating girls. In his opinion, "They only ended up pregnant sooner or later." And so, as became commonplace on many key matters concerning his children, he remained locked out, absolute in his ignorance.

Thoughts about the courses I would take kept rattling around in my head. I wondered if I'd made the right choices: Advanced level English, history, and geography in a two-year college program, it would be a stretch. The scope of what I faced! In school, I'd always been good at English. I was a natural, but not a particularly hard-working or disciplined student.

"History involves lots of reading, writing, and analysis," a college graduate advised. Though not possessing the avid curiosity and analytical abilities of a historian, I imagined a decent enough result given sufficient effort. *But geography?* That appeared to be as hard and scary a challenge as I felt equalled to. It involved social and physical, even mathematical, aspects and detail for which I thought myself underprepared. Yet, as a subject, it fascinated as much as a new novel. I felt drawn to the sweep of geography, taking me across massive oceans to foreign lands and immense populations.

Barriers to success at advanced studies stretched up in the form of absent role models and lack of an accessible, quiet place for home study. But reasons for failure never helped anybody, so why rummage around to find them? Normally optimistic, I accepted the reality that obscured my bright, potential-laden future.

In a quiver of relief, I breathed. Yes, the money was right there. I wondered how many books it could actually purchase. English novels tended to be fairly inexpensive, five or six dollars, but geography and history books would be pricier. With effort, I could also acquire a few dated, second-hand texts.

As we waited for a true sign of our new beginnings, our group worked its way around to the front of the main building, anticipating a bell or a bull-horn from the old colonial house. Forceful Francine, I and the edgy throng chattered and milled around, teasing, questioning, gossiping, waiting for the college authorities to launch us onto the next stage of our adolescent theatre. It came just after nine thirty with the sound of a loud voice. The racket stopped as if a precious sculpture had dropped in our midst. Francine grabbed my arm once a bespectacled, middle-aged man with a balding pate began speaking in a rumbling voice that carried across the pebbly courtyard.

"Good morning, ladies and gents. Welcome to the Barbados Community College. My name is Mr. Martin, and I'm the principal at the BCC. You're here to finalize registration, collect timetables, and purchase books for your new courses. Please line up at the main office at the front for confirmation of your registration. At that time, you'll be given timetables, course assignments, and booklists. Once you know exactly what courses you're taking and when, head over to the book room on the far side of the registration desk where books are available for purchase. The entrance is on my left, beside the cafeteria. As you already know, there are no classes scheduled for today. Your classes will begin tomorrow in earnest, so start getting prepared."

With that, he fell silent. The student crowd moved off in the direction of the main office. Even the prospect of enduring eternal lineups, waiting with a few hundred students to finish the day's business, did nothing to dampen our fervour.

In the queue, Francine and I exchanged vacation news and gossiped about the exam results and the hurricane shocks and surprises those induced. Once the school certificate results came in, a few of our friends opted to return to school to repeat their fifth-form year in an effort to upgrade and gain a few more O-levels. Passing five or more certificates translated into instant happiness; we left secondary school behind for work or studies.

"Yeah, Beverley gone back to school for better results in French and math." Francine was always loaded with information; as Bajans would say colloquially, "she was malicious," though never mean.

"Remember Jasmine?" I asked. She left for the States to join her mother. And Rosalind Hinds began working at Services Commission two weeks now, as she passed four subjects."

"But you ain't hear nothing yet, girl. Cheryl Parris pregnant and right now she living with her boyfriend and his family in Station Hill." Francine's neck jerked forward and her eyes searched my face. Behind me, Charmaine jabbed me in the back. "Wunna can' see the line moving. Stop gossiping and move on, do!"

"What wrong with you? You think they sharing food up there or what?" I replied rudely.

"Never mind that. I want to get out of here before midnight." She chupsed long and hard in mock irritation.

I arrived at the desk, confirmed my registration, and received a pack of information. Francine waited for me to catch up, and we crossed the uneven courtyard together arm in arm, single-minded, for the book room. An occasional call rose high above layers of youthful voices. Excitement boosted me up amidst an atmosphere weighted by heavy, humid air, promising late afternoon rain.

Two doors with slatted panels were thrown wide open to the book room. On entry, we saw ten or fifteen students milling around examining stacks of books on shelves and tables set around a neat, medium-sized, light-green room with a high ceiling possessing the atmosphere of a hallowed hall. I imagined the room in a different age of splendid furnishings, grand paintings, and chandelier brilliance. A skinny young woman, business-like in a polyester maroon skirt-suit and high heels, managed the cash register. Her fingers, polished in bright red, worked the till keys with a steady beat. In the midst of the students, a few adults, dressed and confident like college instructors, moved about with lightness. The mutter of intermittent, indistinct whispers broke the hush and click-click of the machine.

My course lists showed required and recommended books and materials. First, I concentrated on a variety of English literature texts. For starters, I needed *Mill on the Floss* by George Eliot, *Tess of the D'Urbervilles* and *Return of the Native* by Thomas Hardy, *Rape of the Lock* by Alexander Pope, *Hamlet* and *Cymbeline* by William Shakespeare, and *The Miller's Tale* by Geoffrey Chaucer. Anticipation rose with each new prize. History and geography books were restricted to two mandatory tomes each. By the time I had a complete collection, my arms were so overloaded that my muscles felt like carpenter's putty. Francine, meanwhile, wandered around the room after choosing her set of English volumes to look for economics books.

Approaching the till, I set the load down unto a desk beside it. The young woman looked up, wearing a slightly harassed expression.

"Are these all for you?" she asked.

"Yeah." I bit my lip to stop a rude retort.

"You want me to ring all of these in?"

"Yeah." Again, the temptation at a surly response was suppressed.

"All right, let me see then—" The machine clicked and sputtered out a tune as the attendant worked the numbers, punching them in with robot-like efficiency. A thin sheen of sweat, invisible to any onlooker, broke out on my forehead. *Did I calculate right?* I'd done a rough mental calculation before approaching the till and the efficient worker. But my heart still fluttered as the books moved from one pile to another. Then, they were ready to be bagged. All mine to be taken home to read, mark, underline, and reread for future assignments, tests, and exams.

"That will be ninety dollars and fifty cents in all." The cashbox pinged loudly, and everything waited in total silence.

I reached into my fob pocket and froze. "That can't be right," I muttered through pressed lips. I reached in deeper, fumbling. Fob pockets were notorious for their unreliability, I knew this all along. I poked some more into the left and then right-side pockets of my fabulous new jeans just in case I'd by accident transferred the money from one pocket to another. But I already knew it wasn't there.

The world hung still for an age. Shock made breathing near impossible. *This can't be happening*, my mind whispered, refusing to be convinced. *It's a trick*. But dig as I would, the hundred-dollar bill handed to me with so much caution and love by my mother had vanished. It had disappeared down that great empty well where all hundred-dollar bills, thrust without care by reckless teens into fob pockets, settle. *What am I going to do?*

"Um, I just had my money. It was right here in my jeans pocket, but I lost it. I don't…um…know how or what happened," I mumbled, senseless, dazed.

Francine approached. "What happen to you?" Her laser-like intensity focused on my tight face.

"I lost the money my mother gave me to buy books." I said, too stunned to feel anything but a consuming numbness.

"What! You lost a hundred dollars?" Francine's face mirrored my own in dumb shock.

"Yeah, I don't know how or where." A veiled curtain existed between me and the world.

"Let we look for it." Francine, alive to possibilities, offered quick help.

"Why don't you step out of the line and make an inquiry at the office. I'll keep the books here for you until you get back," the till operator said with sympathy. She likely didn't see this kind of thing too often.

"But…" My brain galloped ahead, like the horses at the Garrison Savannah on Saturday afternoons during racing season, to the point where I landed at home to face my mother's disappointment.

"You mean to tell me you had nothing better to do than to lost the hundred-dollar bill I gie' you las' night?" Mummy would say. It would be the ultimate letdown; one I could not bear to face. *What would I say? What could I say? How careless could I be?*

An observer till then, a stylish woman in her mid-thirties stepped forward as we, bewildered, turned away in a cloud. The woman's face was alert, lively with a soft smile.

"Hello, I'm Mrs. Howlet, tutor here at the college. Is something the matter? Can I help you young ladies in any way?" Her buoyant charm was lost on me. I was barely able to find my voice.

"I lost my money."

"Oh, really? How much was it?" Mrs. Howlett asked, too cheerful.

"A hundred-dollar bill." Francine and I spoke in unison.

"Okay, here it is." The instructor, as if by some crazy magic, reached into an elegant black skirt pocket and stretched out a hand from which the money dangled.

I hesitated, dumbfounded. "How? What is this?"

"Go on. Here, take it. Someone found this money earlier, about an hour ago, and turned it in at the registration office. My job was to reunite it with its owner. I think that's you."

"Yes, yes! Thank you so very much." In an inexplicable, dreamlike turn, enchantment suffused the air, and all was right with the world again. The stars were indeed aligned in my favour.

The woman smiled and began moving away. "It not me to thank but the honest person who found it and turned it in. You're a very, very fortunate young lady." With that, she strode off, disappearing out the wide doorway.

"Boy, you lucky, lucky, lucky for truth, Clauds! Count you' lucky stars today!" My friend's vigorous repetition, a characteristic Bajan speech trait when excited, hung in the air as a bold banner writ large. I could do nothing but nod in delighted agreement.

"I'm okay wid it!" Together, we bolted to the cash register to pay for my trophies.

Later, we sat on the open deck polishing off fishcake cutters and pop drinks from the small hole-in-the-wall cafeteria among a bantering, energetic crowd of rowdy fellow students. We parted ways for home by late afternoon after final words about the amazing twists of the day.

Most teens, including Francine, headed out the college's main entrance to board public buses or private minivans on a main artery leading into Bridgetown. Once there, they would climb onto connecting buses for destinations around the island parishes of St. Michael, St. James, Christ Church, St. Philip, and elsewhere. I retraced my earlier steps homeward, back through St. Barnabas housing area where my young siblings pined at home for family members to return.

That night, as we sat inside, I was consumed by my own thoughts under the yellow, cozy glow of a cloudy kerosene lamp. I would read and study English literature by the same light. Inside my bosom, I secreted the story of the lost hundred-dollar bill and its propitious reappearance. In my world of low expectations and underappreciated reflections, I judged that many experiences were better left unshared.

It had been forty years since I'd lost and been reunited with my funds at the BCC. In hindsight, I recognized many layers to my story. While someone had tried to steal a few pennies from our backyard, someone else had returned a hundred-dollar bill capable of feeding a family for a week. I had experienced deprivation as a child and teenager, but it must have energized my ambitions toward a fruitful career path and self-determination. I now reaped the rewards of a fulfilling career, living a comfortable life and enjoying the luxury of life in Saarland, a world apart from my humble Barbadian roots, with my husband and daughter.

23. Hairstyling with a Twist

"Don't laugh," I said to Thomas when he saw my head after he'd returned from number crunching at the university.

He stared, stifled laughter, and then offered a quick fix. "Why don't you go out right now to a better hair salon and have another cut?"

I shook my head. "I don't like it but I'll live with it."

Next it was Leandra who paused, horrified by the lack of skill of this someone who'd been audacious enough to advertise her hair salon services. The stylist had succeeded in demonstrating a crude hack job on my head. "Just how difficult is it to use clippers to buzz-cut someone's hair, anyway? And you actually gave her a tip for that, Mum?"

Those were my family's reactions to what I can, in all truth, declare as my worst haircut. A few haircuts I'd had inflicted upon me in Prince Albert, Saskatchewan, back in the mid-90s came really close. My need for a haircut in Germany had been brewing. I inspected a few hair salons in Saarbrücken and Dudweiler. It was a small need, but at the same time, it wasn't.

For more than half my lifetime, I had been resisting the crazed preoccupation, fuss, and bother exhibited by many of my Black female friends and relatives. They fancied fashionable, elaborate hairdos, wigs, weaves, and extensions. Stories about Black women and their hair could fill a compendium I had no interest in writing or reading.

In her thirties and forties, my mother clapped a ridiculous, jet-black wig on her head for Sunday church services and special occasions, sometimes on the hottest of days, and even though her natural hair was fine. Many of her friends did the same. By thirty, I was resolute in side-stepping the latest hairdo fads. I aimed for a tidy, short cut. Nostalgia for the big, wind-rippled afros of my high school and college days and the perms and wet jerry curls of my early career years had yielded to trimmed and neat. Anyone who knew me knew my hairstyle preference. Little expense, no fuss, little bother.

As I judged the city hair shops, one under a dim overhang, another under a posh, bright glare of glass and mirrors, I became more and more reluctant to pay twenty euros (thirty dollars), for a straightforward clipper-cut. I was leery of at best unpredictable and at worst strange results. So, as a trial balloon, I sailed into a modest outfit near Saar-Centre where a shy, serious Turkish man cut my hair for ten euros. He gave me an even cut, doubtless experienced with working over short curly hair. He did an adequate enough job, but Thomas was miffed.

"That was a men's barber shop," he said. "You should go to a proper women's salon." He found the entire exercise humiliating. He must have felt my refusal to pay for an expensive haircut reflected badly on him.

"He did a good job," I said.

"A woman's salon would have been better," he said.

I resolved to turf the meddling Thomas next time I ventured out into the tricky landscape of culturally diverse Saarbrücken hair salons. In March 2014, I took a bold leap by myself. Seeing a slightly more upscale salon, I stepped across the threshold to find I'd trespassed into an Arabic, all-male domain, committing a cultural faux pas. About eight men sat around in chairs, two caped under barbers' hands. An awkward silence held us for a moment as all faces turned toward me, expressionless. Impressions of the room blurred into a haziness of aftershave, mirrors, clippers, towels, chairs, and faces. Someone hurried forward, the boss man perhaps, and pointed me out the door to the next door where Muslim women operated a hair salon for female clients.

Behind the door stood three bored-looking Middle Eastern women wearing headscarves and long beige or grey gowns. They seemed to be familiars, visiting and chatting. Two women left on my arrival the minute the third woman drew near, friendly but hesitant, her face unrevealing, her body stiff.

"Good afternoon."

"Good afternoon. I'd like a short haircut. Can you do it?"

"Yes, yes." She nodded with a tense expression.

I had the feeling I was participating in an experiment.

"Clippers or scissors?" she asked in an accented voice.

"Oh, clippers. You can use number 4, leaving half-inch of hair."

"Okay, yes." I thought she understood English but didn't speak it much. She gestured for me to sit down, straightaway starting the clipper buzzing over my head, shearing away. In front of the chair, no mirrors lined the wall, as in normal salons. She made no attempt to engage in friendly banter as the clipper droned in spurts. The salon's furnishings were basic, tired looking. Spare without being tidy or untidy, the place lacked any defining décor or colour. A nondescript sofa braced one wall, two straight-back chairs the other, and a large stand-alone mirror stood at my left elbow. No windows let in light or air, and I did notice an absence of scented hair products, curling gels, creams, conditioners, and shampoos.

I wonder how many women ever step inside here? How many Black women? In a few minutes it was all over, with most of my salt-and-pepper hair cropped and lying lamely on the floor. To her credit, the hairdresser had not offered me the advantage of a mirror, or invited my reaction, common practice in Canada. I breathed in, thanked the woman, got up, and hoped for the best. She looked pained, almost regretful. After handing over fifteen euros and stepping outside, I reached up to touch what was left of my clipped stubble. My fingers touched a bumpy, uneven landscape. I fingered a hole on one side, a dent on the other, and a strange pointy muff on top.

Only on my arrival at the apartment when I positioned two mirrors to view the hatchet job did the enormity of the butchery hit home. If someone had taken a weed whacker to my head, I could not have witnessed a poorer result. My head was the sorry sight of a mangy dog. I had been robbed. I hoped that other Black women would not be fleeced in the same way by this pretender. Fortunately, hair does regrow, and hats, terrific for sub-zero temperatures, are amazing for bad hair days too.

After this experience, I understood why Black people are hesitant to have their hair cut by people of other ethnicities with straight or wavy hair, unless recommended. Curly hair and Black hair are tricky unless the hair stylist possesses the right training or experience. Black women, like most women everywhere, are very particular about how their hair looks, sometimes to the point of being obsessive. I don't fall into that category, but I do like a haircut that doesn't frighten me when I look in a mirror.

My haircut experience triggered my thinking for the first time about Muslim women and hairstyling. *Do Muslim women cut and style their hair?* The question led me down a path to a religious quagmire of "yes, but —." I encountered terminology such as *haram* (acts prohibited in the religious texts of the Quran and the Sunnah), *fatwa* (a ruling on a point of Islamic law given by a recognized authority), and *kaffir* (having multiple meanings, from a racial slur, to an infidel, to the name of ethnic groups). It proved pretty complex and confusing for a non-religious, Barbados-born, Canadian woman living abroad for a year. Beyond my narrow familiar reaches, the world shaped into so many different and diverse formations depending on such circumstances as place of birth, social standing, education, and gender.

Resisting my husband's repeated urgings, I did not repair my haircut, living with it until it grew out. Not brave enough to risk another bad hair experience in Saarland, I waited until I returned to Nova Scotia for my next haircut.

PART V

24. Reading Matters

After the Volkshochschule course ended in mid-January, I decided to get on with learning German by myself. I lived in a world of German words and still wanted to conquer them. I began going to the German-as-a-foreign-language section in the local public library on the main street. That spotless library was closed Sundays and Mondays, opened Tuesdays through Fridays from 10:00 A.M. to 7:00 P.M., and opened for three hours on Saturdays; it seemed set up for people with flexible schedules, the self-employed, and the unemployed. I paid a family fee to join, not sure how much. It hoarded outdated, inaccessible computers. Those issues apart, several easy German language readers, fiction and non-fiction, lined one bookshelf on the ground floor.

I signed out simple detective tales (*Krimis*) and dramas. Some titles left me tongue-tied: *Tödlicher Irrtum* (*Deadly Error*), *Der Einbruch* (*The Burglary*), *Tod in der Oper* (*Death at the Opera*), *Teufel in Seide* (*Devil in Silk*), *Ein Schuss ins Leere* (*A Shot into the Wind*), *Das Mißverständnis* (*The Misunderstanding*), *Die Überraschung* (*The Surprise*), *Miss Hamburg, Liebe im Mai* (*Miss Hamburg, Love in May*), and *Die Rache des Computers* (*The Computer's Revenge*). By reading popular and older works at a beginner's level, I began to believe I could overcome my foreign language insecurity. It turned out to be more fun than any classroom routine.

I now had time for simple versions of classics like *Faust: das Volksbuch* (*Faust: The Popular Book*), *Werther*, and *Der zerbrochene Krug* (*The Broken Jug*). I had a passing knowledge of *Faust*, the notorious genius, and of *The Sorrows of Young Werther*, a stormy, emotional novel. But it was *The Broken*

Jug that delighted me most, a comedy alluding to the story of Adam and Eve, mocking human failings within the existing system of law.

Thomas, Leandra, and I developed a bedtime routine starting at about 9:30 P.M. on school nights. I'd draw our bedroom blinds, shutting out the dark. Thomas and I would settle into bed, under comfy duvets. I'd double the tiresome feather pillow under my head. A sharp odour of dry heat from the hot-water radiators would mingle with lingering aromas from our suppertime *Frikadellen* (meatballs) or other foods. Leandra would agree to read a bedtime story she'd pick from the easy German detective fiction I'd brought into the household, sitting cross-legged between us. I'd snuggle in, fighting off sleep, doing my best to listen.

For me, it had become a perfect way to end a winter evening, giving Leandra practice in reading and comprehending German. It gave me a casual way to learn and Thomas a way to share his native tongue.

Thomas loved the detective stories, speculating even before Leandra began. "I wonder what happens when she enters that room behind the curtain." And after Leandra got a page in, he'd say, "I think the guy with the curly moustache will do something weird."

Ready to hear the story, I'd say, "Can you stop guessing?"

By the time the murder happened, Thomas would have named every character in the tale as a suspect. He'd vindicate himself at the end by saying something like, "I knew that innocent-looking character was suspicious right from the get-go. Remember when he disappeared from the party, only to reappear with a flimsy alibi?" He was hooked on predicting plot twists while my questions fell into the category of "What does that word mean?" Prompt translations by Thomas and Leandra sparked my brain into connecting plot pieces. It was wonderfully restful to follow a story read to me in German.

Trouble was, every night after my heroics to bat off sleep and stay alert, I'd succumbed by the time Leandra had finished a half-hour spell. Concentrating on German required so much head work. It became a trial to pick up the threads of the story the next night asking: "Leandra, do you mind rereading the end of the last chapter?"

She'd say, "Already read it." True, but that didn't help me any.

"Summarize what happened then?"

Though Thomas always entertained my requests, understanding that new learning involved repetition, Leandra showed no such patience. "I want to go on to the end of the story. I want to know if that character with the alibi did the hunting trip murder." And she would move on, the hot-water radiators sizzling and crackling in the background. "Mum, are you sleeping again?"

I'd murmur, "Hmm?" Comforting amusement and readings were a fool-proof method to deliver me a good night's sleep.

Not competent enough in the language to appreciate German adult novels, I did a search for English books in Saarbrücken that became a downright challenge. I scoured a quaint used bookstore in the downtown and found nothing. I found a few books on the pedestrian zone, in the nearby mall, at the train station, and in the tiny English section of Thalia bookstore.

The local library helped a little; it housed a one-shelf English collection. Beyond that, I waited for family visits to Strasbourg, Frankfurt, and Nancy to find the titles I looked for buried among piles of French and German books. I remembered the year our son had read most as a teenager; his first novel during his gap year in Germany had been *The Book of Negroes* by Lawrence Hill. The best antidote to a woeful lack of conversational skills in a foreign tongue is a good book to escape into.

I ran to reading as a refuge. Cocooned within an apartment that felt more like home after December, I fingered through works by Doris Lessing, Virginia Woolf, and Alice Munro. My picks extended beyond traditional fare, embracing a varied mix designed to rescue me.

I found comfort in Lessing's creative imagination and drive. Independent to a fault and outspoken to the point of being considered rude, she lived life according to her own rules, breaking away from maternal and social restraints, developing literary skill and agency as a woman, single mother, and writer. She broke ground as a writer, shedding light on women's lives, and won the Nobel Prize in Literature in 2007.

I went digging after reading a few available books of Lessing's and found a woman fired by a creative flame and political causes. She campaigned against nuclear arms and was an active opponent of apartheid, which led to her being banned from South Africa and Rhodesia in 1956. When the

Soviet Union invaded Hungary, she left the British Communist Party. In the 1980s, Lessing voiced opposition to Soviet actions in Afghanistan. When she learned she'd been awarded the Nobel Prize, she claimed she'd won all the prizes in Europe, "every bloody one and [I] am delighted." As an artist, she gave infectious expression to her creative writing ideas and had fun wondering what to do with them. That thrilled me. Sadly, I was forced to give up on my obsession to read her unavailable-in-Germany biography.

Anna lent me John Mortimer's *Clinging to the Wreckage*, the title provoking in me a grin. Mortimer had taken his father's advice to heart, becoming a lawyer at the Old Bailey. He pursued writing too, making it as a playwright and creator of the TV character Rumpole. I loved his sardonic wit, but then some of his content reeked of indulgent, old Brit chauvinism. I recounted to Leandra the story about when he got fitted with glasses for near-sightedness. When he arrived at school at the start of his second year wearing Coke-bottle lenses, the head teacher failed to recognize him. Because of acute shyness, he dared not explain, so he ended up repeating his entire first year. Leandra and I laughed so hard we cried. It was a ridiculous story we could relate to, both of us being short-sighted. I declined any more of Mortimer's books because of the generation gap and the sexism evident in some of his "funny" accounts. I'm not sure if Anna understood why I couldn't take any more of Mortimer's work.

I latched onto Virginia Woolf when I came across a reference to her in *Clinging to the Wreckage*. I found a copy of Woolf's *To The Lighthouse* among the library's English collection and loved its literary power. I then bought *Mrs. Dalloway* in Strasbourg, but my fingers couldn't get beyond page ten. That novel felt outdated and irrelevant. My opening brush with the protagonist left me detached.

Filled with Canadian pride after Alice Munro won the 2013 Nobel Prize in Literature, I ran around town to scare up anything in English by her. My search yielded zilch. Even in the serenity of the public library, I held up fistfuls of air. Munro's books were available only in German. That showed international fortune for the new Nobel Laureate but nothing for me, an anglophone looking for a good read. Patience paid off when, on a pre-Christmas visit to Strasbourg, I purchased two collections of Munro's short stories: *Something I've Been Meaning to Tell You* and *Selected Stories*.

Her stories capture a vibrating personal and social energy connecting me to the lives of girls, wives, and everyday women caught in often troubling relational circumstances. My favourite tale was "The Beggar Maid." I loved Munro's rendering of the contradiction consuming Rose from Hanratty and the inability to solve life's nagging social class and relational problems.

The layer I missed in Munro's work showed up when I watched a video interview with Doris Lessing. While Munro declared herself apolitical as a badge of honour, wishing only that people liked her stories and found them entertaining, Lessing made a different point, rendering Munro's statement hollow to me. I thought readers like myself were robbed of an essential critical tool for understanding and valuing our own lives through character depictions and plot conflicts. Did Munro's characters act out their tiny conflicts in small bubbles unaffected by the impact of larger social and political issues? Were they oblivious of their places in the world? I couldn't help but agree with Graham Greene that "to exclude politics from a novel is to exclude a whole aspect of life." Even so, I added to my reading list more books by this champion author like *Runaway* and *The Love of a Good Woman.*

Robertson Davies had never made it onto my must-read Canadian books list. So, I surprised myself when one day I opened up a shabby copy of *Fifth Business*. I had saved it years before from a ruthless book room purge in my high school in Nova Scotia. On a quiet morning, alone in our roomy apartment, I found it still tucked inside a pocket of my suitcase, having made a transatlantic crossing. I curled up on that now familiar hefty sofa and became captivated in a romping tale about Mrs. Dempster, Dunny, Boy, and Paul. After odd and delightful twists in the first novel that started with an unspectacular snowball hit and a runaway to the circus, I wanted to read the next two books in the trilogy. *Will they be as good?* Those two books lay at home in Nova Scotia, meaning only my patience would pay off.

Perhaps the most captivating and difficult read during the time proved to be *Arthur Miller* by Christopher Bigsby. A 670-page doorstopper of sometimes tedious repetition, this biography describes Arthur Miller's life and development as a writer from 1915 to 1962. Miller went on to live another thirty-three years. He wrote some of my favourite plays: *The*

Crucible, *Death of a Salesman*, and *All My Sons*. In all of them, he takes in social and political contexts while drawing complex characters in their full humanity.

I read books in Saarland at home and on road trips. On long car trips, I'd whip out *Sarum* or *High Price* for a spell. I never found a coffee shop to read in for long periods. After January, one favourite spot became the local library in a carrel next to soaring glass windows nearly overlooking the pedestrian zone. Going there gave me a chance to get out, see Saarländer, get lost in the stacks, and peruse. Mostly I read at home, ensconced in the deep-seated armchair. I stayed home many mornings and afternoons, Leandra off to Sarreguemines and Thomas in an office in Dudweiler or digging among forest soils and leaves. On mild winter and spring days, I'd sit on the front balcony, facing the woods, a parking lot, and a start-up business centre. I could hear the traffic whizzing up the hill past Wildpark. I soaked up damp air and, if lucky on a warm day, a few hours of sunshine. With the luxury of time, comfort, and ready supplies of made-to-eat nibbles of cashews, almonds, Haribo gummy bears, and the addictive *erdnuss flippies*—a weird sweet-and-sour, crunchy peanut-flavoured snack unavailable in Nova Scotia—I consumed books.

Why all this reading? It helped to keep me sane and grounded. In 2022, Nicola Sturgeon, Scotland's first minister, said, "A life without books and reading would, for me, be a life not worth living." Same for me. Reading books by Lessing, Munro, and Davies kept me connected to my primary language, to Canada, and to my identity. It became a fallback position that afforded me comfort and solace in Saarland. Reading reached a part of my spirit inaccessible by other actions. It would have been impossible to sustain the same amount of reading and reflection during my school year with full-time work; it was another gift granted by time. Sharing readings of German detective stories with Leandra and Thomas bonded us in our overseas enterprise, cheering us up. It did the pragmatic thing of advancing my language skills in baby steps, affirming that I hadn't given up on a major goal I'd set myself in Saarland.

Reading helped me to live an interior life. Access to a wide spread of German literature remained inaccessible to me. Books in English saved and protected who I was for me.

25. When Are We Going to Germany?

One day, lounging on the sofa, Leandra asked: "When are we going to Germany?" I lowered my glasses and looked her in the eye. "Oh, never mind. We *are* living in Germany." She chuckled and I joined in. I suspect that minor confusion happened because going to school in France, she heard more French than German. Thomas decided to do something about that.

This led to a planned trip to Northern Germany, and other places by car, Copenhagen, Berlin, and Amsterdam. Our chief motivation? A week-long visit with Thomas's mother living in Schleswig-Holstein, near the Baltic Coast, where conversational German would abound.

The town of Eutin was a convenient location from which to visit Thomas's mother. Overjoyed and tearful, she welcomed us with rounds of fierce hugs. At ninety-two, she seemed tireless, keeping up energetic conversations and giving genuine hospitality. I saw my husband's face reflected in hers: a strong nose, hooded eyes, and a receding hairline on a rounded forehead. We never went hungry at Oma's for her favourite English word was "come," as she dished up Kohlrouladen (stuffed cabbage rolls), fresh bread, and potatoes always served hot.

Offering plum and apple pies, tea, coffee, and chocolates, she talked about her experiences during the war years, life as a wife and mother of six boys, and family news. Leandra and I tried to follow her conversations with her youngest, amused when she forgot exact details, substituting in her own particulars. Thomas, a stickler for facts, challenged her, but even he couldn't always match his mother's resoluteness. "When you were a little boy in Travemünde, you would —" she'd start off. "No, Mutti, I was a baby in Travemünde when we moved to Benz," he corrected. Later on, she'd go back sticking to her story of his boyhood in the seaside resort.

One evening, she complained of deteriorating eyesight. At her favourite window spot, she saw not one but two cars, not one woman walking but two women. *"Oh je,"* she moaned. *"Es ist schlimm! Ganz schlimm!"* (It's bad! Really bad!) By our fourth visit, her vision was good again. Germany's medical system had fixed her eyesight problems with a pair of new spectacles. As we approached, she waved from an upstairs window overlooking an idyllic country street. Every day she descended her stairs for a long walk along village sidewalks.

Thomas's deep attachment to his Heimat showed up in a sly way, setting us up for a three-hour tramp. We'd settled in for the night in our Eutin apartment, ten kilometres away from Benz, the village where he'd spent his youth.

"How about tomorrow we walk through Benz?" he suggested.

Leandra looked up from her book. "I'd love to do that, Dad."

We'd been to Benz before and welcomed a revisit.

I raised an eyebrow, suspicious. "How much walking are we talking about?"

"Come now, an hour or so," he said, straight-faced.

Next day, we stood facing a smart residence of wide glass windows and wooden trims in pastel yellow on a green acreage. It looked a newly renovated house on the spot where Thomas's family home once stood.

Beginning the tour of the village, Thomas humoured us with gossip about the lives of old villagers going something like this: "People arrived here as refugees, like our parents, after the Second World War, from far-east Germany and old German settlements in southeast Europe. Many are now gone. They had to find a place to live during those chaotic days, almost seventy years ago." He pointed, "The strongest man in the village lived there, here was where the bullies in grades three and four got me to the ground, trying to make me say sorry, and over there is my old elementary school building, a one-room schoolhouse, now a daycare centre."

We came to the beloved woods about which I'd heard so much over the years. He'd told us he once encountered a wild male boar when walking home through these woods from a horse stable seven kilometres away. On entering the forest, we followed a trail littered with horse droppings. "Oh!" Leandra said, suddenly startled, out in front. "Hey, what's up?" I called. She had almost walked into a line of barbed wire stretched across the trail at eye level.

"Who would do something like that?" I asked, shaken. "You have no idea," Thomas replied, explaining it was intended to stop horse riders from trespassing on private property. He scrambled on, leading the way over a low wire fence and a brook, trekking across a wet field of bumpy corn stubble, ignoring a no-trespassing sign. We walked and walked, Leandra getting tired, I getting cranky. "Dad, is this ever going to end?" "Soon," he replied as we entered a kilometre-long hayfield and I started sneezing. Despite the fact that I was obviously flagging, our leader mounted the curve of another hill before re-entering the woods. At last, after three hours, he gestured at the final stretch, smirking at having planned the entire thing.

I scowled, muttered a few choice phrases, and wanted to know why he had gone two hours overtime, even as I knew the answer. My husband was reliving his past in the village of his youth and the countryside of hilly east Schleswig-Holstein that claimed his heart. Leandra told us she loved the dreamy, romantic landscape. After that, I bore allergic misery from an abundance of swirling European hazelnut pollen, nothing working for my sore sinuses. Spring had arrived earlier than in Nova Scotia and inflicted upon me an uncomfortable burden.

Later on this trip, after a visit to Berlin, we stopped at Magdeburg, capital and seat of the parliament of Saxony-Anhalt, on the Elbe River. Thomas told us, "This city is known to Germans for the seventeenth-century scientist and politician Otto von Guericke. He gave a public show to convince people of the power of a vacuum. It's a classic physics experiment."

"How?" Leandra asked, leaning forward as we drove.

"He pumped the air out of two copper hemispheres held together by a vacuum. Guericke used eight horses on opposite sides to try pulling the hemispheres apart—they failed."

"Nice stunting," she murmured, eyes bright. But that's not why we're stopping in Magdeburg though, right?"

"Right. A different story brings us here," Thomas answered, pulling into a parking lot.

I knew the reason for our detour and explained it: "Remember when a historian in Halifax gave a talk saying St. Maurice was the only Black saint and hero in all of Europe?"

"Maybe...." Leandra wrinkled her brow.

"Legend has it St. Maurice was the leader of a famous Roman legion and became one of the most respected saints for several professions, places, and churches," I said.

So much history lay around us, in fact, right in front of us too, inside the Gothic Cathedral of Saints Maurice and Catherine. It had taken us less than two hours to arrive here from Berlin. Today, the place looked peaceful, deserted almost. We crossed the wide churchyard and stepped inside a dim, silent interior. Underdressed, Leandra and Thomas shivered, whereas I zipped up my coat.

A tall, lean, white-haired man with the free air of a retiree approached us. He spoke to Thomas in German, pointing out wall monuments, sculptures, and statues. He shared facts and showed us documents about St. Maurice, after which we bought postcards and a small book. Thomas told us later that the man emphasized his group's efforts to preserve the cathedral's historical and artistic significance.

In the nave of the chilly cathedral, we walked around the sarcophagus of Otto the Great, German king from 936 and emperor of the Holy Roman Empire of Germany from 962 to 973. A subsequent emperor of the Holy Roman Empire, Friedrich II, had aimed to complete the Holy Empire expansion toward the east that Otto the Great had begun in the tenth century. When Friedrich II visited Magdeburg in 1234, the church created two figures of *Mauritius niger* (Latin for Black Maurice). The statue of Maurice, standing along the south side of the screened choir quarter of Magdeburg Cathedral, retained much of its unique surface detail and flecked paintwork. The statues revered the courage and belief of the African in the Christian mission.

Some mystery surrounds the actual man named St. Maurice, his actions and racial ancestry. I was moved by the sight of an African figure revered as a hero mounted in a cathedral in the heart of Germany dating back 800 years.

26. Freiburg

During our overseas year we became travel warriors, but our travel agenda had to meet the restrictions of Leandra's school schedule. The French system with four vacation periods of two weeks each gave us precious travel time. On regular weekends we did day trips by train, and with holiday Mondays, we sometimes sneaked in a Friday to make a four-day weekend.

So how did we chart our travel campaigns? We did it by design, both planned and hectic. Thomas burned with the desire to travel, stopping overnight at youth hostels. Leandra and I leaned on him; we trusted his knowledge even though he'd told me stories of boarding the wrong train to end up in the right places and vice versa.

Our travel choices beyond Saarland embraced vacationing on the Baltic Coast, and exploring culture and history in cities like Berlin, Lübeck, and Würzburg, to name a few. To add to our travel fever, neighbouring France, Austria, and The Netherlands with castles, museums, and architectural wonders competed for our attention. Paris. Vienna. Copenhagen. Where should we begin?

No other country boasts more youth hostels than Germany or embraces them with more passion. The only other European country coming close to this lodging culture is France. During our year in Germany, we stayed in five hostels in five different cities: Berchtesgaden, Ingolstadt, Würzburg, Freiburg, and Göttingen, all of them of a different flavour. Göttingen was memorable for a friendly African taxi driver who spoke perfect German.

"You must be from Uganda," Thomas said to him. "*Jah,*" he replied, beaming with pride, at which point Thomas launched into a dialogue about his trips to Uganda years ago.

For me, the anticipation of an overnight stay at a youth hostel was almost as exciting as the stay itself. We'd visited the Saarbrücken hostel right away in July 2013 to apply for membership cards. Travelling by train, we did our first youth hostel stay in November; the following March, Thomas booked a family room in the Freiburg hostel. We packed, loaded up a rental with backpacks and snacks, and got ready for another experience in this German institution.

I'd picked Freiburg, Baden-Württemberg. My attraction started on a sunny summer afternoon in 2006 when Thomas, Art, Leandra, and I stepped into a stream of pedestrians in that smart city where everyone and everything looked *so* cool. Its reputation as the sunniest, warmest, most welcoming Germany city appeared writ large and by March 2014, it was high time to go back when planned for two nights' lodging. To save time, we drove Leandra to school on the Friday morning in order to collect her right at the end of her day and set out on the road for Freiburg. "It's nice to have a car. Let's take a spin through the German-French border region," Thomas suggested after dropping her off.

It was a time of academic freedom for him, working on research projects and having already submitted an article on beech forests in Saarland to *Forstarchiv*, a German forestry journal, in early February. (This paper would be accepted for publication in May. It was also in May that he shared his work with the university department that had hosted and supported his efforts.)

We stopped at a charming countryside patisserie, forgetting our map of the region when we left. We passed forests and a carpet of greening fields, sometimes broken up by village settlements and clumps of far-off trees. "Let's visit the European Archaeological Park at Bliesbruck-Reinheim," Thomas said.

"Where's that?"

"It's nearby in the Saarland district of Gersheim and the French district of Bliesbruck, Moselle. Karl took us there in 2011. Remember?"

I shook my head; I tended to forget foreign place names.

We parked in an empty residential street and walked past new, plastered houses in creams and whites with pretty gardens. At a deserted site, a wide archaeological dig opened up to our right and left, a cross-border project resulting in excavations, and the discovery and restoration of Celtic and Roman settlements. Covering an area 1,200 by 600 metres, it looked larger than the Roman baths in Bath, England. The project fascinated me for its size and its findings. The remnants of the tomb of a Celtic princess, a provincial Gallo-Roman settlement, and a Roman villa were all uncovered. I thought it ironic that only forty thousand people visited this impressive site each year (half of them school children), unlike Bath, England, which was visited by a few million every year. Everything around us stayed graveyard-quiet in a location where France's and Germany's distant past still tossed up fascinating secrets.

"Hi, Leandra," I called as she came out her school gate.

"Oh, hi, Mum, Dad." She smiled broadly.

"Ha! Let the weekend begin!" Thomas shouted, clapping and rubbing his hands in glee.

First, we visited the Sarreguemines patisserie, our eyes wide like dinner plates as we filled up on too much French pastry goodness.

Our car tires spun on smooth tarmac, speeding away from Sarreguemines to our destination, 208 kilometres away, would take two and a half hours. Thomas pointed out every single geographical and agricultural feature he could manage—rivers, forested lands, middle mountains, fields of canola and asparagus. Leandra and I minded other things, her nose stuck in an exciting chapter of *The Girl Who Kicked the Hornet's Nest* (French edition), and I gazing out, dazzled by the lacy cherry blossoms dotting the springtime landscape. We arrived in the Schwarzwald, or Black Forest region, and followed a long street through Freiburg to find the hostel half-hidden among spreading trees, beside a river, and framed by a backdrop of dark mountains. *Can anything be more gorgeous?* At the driveway entrance, we passed a group of youths sitting around a campfire. Leandra's eyes fastened on them.

We'd arrived smack at check-in time, 6 P.M. to be greeted by a fresh-faced youngster with a boy-bun at the reception desk who handed us a gift—a long list of rules. Thomas was fine, he likes rules, while Leandra didn't care for her parents took care of things. The employee instructed us to collect our bed linens and make our beds, then strip them and bring down the linens when leaving. We should help ourselves to the buffet breakfast and clean up after eating, though he made no demand that we wash the dishes. Not enough rules? He issued one more: be gone by 9 A.M. daily. Upstairs, we walked into a small, spotless family room with bunk beds, a shower, and a private bathroom for which we paid ninety euros, a generous sum for no-frills accommodation, including breakfast.

Youth hostels are not luxurious accommodation for pampered guests. The super-clean, private bathroom, prized in the world of hostel hospitality, made our cramped quarters splendid. To house large groups of rowdy students with fussing teachers, some rooms fit bunk beds for a dozen or more. This hostel offered a common dining hall, a music cellar, and a field for volleyball and basketball.

Once refreshed, we caught a tram downtown, about three kilometres away, where I stood pinching myself to be here in Freiburg. I felt the stir of an urban setting on quiet streets surrounded by late Baroque, Renaissance, and Gothic buildings rebuilt after the Second World War. Bright storefront window displays cheered up the semi-darkness, pedestrians' shoes scraping cobbled streets in front and behind us. Aromas from a kebab snack bar drifted over and we caught snatches of fleeting conversations. Buildings framed a dismal night sky, but here there were no real skyscrapers. "Do people live downtown?" I asked Thomas.

"Yes, it's a livable city, like Vienna."

Next morning, we enjoyed breakfast in a dining hall ringing with the hullabaloo of batches of early risers.

"What shall we do today?" Thomas asked as we ate.

"How about the market square?" I suggested, turning to Leandra.

"Sure thing," she said.

We couldn't miss the open-air market at Münsterplatz where market vendors had taken over the space. Scores of stalls sold everything, from fresh flowers, fruits, and vegetables, to pastries, wines, and sausages. "How odd. Look at those baby-blue eggs." I felt like a kid in a fairground, moving in with Leandra for a closer look. "Yeah. First time I'm seeing large blue eggs too."

I turned this way and that, eager to soak up the market scene. I took in baskets of roses and green and red wreaths, drawn by their striking colours. Leandra was fascinated by loads of leafy vegetables, fat pumpkins, beets, orange carrots, and fruit displays of quince and plums. Thomas turned to look at varieties of stacked yellow, red, and black jams before we joined him, turning to enjoy spreads of fragrant breads, rolls, and pies. Along the way, stalls of arts and crafts battled against produce. I admired beautiful olive wood bowls, cutting boards, ladles, and then knitted handiworks.

Shoppers jostled, mixing in a medley of German voices. The market lived up to my expectations, so much so I didn't want to leave this feast. Thomas had disappeared for a moment, so I leaned on Leandra. "What shall I buy as a keepsake?"

"How about a pair of olive wood salad spoons from over there?"

"Great, easy to carry and they'll last," I said, digging into my handbag. I asked the vendor how to care for them.

"Just rinse after use and rub on olive oil. No need for soap." I thanked him.

Before lunch, we stumbled upon a small museum off the plaza, the Museum of Nature and Man, blown away by its archeological and historic displays. We learned about a series of prehistoric settlements of pile dwellings (or stilt houses) in and around the Alps built from roughly 5000 to 500 BCE on the edges of lakes, rivers, and wetlands. I found it instructive that the dwellings went farther back in time than the oldest Stonehenge monument.

We circled and scrutinized more natural and cultural displays, some of miniature stone carvings depicting people with large, protruding posteriors. After, we headed back to the farmers' market for Leandra to order for us a white sausage and a beef patty, sandwiched between cuts of crisp French baguette. Thomas passed but later demolished a pizza. The crowd crush reminded me of Saarbrücken's Christmas market minus the Christmas themes. Of all the farmers' markets I've visited, Freiburg's the one I most fancy.

We could no longer ignore the elephant in the square. I wasn't sure I wanted to see another cathedral, but Freiburg Münster did not disappoint with its history dating back to the Middle Ages. A shattered church bell lay on display, another grim reminder of the ruins caused by World War II.

27. To Begin is Easy; to Persist is Art

Arriving at dusk on a Sunday evening, the scenic setting of the small town of Lienz immediately won me over. From Berchtesgaden, we'd driven two and half hours through mountains to get to this medieval town in the Austrian state of Tyrol. Around us, villages were perched on mountainsides; livestock munched and lolled on lofty pastures. Leandra told me later she loved everything about that pretty, mountainous region. Thomas had found our Tyrol accommodation online, unaware of how close we were to the massive Großglockner mountain. We booked into our lodging and strolled through the uncommonly flat, scenic downtown streets, quiet on a Sunday. For supper we entered an empty restaurant, roomy and pleasant, waiters in formal black-and-white attire.

From the upstairs windows of our lodgings, we viewed distant high meadows dotted with pine lodges and snow-capped mountains. The renovated furnished apartment suited our needs perfectly, having a well-equipped kitchen, two bedrooms, a comfortable sitting room, and a bathroom with a bathtub. For a six-night stay, we had plenty of time to explore and discover Alpine highlands within easy driving distance.

Next day, we drove for hours, exploring the region—mountains and more mountains. Thomas wanted to drive the famous Großglockner High Alpine Road, the highest surfaced mountain pass in Austria. We discovered that a harsh winter and heavy snowfall had delayed opening for the summer. In early May, we were ahead of the season, so instead, we drove toward Großglockner up steep and winding roads following dizzying hairpin bends. Back down at one thousand metres, we parked to regard breathtaking scenery and capture photos of hamlets, sheep, and goats far below.

That's when Thomas floated the idea of a mountain hike.

"Wait a minute, lemme get this straight," I interrupted. "You're asking me to climb a mountain that I'm too scared to go up by car? There'll be nothing between me and a sudden steep drop. I'd be unprotected hiking up on foot. What madness." We were well below Großglockner's peak of 3798 metres, but goats down below still looked like silverfish.

Leandra, who had been snapping photos, cracked up. Her laughter broke the fear that clawed at my throat every time I looked down.

"Come now, I'm not saying we do the entire thing. We drive, park, and then walk the rest."

"But that's the toughest part." I shook my head.

"Yes, but there's no rush to get up. We can take our time, nah." Thomas was determined, his tone persuasive.

"I would *have* to take my time. You see how high that peak is?"

"You won't have to go to the peak, plus we'll get to Lucknerhaus in time for lunch. Come on, give it a try. They serve delicious meals up there, you know." He gave a crafty smile.

"I knew there'd be a bribe in there. What do you think, Leandra?" I turned to her; eyebrows raised.

"Love it. Sounds like fun. Look at this view." She giggled, hands gesturing wide. Thomas suggested I stay on at the Luckner restaurant while he and Leandra went higher.

Outvoted, I caved in. "All right." At fifty-seven, on a trip of a lifetime, I had to be game for an adventure worth talking about when I got back home.

Next morning, we stuffed snacks and water bottles into our backpacks. Again, just arriving at the parking spot, well below the peak, required us to manoeuvre upland S-bends. At lower levels, the width of the road barely allows for counter traffic. Higher up, a sliver of a trail forced one driver to give way on a precarious cliff. I saw visions of our car careening off a precipice, bravely trying to stay calm and carry on as my heart raced.

"How do local drivers manage in winter?" I asked.

"They must be the world's best drivers," Thomas answered. Parking at one thousand metres, we started off on foot.

Hints of spring perfumed the fresh air. I became fascinated by the sight of numerous tiny snails on the mountainside that had sealed the openings of their shells, with a secretion containing lime, to survive frosty winter temperatures. When I palmed them, some were so light, it was as if there was nobody at home.

I kept to the left, leaning toward the secure, solid rock face, away from cliff edges. Soon we left the road to follow wood-trail signs pointing toward Lucknerhaus, that being safer than dodging traffic. Breathless and staggering upwards, I feared a stumble could send me flying downhill. For the first half-hour, pushing upwards sapped all my energy, even the power to form a single rational thought escaped me. Thomas found a sturdy, fallen branch and fashioned a walking stick for me. "Here, this should help." I showed gratitude with a tired smile. He made another, asking, "Leandra, want a stick?" She said no, so he kept it for himself. She led us both, as if she already knew the way. Taking the wooded trail offered us a shorter route than the zigzag road up the heights. The trail drew us across grassy, open fields where we encountered herds of goats tied with small tinkling bells. They stopped cropping grasses to inspect us, human interlopers.

"This reminds me of Heidi and the goatherd in the Swiss Alps," Leandra said as we watched them closeup.

Sometimes we teetered so close to an edge that my courage plunged to my toes. *How about turning back? How about planting myself here and not moving forward?* But going back was now equal to going on, so I hauled myself up bit by bit.

I paused to look back at the view behind and to distract myself from present pains and perils, Thomas steaming ahead, Leandra in the middle, and me trailing. *How did I get here? Whose idea was this?*

I hollered to Thomas and Leandra, waving my stick. "Wait up you two. How about stopping for a bite?" On a pine bench, beside spruce trees, we sat to break out brie, mustard, and prosciutto sandwiches. In cool Alpine air, halfway through a vigorous workout, the food took on an uncanny deliciousness. Too soon, Thomas jumped up, eager to go again.

"Can we stay here forever?" I teased, flopping my body back.

"Okay," he agreed, "let's take another ten minutes or so. How about you, Leandra?" With the slightest encouragement, I'd have made a bed of pine needles in open air.

"I'll be ready when you are," she said, leaning back on the bench and closing her eyes. Behind us and to the right, mind-bending green ravines spun. In front were thinning spruce and larch. Soon, we went on, me struggling to keep step with my pace setters, but falling further behind, sometimes resting gratefully on my walking stick, my lungs about ready to burst. Yet, on and on my husband and daughter pushed to where a ribbon trail met a logging road.

"Where is this Großglockner resort, anyway?" I wheezed.

"Just take your time. It's up there," Thomas replied, pointing. "We're more than halfway." Suddenly he stopped, exclaiming, "Look at this!" He was a good five minutes ahead and I approached, picking my way through a litter of shale.

"What's this?" Leandra asked, as our eyes scanned the rubble.

"It's erosion, but look here." Thomas rubbed rust-red veins of rocks on the cliff side, making bits cascade to his feet. He pointed out that the position of huge shale plates, laid down flat on sea beds hundreds of thousands, perhaps even millions of years ago, now pointed skyward on the mountains, evidence of the earth's plates and the collision of continents. *What a geography lesson.* I'd never seen better signs of the tectonic-plates theory.

I rotated, struck by the sound of silence, for even the wind had taken a break. Far off surrounding us, spruce and larch blanketed Alpine slopes next to clear-cut patches. In the highest regions, no trees grew at all, only bare rock and snow. Up here among giant mountains, my lungs took in deep breaths of clean, sharp oxygen, making my head reel and my spirits soar. Equal to the scenery was a perfect mountain lodge perched lonely amid the clouds. A hearty push might dislodge it. "Who lives here? How did they do that?" I asked nobody, baffled. I was caught by the sheer, long drop to one side, as together, we gazed in wonder, transfixed by the sight.

Further on in the distance, a miniature van wound its way around a craggy corkscrew road, disappearing and reappearing nearer our destination. For the first time, Leandra started to tire, looking flushed and annoyed; she began to low-key swear under her breath. Meanwhile, I was high-key cursing my bad luck, at any moment about to suffer a heart attack on this mountain as sweat lines coursed down my back. How did Thomas succeed in getting me into this hike, making it sound so attractive? I could kick my worn-out, sorry self for agreeing.

"Why didn't I just say no and drive up here instead?" I yelled loudly, but Leandra didn't answer, and Thomas was too far off to engage. "Are we there yet? How far do we still have to go?" I panted, grumpy. Thomas appeared tireless, bolstered by the ascent, one of his evident contradictions, most hyper when most tired. *How is that even possible, with me about to die on this hill?* He came to a standstill, waving energetically at me. "See that ridge up there? The resort should be on the other side."

"Oh great, another ridge." I groaned, pausing and pretending to tie my shoelaces again, just to grab a break.

I followed Thomas's and Leandra's lead, unsteady and drained. I lurched onto a trail beside a log cabin's roof fixed into a slope. Then, without warning, the trail opened up and a two-storey, half-shingled and plastered pine lodge confronted us, fringed by beds of bright red flowers and green lawns, and facing a parking lot with large trail signs. For the first time since starting out, we passed people, a group of fit, jolly folks in pristine ski gear heading down.

Goodness, I'd made it up a thousand metres, and even though it had taken us three hours, to me it smacked of eternity.

Thomas's eyes followed the trail toward the highest mountain peak. "Groβglockner's up there," he said. I hastened towards the lodge, the Alpengasthof Lucknerhaus, mounted pine steps, and entered a cozy, lit dining room.

"What a pretty lodge," Leandra said, struck by the restaurant and inn's décor. I caught glimpses of taxidermy mounted on knotty pine walls, a bighorn mountain goat and birds of prey. A smart looking, dark-haired waiter welcomed us and ushered us to corner seats beside picture windows. I relished the relief of sitting.

"Want to take the higher trail after lunch?" Thomas asked. Without hesitating, Leandra said, "Yep," while I declined.

I could not find the right words to describe the beauty of the natural setting. The sweet mountain air, warm alpine lodge, and spirited exercise improved my mood and appetite. When the pleasant waiter bustled over with menus, we selected the feast we deserved. Thomas coaxed the shy man into revealing his Croatian origins. He returned carrying hot skillets of wild veal in a rich, creamy sauce, golden brown fried potatoes, and red cabbage sauerkraut for Thomas and me. Leandra had breaded pork schnitzel with crispy fries and vegetables. For dessert, Leandra and I ordered apple strudel under a cloak of smooth, warm vanilla sauce, while Thomas chose *Germknödel*, a warm yeast dumpling strewn with poppy seeds, filled with plum purée, and topped with whipped cream. As we ate and chatted about the day's feat, the Großglockner peak, up to now shrouded in mists, broke through the haze to reveal itself as a shining tower of stone and ice.

After Leandra and Thomas set off along the higher path to Groβglockner, I kept my own company, settling into a plush leather armchair, my toes pointing toward the orange flames of a wood stove. Another hour and Thomas and Leandra returned, reporting heavy snow on upper trails. In the fields they spied carpets of crocuses, green stems contrasted against white and purple petals and, in the centre, startling bursts of yellow. They encountered alpine marmots, gopher-like creatures, popping up like sentinels. Saying goodbye to the Großglockner, we retraced the route we'd hours before ascended. What had taken us half a morning to ascend took us a mere hour to descend under my lead.

After visiting Ljubljana, capital of Slovenia, on a whim and tearing across northeastern Italy for Verona, we arrived in Venice.

"Look at this doorknob," Thomas said. When Leandra and I examined it, we saw a head, archetypal of Africans, carved into the doorknob. I learned about similar carvings on tavern and house knockers around this ancient city. A complicated history of African representation in Italy in various art forms ranged from religious statues to paintings and jewellery. Depictions were as capricious as the exotic African, the brave soldier, and the abject slave. I found these representations both intriguing and baffling. They spoke of an astonishing hidden history, secret to me and most tourists and travellers in Italy. They connected me to Africa, Africans, and Black people in the European and German history I'd become rapidly acquainted with in Saarland.

We turned and hurtled northward across the Brenner Pass, through Austria, and into Germany, our wanderlust not yet satisfied. The Brenner Pass along the border of Austria and Italy, with the *Europabrücke* (Bridge of Europe) on the northern end, cast a spell. *Who lives down below this whistling pass?* In the heart of grand mountain country, we experienced a temperature drop from fifteen to five degrees Celsius, ice clouds hanging within reach. "See how travelling into high terrain causes climate changes like travelling further north?" Thomas remarked, eyes glued to the road. It was another tangible geography lesson.

Once again in Germany, Thomas pulled into a perfect, leafy parking lot for an overnight stay at a historic building, a youth hostel in Ingolstadt on the Danube River. Seeing the beautiful two-level, red-brown brick building, I thought we'd arrived at a castle. A central round tower displayed rows of windows. This hostel lies an hour from Nürnberg, which we intended to visit the following day. Leandra fell for our spacious, high-ceilinged dorm. She said this early nineteenth-century building, which once housed a royal Bavarian regiment, made her think of Hogwarts School of Witchcraft and Wizardry in the Harry Potter series. After settling into our room with its four bunk beds, she began scribbling madly in her journal, inspired. In the evening air, we heard scuffling car tires and distant, soft voices of hostel guests. I slept soundly.

At another time and place, I'd have given more time to Nürnberg and nearby Rothenburg ob der Tauber, but they came at the end of our grand tour. Nürnberg exerted a magnetic pull, like none other, from which I didn't want to be released. We started at a market square so wide that if Leandra and Thomas had stood at one end and yelled to me at the other, I wouldn't have heard them. A steep uphill climb brought us to the city castle on a sandstone ridge dominating the historical center. On our way down, we passed some American teenage girls lugging too much baggage up cobblestones, laughing. They must have stayed at one of the largest and most modern youth hostels in Germany, located in the former Imperial Stables of the castle. I felt thwarted at the Albrecht Dürer House, where a notice on the door read: "Closed on Mondays." Dürer—painter, printmaker, and writer—was regarded as Germany's greatest Renaissance artist for his realism.

"Too bad," Leandra moaned, peeking through dim windows. She, too, shared an interest in Dürer's work. Thomas shrugged and moved on.

As we sprinted across the market square to leave, Thomas leading, a quintet of male singers stopped us, singing in bold operatic voices. Captivated, we joined a waxing, silent crowd. They were the Belo-Mir singers, a group from Minsk, Belarus, so good Thomas bought a CD. I could have stayed to listen for another hour, but instead we began to run away again. This time, Thomas got captured by a man promoting his effort to save a historic Nürnberg building. Uninterested and forced into waiting, Leandra and I gazed at an intricately fashioned, fourteenth-century fountain, the Schöner Brunnen. Then, at the stroke of noon, loud tolling from an aged church bell at the far end of the square drew our eyes forward. High on the clock face of the *Frauenkirche*, Church of Our Lady, near the church spire, seven puppet bodies revolved three times around a seated figure. The mechanical marvel lasted five minutes.

We tore ourselves away and headed to Rothenburg ob der Tauber. *I loved the names and sounds of many German towns. Now, if only I could get my Bajan tongue to obey me and pronounce them correctly.* A town in the Franconia region of Bavaria, it lies eighty kilometres west of Nürnberg. The name Rothenburg ob der Tauber—red fortress on the Tauber—came from the town's location on a plateau overlooking the Tauber River. Thomas steered us through cobblestoned lanes. "See these half-timbered houses still intact?" The buildings were in superb shape. "The old town walls ahead have preserved gatehouses and towers and a covered walkway on top," making the town famous.

In a growing haze of weariness, I pushed on, Leandra dragged a bit, while her dad wielded a new burst of energy like a sword. I was thankful I did, for the history of the city was fascinating, shaped as it was by the Black Plague, the fate of its Jewish citizens, the Thirty Years War (1618–1648), Nazi ideology, and the pragmatism of the people in saving their city from total destruction toward the end of the Second World War. By the time we had circled the city to take in its medieval architecture, it was high time to return home.

I bought a pretty blue umbrella with depictions of German towns, cities, and landmarks: Dresden, Munich, Rothenburg ob der Tauber, Cologne, Schloss Neuschwanstein, Heidelberg, Schwarzwald, Hamburg, Schwerin, Passau, Bamberg, Berlin, Königssee, Nürnberg, and Bodensee. When Thomas offered a visit to Würzburg, I said no. I had rubber for legs, and Leandra drooped. *Enough!* It was a worthy goal, but *Ich hatte keine Lust mehr* (I had no more desire), as Germans say, to visit yet another city with its steady diet of museums, icons, and cultural and historic structures. In a huff, Thomas was unhappy but held his tongue. In the car, five minutes into our return trip, Leandra expressed gratitude for our abridged tour by sending soft snores in my direction.

As we darted the 287 kilometres back to Saarland, we stopped only for food and restrooms. I felt terrific getting back home in bright sunshine on Monday, May 5. I launched into bed well before the wee morning hours, having the rest of the week to relax and catch up on journal writing, reading, and rambles before another excursion. Leandra went directly to her bedroom without even *pickin' she teet*, shutting the door with a decisive snap. It signalled her self-imposed, much-needed time out.

In Europe, I was beginning to better understand my life narrative and the lion's share travel took up in my story. A renewed vigour took hold of me during our wide-ranging trips. I treasured the opportunity to see Europe's and Germany's historic sites and learn about their cultural variety, though things did not always go perfectly. Thomas knew a lot about the features and weight of his country's history, cultural traditions, and landscapes—they remained alive in him. All the places he propelled us toward held much more meaning for him than they did for us. He found this irritating; I shrugged.

My Großglockner mountain climb held symbolic value. Scaling an actual mountain was not unlike facing and overcoming tough personal and family matters in Saarland. It translated into heaving uphill and conquering life's hurdles. Over the previous ten months, Leandra and I had faced and fought different battles, hers related to teenage and academic anxieties in a new social environment and mine linked to failing at acquiring a decent amount of conversational German and concerns about making a meaningful life for myself in a foreign land. We were emerging on the other side reinforced, encouraged, and strengthened by hope and determination to push on.

28. The Mensa, a University Tradition

Thomas and I darted through the forest to the university and the Mensa on Wednesdays at noon, Leandra joining us on the odd day off school. She and I had paid an upfront ten euros each for our Mensa debit cards in August during the language course, and Thomas soon acquired a guest card. The automated payment system relied on diners loading up their cards. For our time in Saarland, even with the university language classes well in the rear, those Mensa debit cards turned into gold.

Anyone can complain about anything, especially cafeteria food. "But a system that feeds thousands of students and university staff daily for a few euros with the support of university, government, and industry has not been matched outside Germany," Thomas once declared with pride. At this very moment, it's possible to go online and find detailed, planned Mensa menus, for any university in Germany, with appealing features for a variety of tastes.

Inside the Mensa's entrance, Thomas and I joined a crowd of university students, staff, and guests looking up at the day's offerings on electronic screens. We chose from menu options A, B, or C with Option A offering a complete meal from soup to dessert, option B a vegetarian dish of the day, and C a meat dish with fries. All options included a vegetable salad and a quark or pudding dessert. If these choices were unattractive, a free-flow zone where dishes varied among an assortment of mains, sides, and vegetables, priced by type and weight, allowed people to pick and choose meals. If none of the options upstairs tempted the appetite, people could resort to the pricier cafeteria downstairs for vegetarian or meat choices, coupled with desserts, especially freshly made crêpes layered with Nutella or jams and whipped cream. I thought the prices, food quality, and variety grand compared to Nova Scotia.

My meals from the complete menu typically amounted to about ten dollars Canadian. As a guest scientist, Thomas paid more than a student, but students could purchase a warm meal at the Mensa for the equivalent of five to ten dollars.

Apart from the food, I enjoyed the buzz of the place, a spectacle of ritualized acts. A noisy atmosphere built up to a crescendo by 1 P.M., before ebbing to a subdued drone when students wandered off. Once university operated in full swing, a more vibrant spot could not be found on campus than the Mensa between 11 A.M. and 2 P.M. I loved the hubbub as it made me feel young again—a throwback to my university days in Fredericton and Vancouver. As a teacher in Halifax, I ate lunch among a quieter, sociable bunch of colleagues.

I could see from Thomas's face and body language the lively student atmosphere energized and lifted his spirits too. When not in our apartment or on family outings, he spent many hours in a university office, reviewing literature, crunching numbers, and writing up his findings and conclusions. Uninterrupted in his research projects by the demands of a busy teaching schedule, he completed a second scientific paper in May about tree diversity and fired it off to *Ecological Indicators*; he'd done that work during March and April. The Mensa brought him back to an academic setting, reviving memories of years of student life spent at the Georg August University in Göttingen.

Upstairs, hundreds of students would stream through beneath high ceilings, packing seats squished between square concrete pillars decorated with bright, angular motifs. People moved in smooth lines from five different vantage points. German and international students ate at tables with friends or strangers, chatting out of curiosity or politeness, or keeping silent. When done, everyone gathered up their dishes on trays and returned them to the kitchen staff on a conveyor belt. Seldom ever did orphaned food trays or dishes remain neglected after an army of youths filed through. Mensa staff would wipe down tables and sweep floors at the end of shifts, to keep everything clean and in good order.

It was wonderful for me to see young people act so civilized and considerate of the cafeteria staff. I loved that nobody piled messy tables, trash, and garbage high for workers to clean up. A colleague who visited Germany after her retirement in 2017 observed similar behaviour on trains: "We sat across from polite, tidy young people. They drank their sparkling water, ate their candy bars and snacks, and stashed away their wrappers. When they left, the spaces they'd occupied were as spotless as when they first sat down. I was stunned." I'd seen the opposite behaviour at my high school and two local universities. The thoughtful behaviour of the German youth recalled the image of Germany as symphony. For the greater good, that of social harmony, the individual preference was subdued and the presence of a conductor wasn't even needed to make it happen.

29. A Life Worth Living

One Saturday in May, Leandra, Thomas, and I arrived at a low, nondescript building on the eastern edge of Saarbrücken, the East Hall near an old Roman fort. The area looked like a shady, somewhat disreputable part of town, near a business park. Our event started at 7:30 P.M. and we had arrived half an hour early. People hung around outside in clusters, dressed in jeans, t-shirts, and layered, multicoloured skirts and dresses. A hippie vibe permeated the air, creating the joyful mood of a fringe festival on a warm spring evening. We entered a large gym-like room with risers and chairs to the right, facing a stage with a mounted screen.

At Anna's suggestion, we had chosen to attend Festival Perspectives, a German- and French-language festival of contemporary stage art. For more than thirty years, the festival had combined theatre, dance, music, and circus acts, blurring the lines between art forms.

Quality Control stood out among the dramatic performances of Festival Perspectives. Nothing had prepared me for the searching life portrait of Ms. Hallwachs' life. With the help of theatrical delivery and stage craft, Maria-Cristina Hallwachs gripped the attention of all present with her very first words and never let go until she stopped. She offered up a strong lens for seeing into a different world than that of every complacent able-bodied person sitting in the audience. Her words sketched a way of being as different as living on a weird planet where someone's body could be as light as a sheet of paper, refusing to carry out the simplest commands.

Even though she spoke every word in German, I understood her heart-wrenching loss of opportunities. I leaned forward in my seat, hanging onto her voice in the dark auditorium to grasp the full scope of what it conveyed. Video images shared on the big screen helped my understanding. The main character was not acting; she was presenting a life drama, inspiring in its scope and authenticity.

Maria-Cristina is a person with quadriplegia, the result of an injury that happened when she was nineteen. At the end of an exciting Abitur school year, her parents gave her a gift of a trip to Crete. The high-spirited teenager, bursting with joy and love of life, took the last jump of her life when she spontaneously dove into the resort's pool at the shallow end, breaking her neck, causing complete respiratory paralysis. After her father rescued and resuscitated her, she endured a long rehabilitation period, akin to coming back from the dead.

She lives today in Stuttgart in her own apartment with twenty-four-hour caregivers. She writes with the help of a gadget held in her mouth, reads books, flies in planes, goes to soccer games, clubs, and restaurants. But she's unable to breathe on her own, for her diaphragm, like most muscles in her body, no longer carries out the commands of her brain. Blood still flows through her limbs, and the wonders of modern medicine have unknotted the worrisome kinks associated with bladder and bowel issues that many people with quadriplegia died from as recently as fifty years ago. Ventilation allows her to live. I was inspired by her heart, living with the motto: "There is always a way."

What is a meaningful life? And who gets to decide about that? Those two questions posed in that powerhouse theatre exposition fired my reflections. Could the scriptwriter have posed more difficult questions? But it was the story of Maria-Cristina's baby sister that broke my heart.

What causes a normal, healthy child to stop developing cognitively at age two? No one knew the answer and no medical specialists could clear up the darkness descending upon the parents as to why that affliction settled on their second daughter. A genetic flaw gripped their child's brain, gradually erasing all sense of self, identity, and mental capabilities that children exhibit as they grow and develop. This child began slipping away from her family as if her body vanished before them. Losing the ability to speak, she retained her innocent laugh. She could not voice the smallest wish or do the most basic tasks for herself. As her body grew, she lost her concept of self. Unlike Maria-Cristina, her sister lives in a group home.

The theatre performance drew on collective memory and the horror of the "unwanteds" in Nazi Germany. During that time, medical authorities charged with saving lives killed many, including the mentally and physically challenged. Today, the routine elimination of people categorized as unwanted is too horrible to contemplate. If people are asked, "Are such lives meaningful, worth living?" many, perhaps even a majority, would give a resounding *yes*.

People who are disabled are cared for in Germany and other wealthy countries. Maria-Cristina can enjoy many of the activities able-bodied people can. She can't make her body rise and walk, her arms and legs move, or her lungs breathe. On the other hand, while her sister is physically "able," her disease is as cruel and crippling as her older sibling's. Unlike Maria-Cristina, her sister cannot talk, read, or write a poem; nonetheless, the worth of both of their lives may be measured in their smiles of joy.

Who has the right to decide if a life is meaningful? Maria-Cristina's theatre piece drew on the promise of the future. The suggestion was that views on this question will also change, because societies keep changing, advancing. More technological and medical advancements may hold answers for much of the current limitations of bodily incapacitated adults. Who knows if and when a miracle cure for broken spines will become available? Even a woman in similar circumstances to Maria-Cristina in the far distant future who desires to bear a child may have her wish fulfilled through science and technology. I was amazed by the audacity of this woman's spirit and hopefulness.

Aside from the difficult, enduring quality-of-life questions, I paused to think of the financial costs of such a high-maintenance life, an issue not easily raised. In poorer, developing countries like Barbados, for instance, Maria-Cristina might well have died as a result of the severity of her injuries unless her parents had enough wealth to engineer her survival. Decades ago, a friend from West Africa living in Saskatchewan said to me, "When someone falls critically ill, requiring unaffordable intensive medical treatments, we pray for them to die." This raised the question about the West's obsession with life at any cost, even though it is an idea not applied evenly or fairly.

"Is it ethical to devote so much of a society's resources to one single individual, enabling her to live independently, requiring expensive technological gadgetry and twenty-four-hour care?" I asked Thomas and Leandra. We were waiting at the tram stop in a slant of early evening light. *The performer's sister's case appears more clear-cut.* No civil society nowadays sanctions ending people's lives because of mental deficiencies. Maria-Cristina's sister is able to live on, accommodated, either in a group home or with family, supported by state and or private care.

"In societies where we see obscene wealth, to the extent that people drive Porsches, Lamborghinis and Rolls-Royces down city streets, it's irrelevant to raise the issue of costs." I knew well my husband's views on wealth disparities, when his eyes flashed with intensity. "But it would never be a life for me, nor would I wish such an existence on any family member. I know exactly what I would do with that marvellous electric wheelchair if I had to sit in it." His gaze was steady.

I reflected for a moment on attitudes back in Nova Scotia and Barbados. Many people I knew (among them young students attracted to sexy cars) would argue that if people can afford luxury items, they have the right to purchase them, unhindered by any other considerations, even though others live in dire need. An individual's freedom to act on any opportunity to purchase and use products in the marketplace of capitalist societies pretty much prevails as a sacred tenet. I felt compelled for the time to pursue an answer to this ethical dilemma that could fit into my life philosophy.

Turning to Leandra, I asked, "What do you think?" She seemed to struggle to say what she thought at first.

"I was surprised and disgusted at the hospital ethics committee talking end of life beside the paralyzed girl. She could hear them but was unable to say anything at the beginning of her ordeal." She frowned in annoyance.

"Is that what happened?" Me missing that was another example of Leandra's German being better than mine.

"The ethics committee asked the end-of-life question to the parents, who jerked back as if stung," she added.

"They were torn about what to do when the prognosis sank in," Thomas said. "Imagine being hooked up to a diaphragm machine for life. No hope of ever walking again. The need for long-term, round-the-clock care terrified them."

"Yes, of course," I responded. By talking together about what Maria-Cristina had presented, I was understanding more about the parents' misery. They had wondered if such an existence was worth living. Should someone pull the plug? The father had hoped that the plane airlifting them from Greece to Germany would crash and end their agony. If mental incapacity had been coupled with the physical disability, her father had favoured bringing her life to a quick, merciful end. By comparison, her grandpa refused to accept the reality of any disabled people in his own worldview. Relatives reacted with heartbroken grief at what amounted to a prodigious tragedy. Someone on the committee recommended asking the patient if she wanted to live. Once she said *yes*, her parents fought for the insurance company to provide the means for their daughter to live on her own with caregivers.

"I think Maria-Cristina has meaning in her life. She can still do some things for herself and others, counselling people with quadriplegia, reading, writing, and presenting her story," Leandra said with insight. She'd worked out the dilemma for herself.

"I like that she continues her life with purpose," I nodded, agreeing.

There was something powerful about Maria-Cristina using her voice because too often, in society, we relegate people with severe disabilities to the shadows. By presenting her story, Maria-Cristina made the audience reckon with her reality representing a powerful lesson I absorbed in Saarland about quality of life, technological advances, and medical-ethical dilemmas. As a teacher, I'd debated topics with my high school students like the right to die, end-of-life care and legislation, and the state's and doctors' ambiguous role. For the first time, I'd gone beyond a theoretical frame into presentation of a real-life experience where the issues related to the presenter herself, moving me beyond words.

30. Down Memory Lane

"A bridging weekend. Yeh!" Leandra fist pumped, and I applauded, sharing her high anticipation. We were sitting at our Wednesday confectionary haunt before piano lessons, clinking dishes and cutlery punctuated a blanket of soft voices. Leandra had paid the price of early mornings and long days, and deserved a four-day break making her next school day the coming Monday. "Let's get an early start," Thomas reminded us, his fork poised over blue-black plum cake, coated in vanilla sauce and cream.

Next day, Thursday, May 29, was Ascension Day, a public holiday in France and Germany. We would seize the unofficial practice of the "bridging weekend," for Friday was really still a school day. As Canadians, we found it amusing how officialdom looked the other way while teachers announced to their students not to expect a normal Friday routine. We thanked the deep influences of the dominant Catholic traditions in the region.

On a forty-euro family train ticket, we left Saarbrücken at 8:20 A.M. in high spirits under a forever blue, cloudless sky. Undaunted by several milk-run stops, we changed trains twice, once in Frankfurt and then in Kassel, the train passing through an ocean of forests, pastures, vineyards, and crop fields. Travelling alongside the familiar Nahe River at first, we crossed the Rhine River at Mainz, now a familiar train route.

True to form, Thomas said, "We're passing through the German middle mountains region with leftovers of dead volcanoes." Then he added, "See those two mountain peaks? They're called Die Gleichen, the equals, because they look the same. Old castle ruins dating back to the twelfth century are up there." I caught a glimpse of the mountains, but no sign of castles.

Not long past Marburg, he pointed. "There's Amöneburg—a small town on top of a mountain, built around a castle of the same name."

"That's interesting," I murmured, fighting sleep.

Thomas frowned, asking, "Why do I even bother?" He could never give up on his mission to teach German geography to his less-than-enthusiastic family.

At Frankfurt, we stored our bags deep inside a train station locker. The architecture of the station is a combination of Neo-Renaissance and later neoclassical features. Exiting the iconic eastern façade of the reception hall, we stepped into clamouring street noises for a brief sight-see.

Home to the European Central Bank, Frankfurt is the financial centre of Germany. And because it's located in the middle of Germany and is used as a transport hub for long and short haul travelling, its train station is regarded as one of the most important in the country. The previous November, we'd visited the world's largest book fair in Frankfurt. A few years later, I read that more than 7,300 exhibitors from over 100 countries and more than 286,000 visitors participated in the 2017 book fair. When I walked around the book fair in 2013 amid thousands of people, some dressed in character costumes, my head whirled at its size. I remember buying at least two books in English, biographies of Arthur Miller and Charlotte Brontë. It proved harder than I thought to find English books.

Returning to the train station, we bought refreshments before starting our second leg. Frankfurt train station is built to prevent trains from passing straight through, as in Hamburg, enabling a cozier and less drafty station, particularly in winter. Leandra and I looked around with interest while Thomas walked casually. Here gathered a bachelorette party with a young woman wearing a white veil, there stood a group of East Africans dressed in finery, as if off to a wedding, and farther off parked sets of young men and women, as if assembling before heading off to a game. A feeling of gaiety soared.

"I need the toilet," Leandra announced.

"I'll join," I said.

"Here are two euros." Thomas handed over coins for the turnstiles from which we'd each get back fifty eurocent vouchers.

Leandra and I knew the deal, that the washroom was a bit of a rough scene, with a bother having broken out once before when we'd ventured in. Two personnel of African origin, a lady for the women's toilets and a man for the men's, supervised.

For train station toilets, people paid before using the facilities, here one euro, meaning the price could be a bit much for some with little money. Nevertheless, practical sense said if you could afford to go by train or hang around train stations, you should be able to pay to use the toilets.

This situation must be common at train stations in Germany. For youth with little money, one euro each time to pee quickly added up; besides, not all shop owners accepted the toilet coupons. Most declared that a purchase of at least €2,50 be made per voucher and only one person per voucher each time making for a sticky situation. I realized that, as with most things in Germany, there were right and wrong ways to observe toilet etiquette, but like youths everywhere, some were busy breaking the rules. For a country with so many social supports, I didn't understand why people needed to pay for lavatory use, but Thomas said train station hygiene had much improved over the decades with the user pay system.

I plugged all the money in and waited.

"Mum, go in quick!" Leandra pressed me. The voucher machine spat out two fifty-cent vouchers but released the glass stop-door for only my entry.

An advancing Leandra stood blocked, holding two vouchers. Two teenage girls snuck under ahead of Leandra and disappeared before she twitched a muscle.

"What just happened?" I asked, confused.

"Never mind. We have to wait."

An advancing, much-harassed toilet attendant waved at us, having seen the action.

Leandra showed her the vouchers as evidence of payment, and the woman's face creased in irritation. If she'd been a Bajan woman, she would've chupsed so hard about teens passing through for free it'd be heard clear across the Atlantic. Instead, she exercised restraint, freed the glass partition, and signalled Leandra through. It's unlikely she made a habit of chasing cheeky youths through the Frankfurt train station, toilet brush in hand.

Inside, Leandra explained. "Mum, you need to put in the euros one at a time and wait for the voucher."

"Ohh." How could I be blamed for my small-city (and small-island) ignorance?

We arrived in Göttingen at 4:30 P.M. having covered a distance of 400 kilometres. After being transported by taxi over jarring basalt cobblestoned lanes, we arrived at a beautiful acreage, our youth hostel accommodation, where young people sprawled out on the lawn. Inside an immaculate, bright lobby, a young woman assisted us in storing our luggage until check-in time at 6 P.M. after which we turned to make our way downhill through hedgerows.

We passed through a wide white archway into a beer garden area and sat under a blue umbrella next to two other tables occupied by couples. A mature, monosyllabic waiter took our orders in a crusty manner, but we were happy. A visit to this city called for a call at this historic eatery, Potis. Before long, the waiter laid plates of gyros before us, a Greek dish of tender pork loin, grilled to a miraculous crisp and accompanied by roasted potatoes, Greek salad, and a herby tzatziki dressing, one of Thomas's favourite meals during his university years. For me, eating it was sheer indulgence.

Next day, we toured the grounds of the Georg August University of Göttingen—a university that has so far produced forty-five Nobel Prize winners. We wandered through nearby forests and botanical gardens, strolled the main drag, where Thomas had lounged outside drinking beer during his student days, and rummaged through a bookstore. Leandra liked this university town so much she asked her dad, "Why didn't you stay here after graduation?"

"Little prospect of work in forest science as nobody I knew ever got work here," he replied. "Plus, if I'd stayed here, I'd never have met your mother, and you wouldn't be around."

She thought about it for a bit and said, "Must have been a big change into English-speaking Canada."

"That's true, but I've learned a lot of English from your mother."

I smiled. "You give me too much credit."

"It's true, though."

For Thomas, Göttingen served as another waltz down memory lane. It complemented the earlier visit to his old high school in Eutin, highlighting parts of the childhood and youth he'd left behind for life in Canada. Every time we accompanied him on these tours, we learned not just about Germany's places, history, and culture, but also about his past. When we met in 1990, everything had changed not just for me but for him, too.

PART VI

31. Passings and Birthdays

On a chilly January day, Thomas and I sat among others facing a simple, adorned altar in a tiny, wooden village chapel. Furnishings amounted to ten pews, five on each side of the aisle, and a podium to the left. I tugged my black cardigan tight against a wind blowing in through the open doorway.

Thomas's friend Karl had been seriously ill for many years. Now, white-faced with grief, one of Karl's closest colleagues struggled to deliver his eulogy. About ten wreaths, each a metre or more in diameter, crowded the area in front of the altar.

We'd gathered to pay our respects to a husband, brother, friend, and colleague. Everyone who had known Karl expected this end, but it had arrived too soon—a shock but not a surprise. Thomas had shown a solemn, reflective mood. I thought of Karl with fondness, his cheerfulness toward me whenever we met and his kindness with the loan of a TV.

After a brief, subdued service—Karl was not a religious man—we had walked through an aged old cemetery for the burial. Karl's widow, Julia, sad-eyed but composed, hugged everyone, mentioning being buried in the same grave as her husband. At the village pub, a generous spread of pies, cakes, and open-faced sandwiches lay before us, most of it remaining untouched. I was humbled by the sober restraint of the funeral service.

"Isn't it ironic that Karl passed away the very year we were here?" I'd said to Thomas after the funeral.

"Actually, yes." He didn't want to speak of it.

So, now Thomas's old friend lay buried in a village graveyard. Living life in a foreign country meant hurrying toward anticipated good times and slowing to a crawl for unforeseen shocks and surprises. Karl's friendship and presence in Saarland had made Thomas's study leave there possible and attractive. He'd died in winter's coldest month after fighting a ten-year battle with leukemia. Doctors had achieved a medical triumph by transplanting Karl with his bone marrow cells, extending his life by a decade. His last conversation with Thomas was strange, with incoherent ramblings foreshadowing his demise.

Karl's widow faced the challenges of living alone and managing household and financial matters that had always fallen to a loving husband.

"What do you think of meeting with Julia once a week to help her through her grief?" Thomas suggested.

"That's a kind thought. Where?" It was a few weeks after Karl's funeral. We watched Leandra feed a bag of acorns to greedy boar in Wildpark; close by, two small children squealed in glee at the goats.

"How about meeting her for coffee at the Brasserie on the pedestrian strip?"

"I think she'd like that."

With time, our coffee dates delighted the three of us. I saw first-hand how the outings distracted and helped Julia.

Most Wednesdays, we met at ten o'clock and nattered away until noon at whatever caught our fancy. Julia wore woollen cardigans, bright, colourful shawls, and long floral skirts or slacks, hippie-like. She had a fine, delicate face framed by chestnut curls and set with watery-blue eyes and dimples when she smiled. Of a gentle and sympathetic disposition, Julia was grateful for the loving kindness that had been showered on her by her deceased spouse.

"I don't have many friends, but I value the ones I have," she said. Demonstrative and tender, in our chats she unearthed memories of a harsh, religious mother. "I have a diary full of my own poems and expressions that I've kept over the years. I read and reread them." Karl had written in her diary. Perusing his healing comments meant the world to her as Julia transitioned into a new life phase.

Some months later, in spring 2014, Anna's mother died in her early nineties. In conversations with Anna, I learned that Saarland's care homes for elders functioned by requiring families to take responsibility for much of the daily caregiving and support of their seniors.

"No regular-income family in Saarland, or Germany, can afford the sky-high costs of full-time, twenty-four-hour care for the elderly and sick," Anna stressed. It came as an insight that the "subsidiarity principle," well-known in Barbados as a key characteristic of a well-knit society, is also upheld in a wealthy country like Germany. *Collins English Dictionary* defines subsidiarity as "a principle of social doctrine that all social bodies exist for the sake of the individual so that what individuals are able to do, society should not take over, and what small societies can do, larger societies should not take over." As a traditional family man, Thomas loved the idea that "regardless of economic status, family remains the glue of nationhood everywhere."

In June, Julia invited friends for her birthday party, a small, intimate affair with a French-German couple, Thomas and me, and a dear Saarland friend. Though thrown together with the others for the first time, we felt at ease. The party occurred at Julia's large, semi-detached, two-storey home in a peaceful country hamlet. A large picture window overlooked a tranquil cobblestoned street, the back door leading into a generous, fenced yard. Almost untidy, the overrun yard surprised onlookers with flower and vegetable beds, grapevines, and fruit trees—plums and different kinds of apples. Before it became Julia's and Karl's home, the downstairs had functioned as a bakery, the rest making up the family home. Julia had confessed on one previous occasion, "If I wanted to clean this entire house, I'd never get it done." It hid a surprising number of rooms, nooks, and crannies, some shadowy, in crying need of an energetic overhaul.

Helping ourselves to generous slices of sour cherry and bee-sting cake and servings of whipped cream, we listened to an "ethnic German" (*Volksdeutscher*) who had grown up in the former Soviet Union tell stories about his family. His eldest son had undertaken the ambitious feat of biking across Russia.

At the party's end, so much of the cake feast remained untouched that it would have been a shame to throw it out. Julia contacted neighbours who she hoped would accept portions. As we left, Julia said, with hugs and a smile the size of Saarland, "What a wonderful birthday!" her eyes sparkling.

A few weeks later, Anna celebrated her birthday with a squad of eight at her home. Thomas and I joined Anna's sister Clair, a young Brazilian-German couple with a bouncy three-year-old, and a shy female friend of Anna's from Italian language classes. We spent a jovial afternoon in an easy family atmosphere, sharing and learning a bit about each other, recognizing Anna's knack for bringing people together.

"Have some more cake, Claudette, Thomas," Anna encouraged. We fed our faces with strawberry torte, Kuchen and coffee, after raising celebratory glasses of wine to Anna. Wise woman that she was, she had split her birthday revelries into two parties, having entertained a group of close women friends the previous evening. I was grateful to share in Julia's and Anna's birthday parties, wrapped up in warm Saarland hospitality.

32. Strange Telephone Links

Émilie had warned us not to use our apartment phone for long-distance calls, as those would be very expensive. This caution, translated into English, sounded exaggerated, so I ignored it.

Receipt of the first telephone bill in September lulled me into thinking Émilie's warning had been false. Then a November statement arrived; we owed the equivalent of about five hundred dollars for overseas calls. Thomas had made calls to Canada about our home insurance, and I'd made a few to Barbados, so we paid the balance owing, though it stung as we really didn't need an additional five-hundred-dollar charge.

Our costs in Saarland added up, but we never went broke. We paid €800 ($1,200) per month for the apartment. Transportation costs, not counting weekend and vacation travel, totalled about €1,800 ($3,000) for the three of us over the year. With more competition among grocery stores than in Nova Scotia, groceries were less expensive in Saarland, perhaps 20 percent less. We probably spent €300–400 per month on groceries, but we never kept close tabs or penny-pinched. Eating out at restaurants is more expensive in Germany than in Canada.

Use of our apartment landline telephone transformed into my most maddening experience, outside of learning German. How could Saarland, a state within this powerhouse nation of Germany, not be up on all kinds of phone technology, electronic gadgets, and long-distance communications? Surely, they should have as easy or even easier access around the globe as in Canada.

"Why are the telephone charges copied out in laborious handwriting?" I asked Thomas. "Doesn't the university have a printer?" He didn't know.

The invoice showed reasonable prices for local and long-distance calls to Canada, but Barbados had outrageous prices attached. *What is that about? Some strange test of my inner fortitude?* So instead of running to the nearest Internet café, I inferred that I could still on occasion call my mother in Barbados from our apartment, and Thomas could carry on making calls all across the universe.

After November, each passing month came without a telephone statement.

"I'm beginning to feel nervous," I confessed. *Is an enormous storm surge building?* By March, worried, I made inquiries to poor Émilie, now wedged between two parties, the university and us. It hadn't helped that she broke her foot in winter and spent several weeks away from work. We dared not ask her surly replacement anything—one day Thomas returned early to our apartment and heard her tearing down Émilie about all the work time she was missing. Nevertheless, Émilie promised to pursue the matter at the university, and she did. But the university employee stuck with this matter happened to be on vacation (perhaps on a cruise to Barbados?). The next time Émilie inquired, the employee was on sick leave. That employee was the only one who could fix the matter, which was quickly turning into a problem. By May, Thomas joined me in making gentle requests to Émilie but with no real results. The entire issue appeared surrounded by subterfuge, for which I experienced nothing except frustration. Around mid-June, with the year in Saarland ending, Thomas asserted himself to a mortified Émilie. He demanded an invoice by June 18, no ifs, ands, or buts. Émilie co-operated as usual, promising a miracle.

The situation had grown wings, turning into a strange, gigantic bird about to take flight whenever it saw us coming. Something baffling, frustrating, and, worst-case scenario, embarrassing positioned itself at the heart of this matter. "I am not leaving an unsettled telephone bill behind for my host professor to pay," Thomas said.

Is this happening because someone has to write it out by hand? Perhaps someone hoped to put guest house residents off using the phone so as to avoid the chore. Most normal house guests carried a cellphone 24/7 and had little use for the university's landline. We didn't possess a cellphone—on principle. Leandra wished for a cellphone but would have to wait until age eighteen. *What's wrong with using the apartment telephone and paying the charges?* I wanted to be able to call my mother. How infuriating not to have a more transparent system in place. Leandra was unfazed by our telephone fluster, probably thinking it served us right for not having cells.

When the telephone bill for December to April calls arrived June 16, I noted the expensive Barbados calls. Monthly invoices would have provided us the information we needed instead of prolonging our anxiety. Why could this situation not have been handled earlier?

"We should have listened to Émilie," Thomas said.

"But then we would have needed another option," I answered.

"Yes, the Internet café."

"Or a cell," I said.

"That might not have helped." Neither of us knew why. Did it have to do with Germany's cellphone grid?

To add to my frustration, I had to deal with blocked calls to Barbados from the downtown Internet café too. From July to November, I'd often called from there, but afterwards, from December through February, I'd switched back to the apartment phone. Then in March, without warning, I could make no direct connection from the apartment phone, so again I went back to the Internet café and faced a link problem there too. Either in Saarland or in Barbados, someone had severed a connection. The approachable Kurdish owner-operator of the Internet café tried to explain with limited English that I must be calling a very expensive location, with a Spanish name, perhaps in Mexico, which simply wasn't true.

It didn't make sense that calling long distance from the university apartment telephone was prohibited. I didn't like it one bit. But it was illogical for the link to be cut at the Internet café too. Thomas, however, could make endless international calls to Canada. My telephone problems defied comprehension in today's overconnected world. Why were calls blocked to Barbados from the Internet café where I paid upfront for the service?

In May, through an operator, I reached Barbados from the apartment, apologizing and explaining to my mother that direct and regular calls had become impossible. Stoic, she didn't utter the disappointment her voice betrayed, changing the subject to ask about life in Germany and the family. I felt far removed from Barbados, farther than I'd ever been in my life. In

Nova Scotia, every Sunday I called my mother. It was our time to catch up, to talk about important and trivial things. She anticipated and valued my calls in the same way Thomas's mother in Germany expected and valued his. My mother hardly ever spoke frankly about her deepest feelings, but on this call, I sensed her detachment and hurt, like a tree with a branch lopped off. I experienced the shatter caused by lost, irretrievable time.

I tried to situate my crazy telephone experience within the context of the German obsession with the *Leistungsgesellschaft* (meritocracy), a well-organized, well-run, efficient society. But I came up with only contradictions and questions. It reminded me of the foolish New Year's Eve episode and the ancient, inaccessible computers in the local library. Certain rigid quirks existed within Saarland that puzzled and frustrated Thomas and me. I put the telephone story down to an antiquated system between Saarland University and management of Humboldt House. But perhaps it was the lack of existing telecommunication systems between Germany and the Caribbean region, as the independent Internet café was not a big help either. It was insane that in 2014, I was only able to reach my mother in Barbados using an operator for connection.

I'm not sure that purchasing my cellphone would have helped, but if I'd known my mother would pass away in December 2014, six months after we left Saarland, I would have been more earnest in my efforts to call her more often.

33. Budburst

The tizzy that birds excite in the beginner is a property of the beginner, not of the birds; so those who love the tizzy itself must ever keep beginning things.
– Anne Dillard

Leandra chuckled, saying, "This is the first time I'm actually experiencing a spring." It was a Saturday morning in early March and she glowed, getting ready to meet her friend Sophie for an outing downtown.

"You can break out your shorts soon," I said, matching her light-hearted mood. In Nova Scotia, spring felt a lot like winter until summer arrived to even the score in late June. Spring had arrived early in Saarland, or winter had taken a break. Trendy winter boots selected from Rieker's looked terrific but were relegated to decorating our shoe rack. Anticipated snowdrifts, treacherous ice patches, and slushy mush, so familiar in Nova Scotia's winter landscapes, remained at bay.

That one day in late November, when everyone awoke to a magical world dusted in snow, didn't count, for it had vanished by noon. For one fleeting moment, glinting snowflakes softened the edges of trees, rooftops, and byways. With cheerful expression and a broad grin, our neighbour Arenata, zipped around snatching as many photos as she could. I was happy not having to bundle up against temperatures below minus ten degrees Celsius accompanied by bone-chilling winds. We had traded snowfall and ice pellets, so common in Nova Scotia winters, for Saarland rains.

Those Saarland rains added a soothing hum to our night rhythms, Leandra reading Krimis aloud and me falling off before she'd finished. Yet too many cloudy, damp days among the beech trees tested my sun-deprived soul. Sometimes I lifted my face skywards, imploring the heavens to release some rays of sunshine. The warming trend in early February ushered in shy, dainty snowbells nodding beneath naked forest trees. Their appearance motivated Thomas to check out a 1950s Saarland phenological atlas about flowering plants, which gave him the date of emergence of leaves and flowers in the region. What a clever book.

One day in March, we discovered that our shy resident owl, first sighted in summer 2013, had vanished. Thomas said it was nesting somewhere else, to return in the summer. How long do owls live? My husband said he didn't know; he has always been more interested in trees than animals. Wikipedia answered: twenty years is the average maximum lifespan for most owls. This question had never occurred to me before.

Spring blooms from sour cherry trees popped, turning a frilly white amidst a soft April green. Soon they floated down in a glut of snowflake petals, a blessing from higher spaces.

Ah, the secret life of woodlands and their inhabitants. With spring, our forest outings boosted my spirits as buds burst, flowers blossomed, and leaves flushed. As a lifelong student of forests, Thomas never sleep-walked through woods half-aware, not seeing the trees for the forest. Each new day, his woody plant friends offered a different aspect or unique mark of nature, his observation powers tuned into nature, alert in ways I never matched.

Walking through the woods, Thomas summed up the abundant forms and functions of plants and trees. Trees desired him to estimate their height, girth, lumber volume, and quality. Tree rings begged him to count them, and trunk-slashes by forestry personnel cried out for his description and explanation. Leaves beckoned him to examine them, and flowers asked that he scrutinize and appreciate their true colours, petal shapes, faces, and profiles. Creeks hurtling through the forest floor, like the blood flowing through our veins, wanted him to yield up their pH values.

"This tree here was cut down by the forestry personnel; that one there got marked for felling years ago but was never removed. See how the notch grew?" he indicated, as if revealing wonders of the forest universe. "Those beech trees are part of forest thinning. Doing these things means this forest will regenerate for ages. Cut the trees, not the forests!"

He criticized the lack of proper silvicultural practices in Canada where pulp and paper mills landed access to enormous strips of forested lands. Government–industry deals resulted in clear-cutting, causing long-term adverse environmental effects such as destruction of forest ecosystems, depriving wildlife of natural habitats and decreasing biodiversity; increased risks of soil erosion; and nutrient leakage to water bodies. He'd told me Germany practised sustainable forestry, after learning from centuries of deforestation.

"Too much clear-cutting goes on in Canadian forestry operations." He paused to touch a thick tree trunk. A chainsaw wailed as we passed forestry workers half-hidden up slopes. A scent of bark, moss, and sawdust infused the air.

"Those men are Romanians. There's a long history of people coming to work in Germany's forestry from as far away as Romania."

One day, we stopped to inspect logged trees, swept down as if by some giant hand. They waited high up on hills for the hauling needed to heave, pile, and sort them for dispatch. Another day, Thomas paused to engage a lumberjack on break after he and fellow workers had cut down hefty oak trunks on the north side of the Schwarzenberg.

Thomas addressed the sturdy fellow with a hearty, *"Guten Tag."*

In resin-stained overalls, covered in sawdust, the worker and his partners had spread out their lunches. The aroma of strong dark-roast coffee escaped a nearby percolating pot. Startled by an unsolicited greeting, the man's face clouded over in uneasiness, ill at ease. Later, Thomas credited his reserve to not being fluent in German. Felling and hauling logs did not require him to master fine points of conversational German. Thomas beamed with irrepressible admiration for the tough grit of those hard-working labourers cutting and heaving timber, chain sawing their way through massive tree trunks like sous chefs slicing tomatoes.

"Coltsfoot, snowbells, and crocuses are among the first spring plants to appear. Here, that happens earlier than in Nova Scotia," Thomas said.

I didn't recall seeing as many spring flowers in our woods. "Are there more forest flowers here than at home?" I asked.

"Actually, no. In this old-growth forest, wild plants or flowers wouldn't get enough light. But some wildflowers grow around the edges." My eyes scanned the ground.

The leaves of beech, oak, and cherry trees sprouted and unfurled in April, revealing a soft, delicate green, wildflowers competing for our attention. After the nodding snowbells came purple violets, which were chased off by pink anemones. All charting their course, May bells, Solomon's seal, and much later, foxgloves, and then pale-yellow impatiens followed in late spring. By late May, the wild lily of the valley showed up with its small stem covered in tiny, delicate white flowers, accompanied by showier lavender lupines. Each plant vied for its brief theatrical moment in the limelight, before being nudged off stage until next spring.

"Look, a prey bird, a buzzard or hawk." Thomas pointed as it arced high above the trees.

A swift, black thing flew by me, and I jumped, covering my head. "Oh, what was that?"

"Another prey bird."

"It was so low and went arrow-straight even through these trees!" I was awed by the grace of the moving predator, its large, agile wings missing tree trunks and branches.

Birds sang longer and sweeter in Saarland forests, in support of spring, non-stop twitters and chirpings meshing the air.

One Saturday morning, Leandra complained, "I wanted to sleep in, but some annoying birds—probably chickadees—kept me awake, chirping outside my bedroom window. Even with my window shut, I could hear them going on non-stop."

"Are birds louder here?" I wondered aloud.

"Yeah, sure," she laughed. "Mum, we *are* living in the middle of a forest."

As I walked among the brush, I heard a tweet as sparrow-like wings fluttered and vanished. The world was whirring alive where an ensemble of birds cheeped and whistled overhead and in the shrubbery. Larks and finches inhabited nearby places, and warblers maintained safe distances while chickadees flashed about. Flitting their wings and catching insects, the jumpy golden-crowned kinglets were easy to spot, their high pitches dropping to a quick chatter. Thomas often got lost in a reverie of tree-ness; I became attracted by any forest-creature movement or sound.

Lying in bed one morning, about to rise, I paused to listen to a startling melody. The others had already slipped out for office and school. I closed my eyes, waiting, paying attention to a call I'd never isolated before in the blend of bird calls. The bird emitted a series of rhythmic tweets, chirps, and whistles followed by a long, resonant churl at the end, a musical arrangement. I waited for that churl-like flourish at the end of a musical composition. I never found out what bird made such a beautiful sound.

On Mother's Day, as Thomas and I rounded a bend on the forest trail, a rambler emerged, binoculars in hand. This slender woman, bearing a focused air, was one of our apartment neighbours taken, like me, by the peeps and whistles of our feathered friends. "I love birdwatching," she admitted in Eastern European accented-English, "but I'm a mere beginner." I told her I'd probably never get past the beginner stage.

One day in late May, walking near the pretty, half-secluded Scheidt village, we spotted a bird on the ground, half-hidden in the shrubbery.

"It's young, not yet a strong flyer," Thomas said, as we stopped, looking harder.

"Yeah, feathers soft and fluffy."

We rested to get a good look while the fledging stayed, trembling. Then out of nowhere, a larger, mature bird flew up to where we stood, taking in the sight, catching our attention. It then took off half-hopping, half-fluttering, low along the path in front for a few feet at a time as if to say, "Here, follow me." We did just that. After a minute of this peculiar behaviour, it flew off to the side, disappearing into the thicket. It was one of the cutest shows of nature I'd witnessed anywhere. We concluded that the parent-bird, seeing our initial interest, pretended injury in order to distract us away from its young. We'd seen a priceless demonstration of a bird's innate intelligence.

By May, I saw the entire mature Schwarzenberg beech wood forest flushed with leaves, revealing an avocado-green canopy when we craned our necks. Thick grey-green trunks climbed skyward; lines broken by intermittent leafy branches stretched in spiny arms spread wide throughout sometimes dense foliage. At the feet of these soaring beeches lay a riot of new understory growth, a regeneration of feisty beech seedlings. Like new hatchlings, seeds that had survived a few winters mustered stored resources for a big growth spurt. A combination of warm days and sometimes heavy, almost tropical rainfall produced a surge of vitality and growth among plant life I so admired.

While I forest-bathed, keeping silent, the forest revealed itself to me, especially on warm days after night rain. If I asked my forest scientist companion, "What are the mysteries of this forest world?" he wouldn't be able find the right words, so I didn't ask. Passing through those hundred-year-old trunks, I turned my gaze upwards in this cathedral-like place, where a green ceiling way high, soared. Sometimes it would be at an hour when the light descended in a soft yellow. Beams would crack the forest crown to spill below in gold.

"Are there beech forests like this in Canada?" I asked one day, taken by the slanted light effect. Thomas habitually responded to questions, especially those about trees. While he walked in woods, his face relaxed, not folded into intense concentration.

"Not much beech left in Nova Scotia, but we have some decent stands of old eastern hemlock in the North River Wilderness Area of Cape Breton." He thought for a moment. "Remember, this forest was destroyed, cut down, and grew back in the late nineteenth century. It's proof of successful forest sustainability."

"There's something unforgettable about this forest," I beamed.

"Yep, these trees, almost like old friends. I'll miss these beeches when we're back in Nova Scotia," Thomas stated, stopping to examine a fine-grained knot-free trunk.

I'd come full circle, from a dread of entering the dark, frightening Schwarzenberg Forest to embracing its natural wonder. Abundant evidence of plant and animal life thrived everywhere I looked. Ancient human activity had left imprints here in the forms of an old Roman well, still swelling with crystal spring water, and a four-hundred-year-old witches' dance floor that we passed every time we hiked the trail.

Whenever we passed a sign saying *Hexentanzplatz* (witches' dance place), I knew we had half of our walk left. According to legend, at the time of the witch hunts in Europe, the accused held secret meetings on mountains or in fields or forests; the locations where they met were labelled witches' (or devils') dance floors, because it was believed that witches would have gathered there with the devil. I associated the Hexentanzplatz, with Arthur Miller's *The Crucible,* which I read with grade twelve students. This bizarre bit of German history, made tangible in the survival of ancient place names, connected in my mind to familiar American literature.

So much had changed in me since my initial foray into the Saarbrücken forest less than a year earlier. The forest's harmony transformed me when I claimed and absorbed its rewards as evidence of ever-changing life.

34. Entertainment

As I counted my last days in Saarland, I surveyed our supplies in the kitchen cupboards. *What should we use up? What do we still need?* I wanted to reduce the food ending up in the gaping mouth of the dumpster downstairs, crediting my frugality to my mother's influence and Bajan upbringing.

By the end of June, we'd need to munch through seven kilos of wild, brown, and milk-rice. It wasn't going to happen. I grabbed and set straight bags of lentils, fusilli pasta, whole oats, and assorted portions of linseeds, sunflower seeds, and sesame seeds. Several packages of Wasa *Knäckebrot* (crispbreads) lined one shelf, valued for its low calories, long shelf life, and lightness for travel. Loads of packaged teas slouched: specialty black tea flavoured with blueberry, decaffeinated green, rooibos, peppermint, fennel-caraway, elderberry-ginger, ginger-green, and a variety of homeopathic teas. According to the package labels on the homeopathic teas, these herbal brews would clean out the liver and gall bladder, treat coughs and bronchial problems, and flush the kidney and bladder. If so, *what are they still doing here then?* Our departure date in late June meant lots of super-fast eating and drinking or abandoned stockpiles for Émilie's pragmatic verdicts.

Summer arrived full throttle in Saarbrücken with humid weather and temperatures soaring to thirty-six degrees Celsius by June 10, effecting teeming plant life and lifting moods among city and university crowds. By early afternoon that day, I sagged like a wet rag. Next day brought only marginal relief at thirty-four degrees.

What a tropical heat wave descended, at once like sunbathing in the tropics but different for its lack of trade winds relief. It was like being slowly stifled in Bridgetown on the muggiest of days. But what a blessing to finally enjoy some blood-hot temperatures after the restrained Saarland winter. The heat was a robust reminder to me of the previous summer's warmth when we had arrived in Saarland, looking forward to everything.

On the day of my lunch date with my friend Anya from the Volkshochschule, it was probably thirty-four degrees, while half a world away in Halifax, the temperatures barely cracked twenty.

"Hi, Anya." I greeted her at the entrance to our old classroom. Tall and slender, with straight dark-blonde hair tucked behind her ears, she looked elegant.

"Hi, Claudette." She flashed a smile, head balanced on a long, slender neck. She had told me in her native Moldova, people spoke very fast.

"How nice to see you. It's been—how many months since we last met?"

"Almost five." She had continued on to B1 level of German after I'd freed myself from the course. Walking the fifteen minutes from the school building to the old city square felt like wading through soupy air. I sweltered like a pot cover on a stove.

At the Brasserie, where Thomas and I met Julia on Wednesdays, we bypassed red floating umbrellas, in whose shade half a dozen people clasped cool drinks, and entered a dim interior. Just inside the doors, flung wide open, a few patrons looked up as we stepped inside. Others were sitting at round wooden tables set with plush, dark-red upholstered or heavy wooden chairs, some covered with plastic. Booth seats lined the wall on the right opposite a mahogany-like bar to the left, polished to a shine, that ran almost the length of the room. A pleasant waiter approached and took our order. "It's my treat today," I said. "A parting gift."

Anya tried to object. "Oh, don't do that."

"I insist. You can return the favour next time," I said, at which we chuckled knowingly.

We sat chatting and sipping cold water and beer and devouring salads in sticky air against a steady backdrop of pedestrian clamour. Anya was torn between taking more German language classes and focusing on finding a job. Her fiancé worked long hours doing a medical internship at a local hospital. She sparked with ambition knowing that the kind of job she searched for in marketing was not readily available in Saarbrücken. Telling me she'd never met Estella again, even though I'd thought them close friends, we gossiped about people I knew in her classes.

After sitting for three hours, I sensed my cotton cargo pants sticking to me thanks to the plastic on my seat and the humidity. When I tested my legs upon rising to leave, Anya said casually, "I'll walk with you for a while so my pants can dry out."

"Don't worry, I have the same problem." And we both hooted.

Anya hated the sun's scorching heat, because her white skin burned easily and she felt sweaty and yucky. Although I disliked the burning penetration of the sun's rays that made me perspire in buckets, it ushered in welcomed memories of tropical days and nights.

I had known Anya for about nine months, but the smart, determined young woman had quickly impressed me. Among a band of internationals, she proved to be the most motivated and best student in our German classes.

To get to know a Moldovan for the first time and learn about her country and its people, landlocked between Romania and Ukraine, was a stroke of luck brought about by my life in Saarland. Following the collapse of the Soviet Union in 1991, Moldova emerged as an independent republic, regarded as one of the poorest countries in Europe, with its economy relying heavily on agriculture. The capital city, Chişinău (difficult for my tongue), has a population of 2.5 million people.

Before we parted, Anya drew out her purse, saying, "Here's a Leu for you, official currency of Moldova." The memento was worth about seven Canadian cents, but to me it was priceless.

"Why, thank you. That's so nice. And here's a Canadian toonie for you." I handed her the two-dollar coin with a polar bear on one side and we hugged.

At our parting, a wistful sense of loss seized me. I knew this chance encounter on life's train tracks meant we would likely never meet again when we said our *au revoirs*. She walked off resolute and I watched her, curiously reluctant to move away.

"There's a performance of *Die Physiker* in the university auditorium this Saturday evening. Would you like to go?" Thomas asked.

I lifted my head from my book to ask, "Who's putting it on?" I was taking advantage of the warm weather to join him on the front balcony, visited by the occasional bee, ladybug, and beetle. Those creatures were too much for Leandra, who sat safe inside.

"It's in German—put on by drama arts students."

"What about you, Leandra, would you like to go?" I asked over my shoulder.

"Yeah, sure," she said, without any hesitation.

Plays were often a stretch for Thomas, but he was familiar with this one from his school days. I also had a nodding acquaintance with *The Physicists*, having read a translated version six years, one of a list recommended readings for teaching a high school course.

So, on a blissful summer evening, we strode over to the university theatre, passing animated students smashing a volleyball on an outdoor sand court near an oak tree where I'd bagged acorns for the Wildpark boar.

A half-filled auditorium seating three to four hundred people yawned before us as we entered. I'm embarrassed to say I struggled to keep awake during the first part of act one, language being a huge barrier, plus the room must have registered forty degrees Celsius. I suppressed visions of my soul's light being snuffed out amidst an attentive crowd where I became the central spectacle. It was only my scant prior knowledge about the work and pride that prevented my eyelids from fully descending in the darkened room.

Walking back home, Thomas quizzed Leandra about the play. "Did you get it all?" he asked.

"Some of it, but the first part was confusing, and I couldn't hear all the actors," she replied, puckering her forehead.

"True that. Some actors didn't speak loud enough," I said.

"Okay, so the play starts with an investigation of a recent killing at a mental hospital. Three brilliant scientists, Newton, Einstein, and Möbius, are being kept there for insanity. With me so far?" Thomas asked, and Leandra shook her head.

"But these men aren't mad. Two are spies and the third wants to save his scientific knowledge, himself, and mankind from the creep of science put to evil uses. Act one ends with the onstage murder of the nurse. Remember? In act two, the reasons of the crazy pretenders become clear. Did you get how the plot twist works to spoil the plans of the physicists?"

"Oh, that makes sense now." Her face lit up in an *aha!* moment.

"What about the questions about ethics, science, and technology?" I asked, thinking of my class.

"But Mum, I saw you nodding off during the play. Did you see that, Dad?" Leandra asked, chuckling.

"That was only in the first half," I responded with a wink.

Written in the early 1960s during the Cold War, the play is a grim reminder of an era when nuclear war and the real possibility of colossal ruin loomed. It drills down into our fear of what people are capable of and how scientific developments can be used for evil purposes if they fall into powerful, wrong hands.

"I really liked that play," I said. "It's as relevant today as when it first came out. It brings up questions about the objectives of scientific progress and what it means to be human." I was being teacherly.

"Relevant questions," Thomas said, adding, "Dürrenmatt was a politically active leftie."

The Physicists was the second theatre piece we'd attended at Saarland University. We'd seen an English version of *Steel Magnolias* put on by the English department in February. None of us had seen the movie, although Leandra and I knew about it; the upshot was a perfect way to spend a winter evening. A few actors failed to deliver their lines with the force necessary to project for the entire auditorium, but it was still wonderful. And all the more admirable for being performed in English. Where in Halifax, or even Toronto, or Montreal, could Canadians attend theatre in German? I judged *Die Physiker* a better conceived and rendered production, displaying creative imagination delivered through fine acting skills on a craftily, pared-down stage.

Saarbrücken vibrated with a variety of choices for entertainment and social engagement, allowing people like us to choose from an array to suit particular preferences. Thomas and I loved the affordability and convenience of university movies, plays, and musical productions popping up with steady regularity. As a couple, we were able to do all the cool things a university offers without the pressure or grind of attending or teaching classes.

At the city hall and public library, a range of announcements flowered on display boards, calling us to lecture series on science, the environment, and politics, too many fruits for us to harvest. Leaving Leandra at home one evening, Thomas and I attended a public lecture in the city hall about education in Saarland. Never afraid to speak up, Thomas asked the presenters, "Why are so many North American–styled changes coming to the German education system?" They ignored his concerns. He'd shared his skepticism about such changes with me after acknowledging the enormous benefits he'd gained from his traditional Gymnasium education. Back in the day, Thomas had to pass an academic test at age ten to switch from his village school to the *Voß* Gymnasium in the small town of Eutin. A Gymnasium education was designed to prepare students during a nine-year program for obtaining a general maturity certificate as a prerequisite for admission to any regular university program in Germany. He said too many students now aimed for university in a nation that had sustained a formidable apprenticeship system for youth not oriented toward university. Anna had sighed in frustration about the exact same thing to me, she being a retired *Hauptschule* (general school for grades five through nine or ten) teacher.

At other public events, political parties thumped out speeches and students protested university cuts. In one of our last Saturdays in Saarbrücken, we joined an environmental protest with thousands demonstrating against globalization and Monsanto.

Every month, a battery of organizations such as the Saarländische Rundfunk (Saarland Radio) Orchestra and the music school hosted musical performances at locations around the city, including the Saarland concert hall. I loved that the vibrant checkerboard music scene in Saarbrücken offered up a wide variety of choices.

Perhaps the jewel in the crown of cultural events for the Saarbrücken-Sarreguemines region is the annual Festival Perspectives, first launched in 1978, that usually runs for ten days. It was during the May 2014 Festival

Perspectives that we'd attended the poignant *Quality Control* piece. Proudly bilingual, the festival showcases a wide variety of performing arts from musical theatre to multimedia shows. Classic productions at Saarbrücken locations are complemented by light shows, street theatre, and performances at atypical outdoor venues. Theatre houses, auditoriums, and a variety of nightclubs throw open their doors to patrons ready for inspired reflection, entertainment, or straight up escape.

Despite enjoying this cultural smorgasbord, I often had a hard time and was on the brink of giving up altogether, for I understood only a tiny fraction of things said in German. From time to time, I just wanted to hear English. Like Saarbrücken, Halifax offered a banquet of opportunities for people looking for entertainment. Back home, we invited friends and were invited by them, went out for walks and hikes. I joined family and friends for supper, pub, and coffee dates. Leandra and I went to shows at Neptune Theatre, the Rebecca Cohn Auditorium, and in summer at Point Pleasant Park for outdoor performances by Shakespeare by the Sea. I missed all that so much and I was ready to go home.

35. Reflections on a French School

A few years after our overseas adventures, I asked Leandra, "What was the best thing about school in France?"

She replied, "For me, long weekends and four vacation breaks allowing for travels."

"That's like a kid saying 'recess' when asked what she enjoyed best about school." I laughed.

Even if it was hard for me to convince her of it, Leandra's remained a unique story. Here was a Canadian teenager with Bajan and German roots from Nova Scotia who had checked off successful completion of grade ten in eastern France.

"Germans often shivered when they heard I was going to a French school. They described French school as 'militaristic,'" she said. We were sitting on our backyard deck in 2017. Under the July sun, the linden looked greener than green and hemlocks waved tender new shoots. Three years had passed since our Saarland return, and high school and first-year university were behind her.

"What did they mean by militaristic?"

"A clear hierarchy between students and teachers, with the principal at the top. I never saw him at all." We were watching Thomas pile fresh firewood, dust swirling.

"That's unheard of in a Canadian system." The principal at my workplace was a natural extrovert who stood at the school's entrance every morning and walked the halls daily.

"The hierarchy was reinforced by the teachers using the impolite form, *tu*, when speaking to students, while we had to use the polite form, *vous*, when speaking to them."

"Why would that matter?" It had never occurred to me that would make a difference.

"It matters in French. But Sophie, who went through the system her whole life, said that the students would have been uncomfortable to be addressed in the formal way by a teacher because they were so used to the other way."

I shrugged. "Okay. If you say so."

"There was also a lot of annoying lining up, answering attendance, and going to offices to get stamps if I came to class after the hour."

"I remember you being upset by that."

"I wasn't often late, but that *was* at odds with Canadian schools. Also, teachers seemed uninhibited, even rude—one teacher even read off all the students' names and marks for a quiz, calling them either 'very good,' or 'scandalous,' depending on grades."

"Unthinkable in Nova Scotia." I chuckled, wishing I could do that for deserving students.

"Once a teacher just talked off the cuff for two hours about sustainable development during a civic duty class where we were supposed to be learning about the French state."

"How'd that go over?"

"We frigging looked at each other, rolled our eyes, and sat through it."

"What about classroom management?" I asked.

"Most teachers were strict and good in their subjects—two-hour rants aside. But students could also be very blunt, and there were occasional standoffs between a teacher and the sassy student who would 'give it back to them.'"

"Sounds like some classroom scenarios I can relate to."

We watched Thomas upend a wheelbarrow load of wood.

"The grading system was really different. Teachers marked out of twenty, and in a tough class, most people were happy to get a ten, a.k.a. *la moyenne*. As you know, my first marks were eleven, thirteen, along those lines and upsetting coming from the 'pedagogical' system in Canada instead of an old-fashioned, traditional mode of teaching. It was a shit show."

"I do remember that." An image arose of an inconsolable Leandra in Saarbrücken in September 2013.

"Yeah, even gym class was tough because the teacher couldn't give points for effort like here. For a while, my average in France was a lame eleven."

"The grading would have been a big adjustment," I said. In a slight breeze, hemlocks swayed and a dark-eyed junco landed nearby. I had brought back from Saarland an augmented awareness of the natural world, of birds and trees.

"I found the overall French temperament difficult to relate to at first."

"How so?" I asked, eyebrows raised.

"The French students I met were the bluntest people I know, which is often taken for arrogance. Sophie told me that the French are champion *râleurs*, complainers. It took me a while to warm up to classmates whose humour was often putting others down or laughing openly at another's mistakes. I had trouble understanding them because French teens mumbled a lot. Meanwhile, I understood the teachers perfectly. I think it helped that I was from 'America' and 'so nice,' that is, not laughing at people all the time. Who would have thought that makes someone nice? But it gave me novelty status. Eventually, I warmed up to a few students, and I'm still in touch with them."

"Surely you enjoyed learning first-hand about French school?" I caught her face twisting into a wry a smile.

"Did I enjoy the last few months? Almost. I certainly enjoyed not having class in the whole of June due to an unspoken rule that tenth-graders could relax at home while the rest of the school got deep into their baccalaureate exams." She grinned, remembering that freedom.

"What did you like most about coming back?"

"I loved the small size of my school here. Everyone said I had a bit of a French accent and that I showed more confidence. So, I guess some of that French bluntness rubbed off on me."

"What about the workload? Harder, easier, or the same?" I always wondered how Nova Scotia high schools matched up.

"I found the IB program in my two final years challenging, but knowing what students were going through back in France, I didn't pity myself too much and never doubted that I would complete the program after finishing *la seconde*," she said, using the French term for grade ten. In France, after a rough start, she'd surprised everybody and most of all herself with a high class average.

"Was the experience worth it?"

Silent for a beat, her eyes followed her dad throwing bark scraps into a wheelbarrow. "Looking back, it was good to get out of the very small school and social setting. Otherwise, like so many, I may have wanted to leave Carrefour to go to 'an English school' for the big high school experience. I can now say I went to a big high school with twelve hundred students and didn't like its size one bit!"

Race was ever an issue for Art and Leandra, but they both underplayed it until their teen years, when they started openly acknowledging their mixed-race heritage. Art faced a harder time as a Black student in his regular, anglophone public elementary and junior high schools than Leandra. At her schools, Bois-Joli and Carrefour, Leandra was surrounded by a mix of white kids, a few of mixed race, and several students of Lebanese ancestry. Differences popped up between Acadian and non-Acadian (i.e., Quebecois) students, children raised in francophone and English homes, and children from military and non-military households. As with all children, these differences provoked teasing, mocking, and bullying.

When I recounted Leandra's perspective on her French school experience to Thomas, he sighed, after all, the idea of an overseas sabbatical year had been his. He threw a wider vision over it.

"She didn't say anything about being able to take languages not available here, like Latin and German? She liked those courses."

We were relaxing in our living room. I was in a listening mood, trying to be fair, to hold onto both Leandra's and Thomas's views.

"And she faced immediate immersion into the mixture of French and German that people speak in the Saarland-Moselle region. To share the history of these people—what an experience, nah!" His voice rose.

"Remember how she got corrected all the time by other teens?" I asked, grimacing. "I'd have lost patience right away."

Thomas nodded. "Yah, Yah, as a newcomer speaking a cute mix of Quebec and Acadian French, I don't know how she survived those corrections. Did she mention taking the train to school? Here she got on and off a school bus on her very street. Saarland was a different story —public transit all the way, every day," he pointed out.

I saw how Leandra had underplayed the novelty of all that.

"Right. Coming back, I saw her confidence and eagerness to take public transit. Before our trip, she never went anywhere by herself," I noted.

"Remember when we visited Saarland again after she finished grade twelve? She went on the tram alone to see a friend in Sarreguemines." His face creased in worry lines even now, even though Leandra was already eighteen at the time.

"And only told us about it after the fact," I added.

"Another thing, as a foreign student from Canada, she met other international students. So many young people all over the world dream about having such an experience, nah."

I agreed. "So true. I wish I'd been able to do that."

"She met French high school students, and remember the Australian student? She still writes to her."

I nodded. "And her friend Sophie, who wants to come visit."

As a teenager, I'd had at least ten international pen pals, keeping one of them for over forty years. Travelling and living overseas were real-life educational experiences that no books, videos, or talks could ever bestow. That love for travel had brought me to Canada, as it had done for Thomas.

"Remember the movie *Entre les Murs*?" Thomas looked to me for affirmation, and I nodded.

"Remember how those children put their teacher through the wringer in an inner-city Paris school, nah?" His eyes were animated. I smiled wryly.

"I know Leandra's experience was very different, but it makes me think of the movie," he said. He sat straight up as if to rise, and we remained silent for a bit. "In that movie, I admired the French high school." He'd told me the French system seemed to cultivate assertiveness among students, involving them in student–teacher councils and encouraging them to engage in program delivery and student assessment.

In 2020, after she graduated from university, Leandra succumbed to my appeals for a more complete school narrative. I sensed her views would change as she changed. But she never appeased us by openly valuing the experience or even pretending to.

"Mom, don't try to soft peddle this one. From the moment the overseas idea dropped, I feared that a brand-new school in a brand-new city in France would be tough. And, just as I thought, that's exactly what it was." Her body stiffened. "My first week in Sarreguemines released my pent-up fears."

She admitted that, at first, she felt the hell of total social isolation. She had felt helpless in the midst of hundreds of strange teenagers. Thrown onto herself, she had no idea whom to reach out to.

"On the first day, I sat on a bench in the inner courtyard. All these buildings around me. Offices, cafeteria, classrooms, and accommodations for older students in technical courses. And hundreds of students." She paused. "I sat there staring out at everything and nothing, feeling alone. At some point, I should have been lining up to go into a classroom, but because no one told me, I didn't. Then this *surveillant* says, 'Why aren't you lining up?'"

"Lining up for what? Where?"

"He pointed, and I jumped into action. I was so ignorant. Nobody said anything, and I was expected to know frigging everything."

"That's because incoming grade tens would have been introduced to the school and given info the previous year."

"Right, and there I was, Miss Nova Scotia, as unaware as a new puppy."

She told me that on day one, she stumbled around until somehow, she found the right building, the right classroom, the right teacher. It gave her no comfort to know that hundreds of fifteen-year-olds shared similar anxieties, having arrived at a new high school from outlying smaller schools.

"What about asking for help?"

"I didn't want to show how ignorant I was. The students looked so unfriendly, arrogant."

Some of the embarrassing missteps remained a blur, but she remembered missing the bell summoning her to her first Latin class and the ensuing emotional turmoil.

"When I showed up late, the teacher told me sharply me to report to the *surveillant* for a late slip. I saw that as a punishment." She chuckled now at her overreaction. "It was all too much."

By the time she reached the *surveillant*'s office, she was crying. For the first time that day, she encountered a kind reaction. A secretary gently suggested she take a walk and return when she was calm. When she returned to her Latin class, the teacher must have clued in to Leandra's distress and said nothing more. That teacher turned out to be her best for the year.

In my own opinion, French teachers needed not be as 'nice' as in the Canadian way so long as they performed their jobs. In fact, bluntness, sarcasm, and less coddling (there were no substitute teachers when the teacher was absent, and so students had to manage their own time) were helpful features of an education system designed to prepare young adults for the real world.

Thomas and I valued good teaching, rigorous grading, and honest feedback from educators when it matched what we knew about our daughter. Granted, she endured performance pressure, but we left teachers alone to do their work. Her German teacher confirmed that Leandra was a motivated, autonomous learner. No grade inflation flourished at Jean de Pange as it does in many Canadian high schools in so-called regular, academic courses. While at first a shock to Leandra's ego, she survived mediocre marks and recognized, after a few initial meltdowns, the necessity to strive harder to achieve more.

Leandra's personality suffered a jolt from the customary abruptness and plain-spokenness of teachers and peers. The role of the *surveillant* seemed punitive for someone like Leandra who prided herself on punctuality and respect for rules. She discovered that no one looked out for her at school. She wasn't made to feel special; she was just another ordinary student among a sea of faces. Her qualities of shyness, politeness, and kindness took a battering. She'd been protected up to age fifteen, had been liked and admired by a terrific group of friends and teachers. In a new school, she had trouble finding the right friends to fit in with. For her, raw, painful memories sprang up in association with the French school, and revisiting that experience was akin to a survivor of a battle, safely delivered, dredging up old clashes. She'd withstood fateful blows and wanted those memories to stay dormant.

Leandra had returned to high school in Dartmouth, bracing for two tough years ahead in the International Baccalaureate program. She knew after what she'd endured in France, she would reap success on the studious track ahead. Yet the uncomfortable grade ten year had left an indelible mark. At the end of grade twelve, when deciding the path for university, she wavered. It had been her dream ever since age nine to attend Université Laval in Quebec, one thousand kilometres from home. The university required students to be functional in French. She hesitated; her mind filled with a friendless vision, walking isolated among masses of students. Mean-faced *surveillants* still swirled, harassing her about late arrivals. How could she step into a new world again to navigate it by herself? We waited, not pushing.

She did eventually choose to follow her dream and registered at Laval. "What helped you make the leap, Leandra?" I asked her.

"My buddy Kim." Firm friendships have always been key to her sense of well-being, and I suspect they always will be.

Life taught Leandra difficult lessons; however, I don't expect her to promote international student exchanges anytime soon. I don't see her ever acknowledging she enjoyed and freely participated in anything that was gratifying at her Sarreguemines school. Nevertheless, she learned things about herself, other teenagers, teachers, and the world during a rocky adolescent period littered with insecurities, anxieties, and mistakes. She survived a challenging foreign school experience and came out the other side with added knowledge and augmented self-assurance.

Life events, peer support, and our parental backing boosted Leandra's inner motivations and personal resilience. It meant everything to me to be there and to share her life-altering passage. I see it as an invaluable experience in hindsight, more so than in the moment. It made me more intuitive and responsive as a mother and teacher, bringing us closer. We leaned on, depended on, and sustained each other throughout that year, finding out more about ourselves, who we were as individuals and as a family.

36. Hello, Nova Scotia

When does a Canadian immigrant become a Canadian? Perhaps I had always underestimated the strong physical, psychological, and emotional pull of home as country, location, and shelter. Everything that Nova Scotia meant to me as home for the past fifteen years came whistling back to meet me in June 2014. The child in me longed for home—and it wasn't Barbados.

As we checked off the remaining Saarbrücken days on our calendar, I sensed in me an accelerated pace close to panic. It underpinned my mixed emotions and reflections about leaving even as pragmatic matters shoved themselves centre stage. Impatient events crowded in, for example, we had to make immediate decisions about family possessions. We needed to pack boxes for mailing and honour invitations for visits and dinners that barged in, careless of time pressures. A familiar echo of disquieting sentiments got dredged up at the thought of saying goodbye. In my life as an immigrant, I'd stepped into farewell waters several times over, but each departure from family and friends is tinged by its own unique colours, set of experiences, and human interactions.

Haus Brück on Mainzer Straße ran with quiet efficiency, the work of self-assured waiters, all men. A lily-white, nineteenth-century frontage showed a two-storey, gentrified house, once an inn. In the middle of the main floor, eighty seats were arranged whereas on the left, set back, was a glossy bar in wood decorated with a colourful mosaic of stones. Behind that were rooms, one with a fireplace, ideal for social celebrations of a few dozen people. On sunny days, a terrace, shaded and protected by high walls, offered peace and quiet. Anna, Leandra, Thomas, and I chose to sit inside under the subtle light of icy chandeliers.

I had long fallen under the spell of Haus Brück's modest elegance. Outside, sunlight still reigned whilst inside, the air sparkled with a matching array of tables set with twinkling glasses, cutlery, and starched, snowy linen cloths. We were early for supper on a warm afternoon, and only a few tables were occupied by guests speaking in hushed tones. Anna had told me she loved this place, and when Thomas said, "Let's invite Anna for supper at Haus Brück before we leave," I agreed right away.

An attentive waiter offered water and menus.

We made selections, which took a good time to be served. Soon inviting aromas pulled me by the nose.

"So, when are you leaving?" Anna asked as the veteran waiter set down our meals.

"Next week, Wednesday," Thomas said.

"So soon?"

"It's coming fast. We haven't even started packing anything yet," I told her.

Anna spoke about her son's visit to America a decade earlier and a scary experience he had there when, by accident, he trespassed on someone's property and the property owner threatened to shoot him. That incident had burned into her memory. And then she talked about ugly racism, having recently read a shocking magazine article about the Carolinas. Unlike some of Leandra's peers, Anna knew and acknowledged the differences between America and Canada, but she spoke sometimes as if they were the same country. We circled back to our return to Canada, encounters and observations in Saarland, Thomas's research, Leandra's school experiences, and back again to Nova Scotia until time tapped our shoulders.

At the parting, we embraced Anna. I missed her already.

"Thanks ever so much for your warm hospitality, Anna. You helped make my stay in Saarland something special. We will meet again," I reassured her.

"So, you're coming back?" Her eyes brightened.

"Yes, Leandra wants to take another German language course in summer 2016," Thomas told her.

"Wonderful. I look very much forward to seeing you again." Her face matched mine in anticipation.

Next day, we rented a car to visit with Leandra's friend Sophie and her parents. Leandra and I had on previous visits fallen in love with their perfect, right-sized home. Leandra and Sophie spent most of the evening holed up in Sophie's room, chattering, dressing up, and applying makeup. At midnight, Sophie, holder of a new driver's licence, piloted us through dark village roads, tooting a final goodbye as we passed her making tracks for the autobahn toward Saarbrücken.

Visits and dinners aside, we could no longer ignore the business of packing. We bought plenty of boxes and filled them with essentials, books, papers, and knick-knacks before turning to the extra-large suitcases waiting to swallow well-worn favourites and brand-new clothing items. *How was it possible to accumulate so much stuff in one year?* A host of newly acquired books, magazines, papers, and the like vied for luggage space, bent on crossing the Atlantic at whatever cost. Books by Alice Munro, *Sarum* by Edward Rutherfurd, French novels by Molière and Zola, books by Stieg Larsson, German Krimi readers, journals, newspapers, magazines, the popular *Game of Thrones* series, and forest science tomes jostled for space. For two days, we estimated and measured, fretted and sweated, hauled and heaved. Finally, fifteen boxes arose from the mess, packaged like trim gifts, carted off in a Deutsche Post DHL van, to meet us at home. Still more essentials waited for us to stuff empty suitcases by our departure day.

Bright Émilie expressed open regret about the imminent departure of her Humboldt House guests. She joked about joining us: "Put me in your luggage and take me to Canada."

It was she who first told us about the shocking events that happened in Moncton. Details revealed a string of shootings on June 4 in Moncton, New Brunswick, a 260-kilometre drive from Halifax, where a young resident had shot three Royal Canadian Mounted Police (RCMP) officers and injured two. From distant Saarland, that horrific incident froze me into disbelief. It was hard to form a reply to that report. I wondered if our home country had changed so drastically in one year. Perhaps Émilie was deluded about Canada.

Even in the rush of preparations for departure, a brief period of reflection nestled inside me like a mother bluebird incubating a hatchling. I thought of the special German term *Heimat* and its meaning of "birthplace" or "homeland." The idea of Heimat emerged a few times during our stay when, for instance, Leandra made her claim to being Canadian. A German language instructor at the Saarland University presumed her looks not to fit his image of a Canadian. And I felt forced to explain at the Volkshochschule that while I had arrived from Canada and was a Canadian citizen, I was born and raised in Barbados and thus boasted dual citizenship. As a German national, Thomas had arrived home but far from his familiar Baltic Coast, Saarland's regional character at once setting him apart, though not as a foreigner like me. Issues of identity deeply embedded in our three different perspectives and experiences had surfaced throughout our stay. Had we all joined in a life-changing experience? Was the real story of Saarland about self-discovery? What rewards did each family member gain from a year spent in Germany?

For Thomas, it meant the gift of extended time to put distance between his routine workload so as to undertake forest research. He had wished to accomplish that much during a sabbatical year. Knocked sideways for a month in September by a mysterious illness, he recuperated, gathered energy, and followed through on data collection in four old beech woods.

As Thomas said, "A great public transport system, buses, trams, and trains gave me easy access to selected forest locations." He loved that in Kirkel, he chanced upon a historic fort and in Ormesheim, municipality of Mandelbachtal, he visited a legendary shrine. January marked his fiercest stretch as he struggled to figure out how best to abstract, organize, and compose the results of his work. By February, a journal had given him positive feedback on his submission and conditional acceptance with recommended minor revisions. A few months later, he fired off a second paper in the direction of another science journal which secured acceptance within six weeks, again only requiring modest revisions. "What a productive period a year's sabbatical gave me!" he exclaimed happily. Hitting his targets dead-on, two out of two, called for family celebrations.

Thomas admitted he hadn't done it alone. His academic triumph had come from a combination of generosity, offered to him by his host professor, and the gift of genuine scientific freedom to pursue specialist knowledge. This inspired him and triggered a shift in how he planned to work and relate to his colleagues when he returned to Nova Scotia. "I intend to be more independent and autonomous," he vowed.

The year had blossomed into a time of renewal and reacquaintance with Germany for us three. Thomas delighted in speaking his native tongue daily, even if sometimes he didn't understand the Saarländer dialect. He visited with his mother and other family members near the Baltic Sea and revisited high school and university haunts. He frequently walked through mature beech forests he loved and reacquainted himself first-hand with the history and culture of Western Europe.

My husband sometimes remarked how he missed the depth of history and cultural capital available in Germany and the rest of Europe. In Canada, the oldest building at a national historic site had stood for only a few hundred years. Europe possessed locations, monuments, and museums harking back to the prehistoric, Celtic, Roman, medieval, baroque, early-modern, and modern ages. In Germany and France, I joked to Thomas and Leandra, "If we stop to ponder every Roman artifact or quaint, fairy-like, medieval village along the way, we'll never arrive at our destination."

I agreed with Thomas's vision of a four-dimensional Europe teeming with unique cultural landscapes, grand monuments, cathedrals, countless and sometimes tiring museums, Roman and medieval ruins, and romantic or decadent castles, however dubiously afforded.

Jolted by excitement of European travel, Leandra's passion intensified as the year progressed. She settled on England, Vienna, and Slovenia as her most-anticipated and most-loved destinations, although she loved all the travels. A year in a new country and a new school compensated with fresh friendships, stripping her of her initial fears. School chums swore to keep in touch and shared parting gifts with her.

Having survived life in two not too foreign countries and a rigid school system with less pampering than in Nova Scotia, our teenager stepped up to the challenge, exceeding her own expectations. She strengthened her belief in herself as an autonomous learner, made friends, and adopted a new sense of self-possession. A painful initiation into senior high school away from the comfortable customary translated into a pluckier attitude and sufficient transformation to view the year in hindsight as an opportunity afforded to a fortunate few.

As for me, I reclaimed precious daytime freedom, stolen by too many work, family, and social obligations at home. I gave myself guilt-free permission to devote to meeting new people, experiencing the difficulties and intricacies of the German language, and travelling by rail, car, and ferry across Germany and Europe with my family.

Riding the train on weekends and holidays, we crossed several national borders, arriving in lands very different in culture, language, and physical landscapes. When else could we exercise the luxury of taking a fast train to Paris on a whim, arriving there in two hours? Or drive to Vienna for a few days and from there take a train into Slovakia? What about the excitement of standing in the castle district of Bratislava one day and then in Budapest the next? How was it possible to be climbing the mountainous terrain of Großglockner in Austria one fine morning and then, a week later, be walking the Piazza San Marco in Venice or visiting La Casa di Giulietta in Verona? Though my adopted country is blessed with vast stretches of unspoilt wilderness and abundant natural resources, every provincial capital I have surveyed, except for Quebec City, looks like a smaller or bigger version of the previous one.

But it had been the dynamic struggle with the German language that had made the year most exceptional for me. In the end, it hadn't been my skin colour, social background, or gender that defined my Saarland sojourn. I was always going to be perceived first as "other" by mainstream Germany, a Black person first and then a woman, also true in Canada. Had I arrived in Germany to live permanently, I would have sought out a community of open-minded hard-working people for the kind of "entrustment" Jia Tolentino talks about in her 2019 collection of essays, *Trick Mirror: Reflections on Self-Delusion*. I would have accepted my racial identity as a strength in the likeness of Audre Lorde's vision, not merely tolerated but as a "fund of necessary polarities, between which [our] creativity can spark." That designation would have given me the force to pursue a fulfilling life, as I have done in Canada. Based on my year in Saarland, I believe German life would have enabled me to do the same, had I been able to master the language.

My not being able to communicate with confidence in German had made the biggest difference. By being too hard on myself, I felt like a fraud when I tried to speak German. My handicap had barred me from more complete and more meaningful ordinary and extraordinary daily occurrences. I call it *an absence*, a void that opened up like a chasm separating me from ordinary people and much of daily German life. Even the most mundane and insignificant exchanges were unutterable for me. I could only blame myself for not conquering that language mountain, as I had succeeded with Großglockner. But I needed years, not a single year, to win the language battle. I pushed myself to glean what little I could from the buffet table, though I lived with an emptiness at the core.

Failing forward offers its own compensations—life lessons in adaptability, strength, and resilience. A Canadian abroad with deep Barbadian roots, I refused to be defeated by thick language failures and thin word successes, not indulging in self-pity or outright seclusion. Finding ways to deflect letdowns, I fashioned fresh coping methods with new friends, books, travels, and outings, to rise again and thrive with a reawakened vitality.

I hadn't actually lived in the shadowlands of the massive castle of Germany. My husband possessed a key, and I joined him in exploring its treasures. I benefited from theatre shows, classical music concerts (like one by pianist Sebastian di Bin), museum interpretations in Saarland and Berlin, and more. Even without the capacity to enjoy light conversations in the marketplace, I participated in weightier cultural arts performances like *Die Fledermaus* and *Die Physiker*. With aplomb, Thomas translated the news on the TV news programs and written communication in letters, newspapers, and running announcements on trains. Invitations from new and old friends and acquaintances called me into a fold of warm hospitality.

I leaned on myself and my family, doubling down on inner reserves I'd tapped into back in 1986 when I first landed on Canadian soil. My openness to taking some risks had prompted personal and professional grit and growth back then, as much as it did in Germany.

One night, a few days before our departure date, I had a frightening dream. I was swept up into whirlpools, waves of uncertainty, fear, and dread. When Thomas appeared with Leandra, I knew where I was. I was standing in the Schwarzenberg Forest near the witches' dance floor. A time shift fast-forwarded me to Rainbow Haven Beach in Nova Scotia, facing the Atlantic with Art, Leandra, and Thomas. I whispered, "Hello, Nova Scotia" when I woke up. Security is the vision and experience of a safe place called home.

In the predawn hours, I waited downstairs in the postage-stamp parking lot for the taxi to the train station. A single light from the start-up business building cast a yellow halo, defying the darkness. A pensive sadness filled the borders of my throat, matching my final view of the unadorned, concrete guesthouse with its hanging balconies amid woody environs. A vehicle's tires droned on the pavement up toward the university.

Thomas and Leandra struggled with unyielding baggage down fifty-six steps, arriving panting, and depositing pieces at my feet.

"How dark it is," Leandra muttered. "When's the taxi?"

"Yeah. It's only four thirty. Should be here in fifteen minutes."

"I'll go up again for a last look," Thomas announced, hurrying away.

Leandra appeared to be half-asleep standing up.

What would I miss most about leaving this apartment, this city?

I would miss seeing Leandra's face beam when visiting the adorable goats, greedy wild boars, and calm donkeys straight across the way in Wildpark. My heart skipped a beat as I thought of the Saarländer I'd come to know and wanted to keep as friends, like Anna, Antje, and Julia, who had embraced me in ways I could only ever dream of reciprocating. I'd long for the people, numerous colourful acquaintances made during the university Sprachkurs and at the Volkshochschule where I'd known failure as an adult but not defeat. Who knew if I'd ever meet or talk to Anya again?

As we were transported from our driveway, the young taxi driver, stocky, affable and sporting short-cropped dark hair and rolled-up sleeves, chatted with Thomas. In cool morning air, the streets were so empty we glided along as if by magic. The Saarbrücken Central Station ahead looked like a lit-up palace. Inside, the bakery workers were ready, wide awake, for purchases of coffee and pastries so fresh they radiated a warm fragrance.

A surprising bustle already marked the shops, including a supermarket, fast-food restaurant, newsagents and stationers, and tobacconists. We'd begun the wide arc back to where we'd come from. We were retracing the route, starting at the Saarbrücken train station and then on to Frankfurt's cavernous, bustling airport. The long-nosed white train with a red stripe murmured as it awaited departure.

"Ha! We're on our way," Thomas declared exuberantly after we'd settled into four facing seats on a nearly empty train, table in between. It would be full by the time we arrived at the airport station. Leandra snuggled into the headrest of her window seat for some shut-eye even before the train glided off. At the airport, we checked in early and slowed to a crawl. Sauntering past duty-free shops, cafés, and restaurants, we gauged fellow travellers on the move or lounging, restless or relaxed. I watched as if from a distance. Finally, in a fluttery state, we boarded for the flight home.

"I can't wait to see Kim, Emily, and Maya." Leandra said, almost trembling with anticipation. "What's the thing you most want to see or do at home, Mum?"

"After crashing in my bed, tomorrow morning I'll step barefoot into the backyard to see if our resident robins still live there. Perhaps the juncos flit in our hemlocks and the northern flicker pecks on our lawn."

"Oh, that's nice. And you, Dad?" She turned to him.

"To give the house a going over and see that everything's still in good order."

"Oh, Dad," she said, in mock surprise.

When our plane touched down in Halifax, I could barely restrain a giant urge to push fellow passengers aside, dash out, and kiss the earth below my feet. But I had to wait for baggage carousels to give up our luggage and for pleasant customs officers to read our travel declarations and ask us pesky questions. It was 9:00 P.M. and we'd been travelling for about twenty hours. My face shone with tired happiness to be back home in Nova Scotia. I could see Leandra's wide grin even as her eyes glazed over with fatigue. Thomas, as usual, most energetic when most tired, scurried off to arrange the taxi home.

On the wings of memories, our family will return to Saarland when we recount our treasury of experiences together and share them with Canadians who've lived in Germany. We've met numerous members of military families in Nova Scotia who resided in Germany while serving on Canadian Forces Bases Lahr and Baden-Soellingen. To a person, they've praised the lives they enjoyed during their overseas stays. They depicted a material and immaterial quality of life found nowhere else. Perhaps it's evidence of the beating heart of the generous German cultural buffet, or the vibrancy of a symphony not loud but ever alive and breathing life into a society of instrumentalists, each one playing their part and striving for harmony.

Memories of our three common but distinct intercultural experiences live on in us; Thomas's easy immersion as a Northern German into Frankish and autonomous Saarland; me relying on too-cautious conduct and perception rather than verbal communication; and Leandra, whose intercultural experience was not that of a light-hearted, laid-back vacationer, but that of a student. The year gave her and me an opportunity to experience and live in Thomas's native land, a nation of unity deeply rooted in diversity.

Short-term, long-term, and permanent country moves can cause migrants to lose their social and psychological moorings. The seduction of a year in Saarland, an unknown country. threw me back upon myself and in that moment, to change my life, I tried to change my language. As a Black Canadian woman of Barbadian origins, I felt my firm footing give way, and I lost sight of the shore when I tried to assume a foreign tongue. The German language felt coarse on my tongue. A foreign language is a strange new country, breathing beneath the weight of green beginnings, trials, failings, and modest successes. I'm forever changed from when I left Canada to breathe in the Saarland's forest air, experience its culture, and live for a time in the German fortress, taking slim pickings from a cultural feast.

Where Thomas and I stood in life in 2014 was a testament to how far we'd come as a couple. We were a working couple with two dependants, a twenty-three-year-old and a sixteen-year-old. By putting a realistic financial plan in place, we'd managed to pull off a successful year in Saarland.

How fortunate we were to share a relationship where creative financial planning allowed us a year abroad. We'd cultivated family life and established optimistic goals with purpose. I had taken risks in choosing life in Canada over Barbados and agreeing to live in Germany for an extended stay, but the hazards were investments in the promise of a rewarding family life.

Thomas and I ended up loving the allure of that Humboldt House tucked amongst the beech woods, in the green, so much that in the summer of 2016 we stayed there again. That second time, we occupied a bachelor apartment for a month. As a new high school grad, Leandra had signed up for Saarland University's language course again, living her best life in her own private room in student residence, priming her for a move to Laval University in a spirit of liberty that fall. I said to Thomas the guesthouse and its surroundings looked just the same in 2016 as in 2013–14. And in his conservative spirit, he replied he loved it just so. On our first Sunday back, he said, "Let's head through the woods to Ilseplatz for Kaffee und Kuchen." I had no power to resist such temptation for visiting the sumptuous buffet that is Germany meant enjoying its perfect sweetmeats, and I embraced the thrill of our nature walk to reach them.

Printed in the USA
CPSIA information can be obtained
at www.ICGtesting.com
CBHW030543070724
11222CB00010B/113

9 781038 301697